SIZE AND SURVIVAL

SIZE AND SURVIVAL:
The Politics of Security in the Caribbean and the Pacific

edited by

PAUL SUTTON and ANTHONY PAYNE

Routledge
Taylor & Francis Group

LONDON AND NEW YORK

First published 1993 by
FRANK CASS AND COMPANY LIMITED

2 Park Square, Milton Park, Abingdon, Oxon OX14 4RN
711 Third Avenue, New York, NY 10017, USA

*Routledge is an imprint of the Taylor & Francis Group,
an informa business*

First issued in paperback 2016

British Library Cataloguing in Publication Data
Size and Survival: Politics of Security in the Caribbean and
the Pacific
I. Sutton, Paul   II. Payne, Anthony

ISBN 978-1-138-98199-7 (pbk)
ISBN 978-0-7146-4532-2 (hbk)

Library of Congress Cataloging-in-Publication Data
Size and survival: the politics of security in the
Caribbean and the Pacific / edited by Paul Sutton
and Anthony Payne.
p.   cm.
Includes bibliographical references.
1. National security – Caribbean Area. 2. National
security – Pacific Area. I. Sutton, Paul K.
II. Payne, Anthony, 1952-   .
UA609.S59   1993
355'.0330729 – dc20   93-7279
CIP

This group of studies first appeared in a Special Issue of *The
Journal of Commonwealth and Comparative Politics*, Vol.
XXXI, No. 2 (July 1993)[Size and Survival: The Politics of
Security in the Caribbean and the Pacific].

Contents

Preface

Small states are not new. Indeed, for most of history they have been the rule rather than the exception. But as objects of international concern, particularly in the last 200 years, they have occupied the agenda only in the context of crisis and imminent war. Then, for a moment, as they did in Grenada ten years ago or more recently Kuwait, they hold the headlines, but attention quickly moves on and away and with it the fortunes of small states are forgotten until the next crisis precipitates them suddenly on to the centre of the stage.

This state of affairs is clearly unsatisfactory to small states. Their security needs are continuous, not contingent, and the international system cannot guarantee their survival (as the tortuous history of the Balkans and the Baltic states so clearly shows). Small states must therefore fashion their own security policies. They can only do so, however, if they are fully aware of the security environment in which they must act and the likely problems they will confront. The studies presented here are contributions toward defining this situation. They take as their starting point the proposition that a coherent security policy for small developing states is important to their well-being and their survival. The analysis also rests on the argument that small island and enclave developing states (SIEDS) are a distinct category of states in security studies. The reasons for treating them as such have been set out by us in an article which appears in the June 1993 issue of *Political Studies* (Vol. 41 No. 2). There we identify a syndrome of five characteristics that many small states share and which identify SIEDS as a particular sub-group of developing states. Here we take this argument further by presenting a study of the two regions in which the greatest concentration of SIEDS are to be found – the Caribbean and the Pacific. For each region we adopt a comparative approach. The recent patterns of security of the Caribbean and the Pacific SIEDS are thus reviewed by us in a common though separate framework. Some of the most important issues we identify are then subject to further consideration in additional invited contributions from scholars active in the study of small states. In the case of the Caribbean these examine the attempted coup in Trinidad and Tobago in 1989, which raises questions of social cohesion; the continuing insurgency in Suriname, which addresses the consequences of needless militarisation; and the explosive issue of drug trafficking and abuse, which now constitutes by far the most important security threat to every state of the region. In the case of the Pacific the focus is on the security vista for Papua New Guinea, which discusses the security response of the state in respect of ongoing political instability and acts of secession; decolonisation and denuclearisation in Micronesia, which highlights the role of extra-regional powers; and the growing threat to the environment, particularly of the smallest island states, posed by climatic change, which calls into question the prospect of sustainable development being realised by some of them. The final chapter brings the various strands together by advancing specific security proposals designed to enhance the security of SIEDS in each region. In so doing we are mindful of the fact that policy relevant research of this sort is consonant with the interests of small states in their search for security in a rapidly evolving international system. It is therefore no surprise to find that such studies have been called for both in the Resolution on the Protection and Security of Small States which was adopted by the UN General Assembly in December 1989 and in the Recommendations of the Workshop on the Protection and Security of Small States which was held in the Maldives in May 1991.

We both wish to acknowledge the assistance of the International Institute for Strategic Studies (IISS) in London for facilitating part of this study. The security dilemmas of small states are not concerns which naturally attract the attention of security analysts focused on the larger issues of the global balance. Yet, small states are not unimportant to the promotion of international order and the simple fact that there are now 45 states with a population of one million or less (36 of which are in the developing world) implies some recognition of their interests, if only by number alone. It is to the credit of the IISS, and the then Director of its Regional Studies programme, John Chipman, that the IISS understood this and supported our study financially (through a grant from the McArthur Foundation). The conclusions we have reached have been enriched by our association with the IISS (although it is in no way responsible for them) and in turn we hope to pass on to others our conviction that the security needs of SIEDS are an interesting and important area for further scholarly research and policy prescription.

Paul Sutton   **Anthony Payne**
University of Hull   *University of Sheffield*

The Politics of Small State Security in the Caribbean

PAUL SUTTON

The geographical definition of the Caribbean area is imprecise. The sea itself was not so named until 1773 and the considerable proliferation of names which held before this time have continued thereafter, varying with colonial power and subject of study. The comprehensive definition of the Caribbean basin held in the United States thus contrasts with the narrower definition of the West Indies held by Britain or the even narrower one of the Antilles favoured in France. Similarly, the complex topography and oceanography of the islands and the sea encountered in physical geography is distinct from the relatively simple two-fold division of cultural geography that defines the Euro-Indian mainland from the Afro-Caribbean rimland. The Caribbean can include a population of some 135 million when defined as a basin or 30 million when defined as islands and enclaves. Similarly, it can have a total water expanse of approximately 1.35 million square miles if the Gulf of Mexico and the Caribbean Sea are combined, yet a land area of only 92,000 square miles if the archipelago alone is counted. Whatever the geographical definition chosen, however, there are, as Thomas Anderson notes, two overriding geopolitical facts: '(1) no other sector of the ocean has so many different political entities adjoining or facing a common water surface and (2) the region lies adjacent to the United States'.[1] Indeed, geopolitics provides the only satisfactory geographic definition of the Caribbean region appropriate to this article. So considered, the Caribbean is broadly conceived as consisting of the 12 island states and 11 island dependencies to be found in or near to the Caribbean Sea and the 12 states and one overseas possession to be found on its littoral in Central America and nearby northern South America.

Equally complex are political definitions. An historical legacy of acute fragmentation has left little in common among all the states and dependencies encompassed above. Shared attributes are few; interaction among all the units generally weak; and recognition of

Paul Sutton is Senior Lecturer in Politics at the University of Hull in England.

themselves as a distinct area non-existent. There is therefore no one system or security complex to which all belong, either in institutional or abstract terms. Instead, there are two historical and contemporary cores focused on Central America on the one hand and the Commonwealth Caribbean on the other. Membership in one or other core (or neither) sets the agenda, determines the processes and colours the outcomes of policy.

All the small island and enclave developing states (SIEDS) in the region except Suriname belong to the Commonwealth Caribbean core comprising Jamaica, Trinidad and Tobago, Guyana, Barbados, the Bahamas, Grenada, Dominica, St Lucia, St Vincent and the Grenadines, Belize, Antigua and Barbuda and St Kitts-Nevis. This sub-region is presently characterised by broadly similar patterns, if not levels, of economic development; a similar social structure; directly comparable political systems; and common membership in many institutions, the most important of which is the Caribbean Community (CARICOM) established by treaty in 1973. Through CARICOM and its associated agencies, as well as more generally in the Caribbean basin and the international system as a whole, the Commonwealth Caribbean presents a common image and a similar set of foreign policy concerns recently identified by Jacqueline Braveboy-Wagner as a search for security (survival of the system, the government, the prevailing value system and peace); economic development (economic survival and if at all possible 'prosperity'); and prestige (achieving some level of international visibility and influence).[2] These, in turn, have specified a series of common objectives and occasioned a pattern of interaction in the region best conceptualised as a series of concentric circles radiating from the innermost English speaking core, including the United States; embracing next Britain, Canada and the Caribbean archipelago, including also Suriname, French Guiana and the respective metropolitan centres; and finally reaching out to Central America and South America as a whole, but with a special focus on Venezuela.

THE REGIONAL SECURITϒ CONTEXT

The security environment of the Caribbean SIEDS is complex. It takes on board both regional and 'extra-regional' factors, lateral and hierarchical dimensions, creating a complex scenario and addressing a variety of issues from the local, through the regional to the international level. At the apex of the hierarchical system, but also in the innermost circle of the regional, lies the United States. Its actions, more than those of any other state, set the essential parameters within which the

Caribbean SIEDS operate. An appreciation of the United States presence and policy in the region is therefore essential to any understanding of Caribbean security. So also is a recognition of the continuing Canadian commitment and European presence in the Caribbean. Contrary to expectations these have not diminished as much in recent years as had been expected. Canada, Britain, France, and to some extent the Netherlands, continue to provide a modest but largely welcome input into economic, political and military affairs. Finally, there is a significant regional dimension, focused on the CARICOM states themselves and their relations with their immediate Latin American neighbours. While relations within CARICOM are highly developed, those with Latin America are not. Considerable barriers to closer cooperation between the two areas exist and are not open to easy solution. While the SIEDS are therefore undeniably physically part of Latin America, politically they remain distant from it.

The US and the Caribbean

United States policy toward the Caribbean basin has at its heart the issue of national security. This has traditionally served two crucial strategic functions: (1) preventing extra-hemispheric powers from posing threats to the US mainland through acquiring military bases or a significant geopolitical presence in the area, and (2) enhancing US capabilities as a global power by ensuring its position as a region from which to draw resources and in which to demonstrate US resolve. The pursuit of these objectives has led, over the years, to a definition of the region as vital to US security, necessitating, in turn, a policy of military intervention as and when the need arises. Both US policy-makers and the US public regard such action as legitimate, even commendable. An image of the region as a deep 'Deep South' has thus grown up in the United States and has served to introduce a strong normative element into US policy, with decision-makers prone to recall previous examples and the US public particularly susceptible to rhetoric when events in the Caribbean command media attention or achieve prominence on the policy agenda. In sum, the Caribbean occupies a particular and singular place in US policy, one which engages domestic interests, Caribbean problems *sui generis*, and global issues, within a matrix defined as much by historical reflex as by rational calculation of interest.[3]

Within this framework global questions are addressed in the Caribbean through a number of specific security issues among the most important of which are access to military bases, strategic raw materials and secure sea lines of communication. The SIEDS in the region play a part in facilitating all three. US bases are to be found in Antigua and the

Bahamas (and until recently also in Barbados, St Lucia, Trinidad and the Turks and Caicos Islands), complementing those in Cuba, Puerto Rico, the US Virgin Islands and Panama.[4] The islands and enclaves are also of major significance to the US as proximate sources of bauxite and as secure sites for refining and transshipment of petroleum. The former consideration relates to Jamaica, Guyana and Suriname (previously also Haiti and the Dominican Republic), and the latter to the Bahamas, the Netherlands Antilles, Puerto Rico, St Lucia, Trinidad and the US Virgin Islands.[5]

Finally, and most importantly, the Caribbean is the region of greatest concentration of maritime routes essential to US commerce and defence. Caribbean sea routes have been assigned a major role in the resupply of NATO from the continental United States should there be conflict in Europe or adjacent theatres. They are also used to transit oil supplies in very large tankers from the Middle East and Africa. In most instances routes pass close by or through territorial water assigned to SIEDS and other Caribbean states, notably the Bahamas, Cuba, the Turks and Caicos Islands, Haiti, the Dominican Republic, Puerto Rico, St Lucia and Trinidad.[6]

The SIEDS are also important with respect to the other matters deemed vital to US strategic calculations in the Caribbean – those of strategic denial and global credibility. The first has sought to prevent both the establishment of Soviet and Cuban bases in the region and the emergence and consolidation of regimes supportive of Soviet and Cuban foreign policy goals. The proof in each case is provided by the hostile policy adopted towards Grenada under the People's Revolutionary Government (PRG). Within weeks of the seizure of power by the PRG in March 1979 the US had expressed displeasure at the development of links with Cuba and soon after was to express alarm at the construction with Cuban assistance of a major international airport with the perceived potential of acting as a forward Soviet/Cuban base. An escalating policy of weakening and containing the Grenada Revolution was set in train culminating in the US-led invasion of October 1983. The other matter has the status of a strategic imperative. It sees the Caribbean basin as a 'backyard' over which the United States must be seen to exercise hegemony if it is to sustain its claim to global power. Weakness here is seen as limiting the ability to act elsewhere. The National Bipartisan Commission on Central America (the Kissinger Commission) argued this explicitly in 1984 when it stated:

> Beyond the issue of U.S. security interests in the Central American-Caribbean region, our credibility world wide is

engaged. The triumph of hostile forces in what the Soviets call the "strategic rear" of the United States would be seen as a sign of U.S. impotence.[7]

It was also the theme of President Reagan's speech on Central America to the Joint Session of Congress in 1983:

> I say to you that tonight there can be no question: the national security of all the Americas is at stake in Central America. If we cannot defend ourselves there we cannot expect to prevail elsewhere. Our credibility would collapse, our alliances would crumble and the safety of our homeland would be put in jeopardy.[8]

Exactly so. Irrespective of a calculus of interest, economic or strategic, the Caribbean basin matters above all as a place in which to demonstrate US power and resolve.

The Caribbean SIEDS are therefore clearly comprehended by and in some instances specifically party to US strategic considerations in the Caribbean. Although small, they are given no special dispensation by virtue of size, political status or developmental constraints. In Washington DC, US defence requirements in the region have been regarded as paramount; sovereignty conditional. The *sui generis* problems of the Caribbean, which are overwhelmingly economic, social and political, are of secondary concern. Nevertheless, it would be wrong to assume they are of no concern at all. A flood of specially commissioned studies and related academic work on the Caribbean basin in the early 1980s pointed to internal factors (not Soviet–Cuban subversion) as the primary cause of instability in the region and recommended urgent attention be given to promoting socioeconomic development and representative democracy throughout the area.[9] The main US response was to launch and sustain the Caribbean Basin Initiative (CBI), an economic recovery programme with trade, investment and aid dimensions. This is not the place to detail the results. The United States government has generally deemed them satisfactory; the beneficiary nations, now including all the SIEDS except Suriname, as less than expected or desired. The economic problems that beset the Commonwealth Caribbean and Suriname at the beginning of the 1980s – low or negative growth rates, high unemployment, acute balance of trade deficits and rising levels of foreign debt – therefore remained in place at the end of the decade, with all this implies for continuing social and economic uncertainty, if not necessarily political instability.

The last caveat is important. Notwithstanding well-founded fears of a 'Central Americanization' of CARICOM as a result of US policy,[10] chronic political instability has generally been avoided. 'Free and fair elections' – the yardstick by which the United States has judged the existence of representative democracy in the region – were a regular feature of the 1980s. The fact that they also, for most of this period and for nearly every country concerned, returned a regime to the right of the one previously in office, was also a welcome relief to the US. It put in power leaders the Reagan Administration felt it could trust and whom it could openly support, notably Edward Seaga in Jamaica, 'Tom' Adams in Barbados and Eugenia Charles in Dominica. They, in turn, sought out and justified closer links with the US in business, politics, the media and in military affairs. A growing interdependence with the United States thus became one of the most significant developments of the decade, tying the Commonwealth Caribbean region more closely to the US than ever before. In reverse, Caribbean questions made their way on to the US domestic policy agenda in respect of two key issues: immigrants and drugs.

Simply to record the dimensions of each is to attest to their significance. Of the three million people who have immigrated to the US from the Caribbean islands alone since 1820, 80 per cent have landed in the last three decades, and over half in the period from 1970, a growing number of which were from the SIEDS. The flow continues unabated, along with an increasing proportion of undocumented illegal immigrants. Miami and New York now contain major concentrations of people of Caribbean origin. Both cities also feature prominently as distribution points in the drug trade which stretches back through the Caribbean to the major source countries in South America and along which some 70 per cent of the cocaine and marijuana entering the United States is thought to travel. The SIEDS are inextricably tied to this as minor producers of marijuana (Belize and Jamaica), way-stations for drug smugglers (especially the Bahamas) and hosts to 'off-shore banks' for convenient money laundering (the Bahamas and the British dependent territories).[11] The 'war on drugs' is now among the most prominent issues in US domestic politics; and international drug trafficking has been designated a national security threat. The 'spill-over' from the Caribbean into the US and vice versa could not be clearer.

The Extra-Regional Powers

Despite formal decolonisation, Europe maintains a significant presence in the Caribbean by virtue of territory, social and cultural legacies, and a wide range of political and economic interests. These are supported by a variety of relations, formal and informal, at transnational, governmental and intergovernmental level, and have come to be valued in recent years by the Caribbean SIEDS as important resources for security and development. Significant effort has therefore gone into preserving links with Europe, resulting in a European profile in the region higher than that which might have been anticipated a decade ago.[12]

This is particularly evident in the economic sphere. The Caribbean SIEDS continue to cultivate trading, investment and aid links with their traditional European partners. Both directly and indirectly through the Lome Conventions, critical support is provided for export agriculture, opportunities for diversification into manufacturing, tourism and services, and a comprehensive network of financial and technical assistance at the national and regional level. Their combined effect is to ameliorate, if not reduce, the vulnerabilities of the Caribbean SIEDS. They are therefore welcome provision. However, in total they are relatively modest in volume and provide no long-term guarantee. Nor is their availability the result of a concerted approach to the Caribbean on the part of the respective metropolitan states or the EC. The links between Europe and the Caribbean characteristically remain vertical and disconnected, running predominantly from the former colonial territory to the historical or contemporary metropole and vice versa. European responsibilities, influence and interests in the region thus remain concentrated and confined: Britain with the Commonwealth Caribbean; the Netherlands with the Netherlands Antilles and Suriname; and France with the Départements Française d'Amérique (DFA).

British involvement in the Commonwealth Caribbean has been renewed in recent years reversing the previous trajectory and expectation of withdrawal. Interests now focus on security, trade, aid, drugs, the dependent territories and Belize. Several of these correspond with US concerns and it is clear that British policy seeks whenever possible to complement that of the United States. British action to combat drug trafficking and money laundering in its dependent territories must be seen in this light, as also should its support for improved police and para-military capabilities in the eastern Caribbean. However, to recognise this is not to discount an important British dimension to policy in its own right, which is especially welcomed by the majority of the SIEDS. This provides a sensitivity to local context and a familiarity of approach which is often lacking in US assistance. The preferred option for military cooperation throughout the Common-wealth Caribbean thus continues to be British. The Bahamas, Barbados, Guyana, Jamaica, Trinidad and the Regional Security

System (RSS) have all benefited in various ways, but especially Belize. The British presence in that country (as a deterrent to possible Guatemalan aggression) is considerable consisting in recent years of an infantry battalion group with appropriate supporting arms and logistical support units, four Harrier ground-attack aircraft, Puma helicopters, Rapier surface-to-air missiles, and a Royal Navy frigate or destroyer permanently on call in the Caribbean.[13] The size and configuration of these forces puts them among the larger extra-regional forces in the Caribbean. It is clear, however, from official pronouncements that Belize constitutes a 'special case' and that a similar British deployment elsewhere in the region is not anticipated.

The Dutch experience to some extent mirrors the British. Having effected the independence of Suriname in 1975 the expectation was of a gradual disengagement from the Netherlands Antilles. This has not proved possible. Nor, given the post-independence traumas of Suriname, has it been feasible to relinquish a concern with that country's affairs. The Netherlands therefore remains physically present in the Caribbean, committed economically, politically and militarily to overseeing the affairs of its Dependencies and, at one remove, Suriname. It does so in as unobtrusive a manner as is possible. The military commitment to the defence of the Netherlands Antilles (under Article 43 of the *Statuut* governing relations between the parties concerned) is discharged through only a token military presence while all military cooperation with Suriname was suspended in the wake of the 1980 coup. Although a Dutch military mission has now returned to Paramaribo it is clear that should military assistance be re-established it will be strictly circumscribed and characteristically modest. It will also be with the understanding and tacit approval of the United States and the neighbouring countries interested in such an arrangement – Brazil, Venezuela and France.[14]

Unlike that of Britain or the Netherlands, the French presence in the Caribbean is regarded as permanent. It is based on two factors. The first is the political status of the DFA as integral parts of France. This provides the rationale for a policy of assimilation and dependence which has led to the integration of nearly every facet of life in the DFA to that of mainland France. The two regions are politically 'one and indivisible' as far as Paris is concerned as well as in the eyes of the greater part of the local population. The legitimacy of the French presence is therefore not currently in question, either in the DFA themselves, or in France, or indeed in the Caribbean as a whole. This provides a firm foundation for the second factor – the geostrategic location of the DFA in relation to mainland France and to French territories elsewhere which allows

France to claim a global military presence. The DFA are conveniently located on the shortest direct route to the French nuclear testing sites in the South Pacific. They are home to a military force up to 9,000 strong with considerable air, naval and ground force capabilities (including the Foreign Legion). But, above all, in the European Space Centre at Kourou, in French Guiana, France controls an important economic and strategic asset. The Centre is ideally located for rocket launching; it has proven commercial significance; and the Ariane space programme permits access to valuable technical knowledge. Its defence is regarded as a national priority; not coincidental to French interest but a vital part of it. In the final analysis, the French presence in the Caribbean is thus linked to its status as a major power and its preference for unilateral action in the region a direct reflection of the DFA's intrinsic importance to France.[15]

Finally, brief note must be taken of the Canadian presence in the Caribbean. For many years policy has accorded a special status and priority to the CARICOM states. An initiative to enhance trade, investment and aid to the region, CARIBCAN, was launched in 1986; outstanding official development assistance debt was forgiven in 1990; and the limited amount of security assistance provided (to the police, the defence forces and, most importantly, the coast guards) increased since the early 1980s.[16] Canada has also maintained a relatively open immigration policy and given diplomatic support to CARICOM priorities in organisations such as the Caribbean Group for Co-operation and Economic Development. The CARICOM states have welcomed this as 'disinterested assistance', that is Canada has no obvious vital interest in the region, so making it seem an ideal donor. However, this consideration also acts to limit Canadian involvement. For example, in the security arena it has declined to support the RSS or provide military assistance to Belize. It has also prudentially distanced itself from military cooperation with Caribbean governments in dispute with the United States. The role Canada plays in the region is thus subject to strict definition and self-limitation. Ottawa will not necessarily take any opportunity to expand its influence or deepen its commitment to the region.

CARICOM and the Caribbean Basin

The most important foreign policy goal of the CARICOM states has been economic development. Regional cooperation among themselves has been largely to this end and has resulted in the creation of a common market; networks of functional cooperation in such areas as health, education, transport and meteorology; and a mechanism for the coordination of foreign policy. Within the CARICOM region, but specific to the smaller states of the eastern Caribbean, an additional body has been created in the Organisation of Eastern Caribbean States (OECS), established by the Treaty of Basseterre in 1981. This provides a common market; a common currency; and a variety of consultative mechanisms, including ones for foreign policy and security.

The existence of these institutions has resulted in the CARICOM countries being generally perceived as sharing common foreign policy positions. They do, in fact, hold much in common and from time to time concert policy in metropolitan capitals where there is a strong CARICOM presence or in selected international organisations such as the ACP and the UN. They also regularly consult on international affairs in the Standing Committee of CARICOM Foreign Ministers and have been active collectively in promoting a number of issues of significance in the international system such as the Law of the Sea Convention and the new international economic order. However, as one of the most experienced diplomats in the region has noted, the CARICOM states do so 'not from the perception of a so-called regional interest but from a close concern with national interest'.[17] The norm for CARICOM states in the formulation and application of foreign policy both inside and outside the region is thus the pursuit of specific national interests through individual state action. The diplomatic infrastructure at home and abroad is designed to reflect this fact above any other.

This singular approach is especially evident in relations between the CARICOM states and their Latin American and Caribbean neighbours. The characteristic pattern is one of selective bilateral relations focused largely on economic questions or highly specific security matters. Relations also tend to be concentrated in only a few states: from the CARICOM side Guyana, Jamaica, Trinidad and Grenada under the PRG; and from the Latin American side Brazil, Cuba, Mexico and Venezuela. Even here, and with the exception of Venezuela, they are of recent origin. There is, in consequence, little sense of continuity or coherence in interaction and relatively little depth. Nor is there much spill-over to be found. Venezuelan diplomacy has had to proceed on the basis of representation in each CARICOM state when a regional approach would have been preferred; while the English-speaking eastern Caribbean has been largely indifferent to the recent conflicts and the search for peace in Central America. A lack of communication abounds on all sides, with misunderstandings arising easily, as over CARICOM support for British action in the Falklands or Latin American suspicion of CARICOM membership in the Commonwealth and the Lome Conventions. In short, there is no natural tendency on the part of either the CARICOM states or their Latin American neighbours to look to each other as neighbours, that is as providers in the first instance of resources, political, economic or military. The most pertinent examples of this in the security arena are that among the CARICOM states only revolutionary Grenada sought close bilateral security ties with a Latin American state (Cuba); while only Trinidad and the Bahamas have become signatories to the Inter-American Treaty of Reciprocal Assistance (Rio Treaty), the major collective security treaty operative in the Americas. It is thus difficult to escape the conclusion that, for the majority of CARICOM states, Latin America is on most counts, certainly security ones, peripheral to their vision and marginal to their concerns.[18]

The only exceptions to this are Cuba and Venezuela. A good deal of suspicion has attached to the foreign policy of the former, but not at the expense of denying Cuba a legitimate interest in Caribbean affairs. This was particularly the case in the mid to late 1970s when Castro's assertion of an 'Afro-Latin' identity for Cuba and his espousal of an active global diplomacy for the Non-Aligned Movement (NAM) coincided with the reformist inclinations of several CARICOM states. However, regime changes in CARICOM, as well as significant Cuban support for revolution in Grenada (and to a more limited extent in Guyana and Suriname), brought about a reassessment of Cuban intentions in the Commonwealth Caribbean in the early 1980s.[19] Diplomatic relations were reduced, technical assistance agreements curtailed, and charges of possible Cuban subversion openly and widely discussed. By the time Grenada was invaded, the Cuban presence in the region was already much diminished and the reputation it had once enjoyed, particularly as a possible development model, was in the process of being reversed. Since then neither Cuba nor CARICOM have deemed it necessary or prudent to restore relations to their former levels, although dialogue between them continues, particularly in regional fora such as the Latin American Economic System and the Caribbean Cooperation and Development Committee of the United Nations Economic Commission for Latin America and the Caribbean.

Venezuela has an economic and security interest in the Caribbean greater than that of any other Latin American mainland state.[20] It pursues an active diplomacy in the region and in recent years it has invested considerable time and effort in winning acceptance, markets and goodwill among the CARICOM states. Venezuela's standing in CARICOM eyes has thus improved, dramatically in some cases in the eastern Caribbean. Nevertheless, elsewhere, particularly in Trinidad and Guyana, doubts remain about Venezuelan motives and long-term commitment to the region. Its relative power *vis-à-vis* CARICOM is also an issue of concern, given that there is still a substantial unresolved territorial claim against Guyana. There is, then, a hesitancy about entering into any deep relationship with Caracas, especially in security matters and especially since government-to-government relations between Venezuela and the CARICOM states remain undeveloped as compared to the dynamic Venezuelan private sector involvement in the region. In sum, Venezuela is welcomed throughout the Commonwealth Caribbean as a commercial presence (which promises to be institutionalised in a free trade area) but not yet as a political partner or potential military ally.

THE THREAT AGENDA

Throughout the 1960s and most of the 1970s the regional security context for the majority of the SIEDS was relatively benign. Major threats to core values were few and confined either to concerns about the preservation of territorial integrity in the cases of Belize, Guyana and several of the multi-island states of the eastern Caribbean; or to the domestic costs of not achieving appropriate levels of development and welfare, particularly in Jamaica and Trinidad. Cuba was not regarded as other than a latent threat and the assistance of the US was only rarely sought in this regard. Indeed, in most instances security was provided by the continued engagement of the extra-regional powers, either through continuing discharge of responsibilities in defence and external affairs or appropriate and varied levels of *ad hoc* provision once independence had been achieved. Military and para-military force levels were correspondingly characteristically low (or embryonic) and public debate on the subject of security, other than in its economic or social dimensions, practically non-existent. Much of this was to be transformed, almost overnight, on 13 March 1979, when 46 lightly armed members of the New Jewel Movement seized power in Grenada in the first successful coup/insurrection in the Commonwealth Caribbean. With this action the perceptions of the majority of the Caribbean SIEDS began to change: security came to be regarded as no longer a question only for military officers and the police but also for politicians. It was to undergo further revision as events redefined the matrix of threat and response throughout the region in the 1980s.

The Experience of the 1980s

The most immediate impact of Grenada was felt in the eastern Caribbean. The new threat scenario was foreshadowed in a

Memorandum of Understanding concluded between Barbados and Trinidad in April 1979 which acknowledged *inter alia* the growing complexity of security problems in the Caribbean and identified 'terrorism, piracy, the use of mercenaries and the introduction into the region of techniques of subversion' as particularly worrying.[21] These themes were to re-emerge in Article 8 of the OECS Treaty concluded in July 1981 which, for the first time in the independent Commonwealth Caribbean, made explicit provision for the establishment of a Defence and Security Committee among member states, the responsibility of which was to coordinate efforts

> for collective defence and the preservation of peace and security against external aggression and for the development of close ties . . . in matters of external defence and security, including measures to combat the activities of mercenaries, operating with or without the support of internal or national elements.

Finally, threats were to be further defined and given explicit effect by the 'Memorandum of Understanding Relating to Security and Military Co-operation' (MOU) concluded between Antigua, Barbados, Dominica, St Lucia and St Vincent in October 1982. This enjoined the signatory parties

> to prepare contingency plans and assist one another on request in national emergencies, prevention of smuggling, search and rescue, immigration control, fisheries protection, customs and excise control, maritime policing duties, protection of off-shore installations, pollution control, natural and other disasters and threats to national security.

After independence St Kitts-Nevis joined in February 1984 and Grenada was admitted in February 1985.

The exclusion of Grenada from the MOU in its early days establishes the real purpose of the MOU and the RSS it created as fear of revolutionary change. The neighbouring SIEDS, particularly the smallest among them, saw themselves as susceptible to take-over or serious public disturbance instigated by, or through the example of, Grenada. As the revolution consolidated itself and as Grenada's ties with Cuba and the USSR became more pronounced, then so the need for a 'loose' collective security system addressing individual vulnerabilities of the smaller neighbouring SIEDS became compelling. However, the RSS was not regarded in itself as a sufficient force to deal with major threats, particularly invasion by other states. In these instances it was to act as a trip-wire, containing a situation until assistance from abroad could be obtained. The prospect for this had been greatly enhanced with the election of Ronald Reagan in 1980. From the outset his administration identified the Caribbean basin as a priority arena and the commitment to a security profile in the eastern Caribbean was signalled in a number of ways, notably in the provision of military assistance to the Barbados Defence Force (established in 1979), the various coast guards (then under consideration) and naval exercises and increased ship visits in the area. The high point of its involvement, however, came with the invasion of Grenada on 25 October 1983. The details of the operation are well known and need not be repeated here.[22] The invasion was carried out at very short notice by some 6,000 US troops and met with only minor resistance from the Grenadian People's Revolutionary Army and Cuban construction workers. The major objectives of the invading forces were therefore quickly secured with comparatively little loss of life. The invasion was welcomed as a 'rescue mission' by the vast majority of Grenadians. It was politically supported by a majority of the Caribbean SIEDS and commanded token military support from Antigua, Barbados, Dominica, Jamaica, St Lucia and St Vincent. It also enjoyed widespread support in the US itself. However, the action was opposed as precipitate by some SIEDS (the Bahamas, Belize, Guyana and Trinidad) and as unnecessary and/or illegal by all the extra-regional powers and most Latin American states. A consensus on US action was therefore not achieved. Neither was it sought. Indeed, the primary lesson drawn from the invasion for the SIEDS and other states in the region was the end of Commonwealth Caribbean 'exceptionality'. By invading Grenada without involving or even informing Britain and its other allies until the last moment the US demonstrated its historical preference for overt unilateral action in support of its interests throughout the Caribbean. Or, as 'Tom' Adams, Prime Minister of Barbados, was to remark before the Royal Commonwealth Society in London shortly afterwards, the Grenada invasion marked 'the watershed year in which the influence of the United States, willy-nilly, came observably to replace that of Great Britain'.[23]

The immediate impact of this new perception was an attempt by Adams to regularise US commitment to the eastern Caribbean through winning its support for the creation of a standing regional defence force. The proposal, as presented to Secretary of State Schultz on his visit to Barbados in February 1984, envisaged a force of 1,800 men, including 700 infantry with the remainder coast guard and support elements. The headquarters would be in Barbados with smaller garrisons of 50 to 90 men on two other islands. The cost would be around US$100 million.

The US reaction to this was unfavourable from the outset, in part because of expense. However, other objections soon began to surface, focusing on the consequences of a needless militarisation of the region when there were many other pressing problems to resolve. James Mitchell, elected as Prime Minister of St Vincent in June 1984, expressed these when he stated that 'the sores of poverty in our region cannot be cured by military therapy . . . the more arms we have available in the country, the greater will be the temptation to solve our problems with a coup'.[24] Other eastern Caribbean leaders, worried by the age-old problem of 'who will guard the guards?' against unwarranted political interference, joined him and by the end of 1984 a consensus had been reached among themselves (and with the US, Britain and Canada) that such a force was not needed. Instead, there was a return to a focus on low-level threats to security – drugs and smuggling, surveillance of waters, protection of fishermen – and the appropriate response to contain them – small para-military forces on each island with a supporting coast guard and a loose-knit RSS.[25]

The next important step in defining threats to the region was taken at the Caribbean colloquium convened in February 1985 as part of the Commonwealth Secretariat's study on the special needs of small states. Compared to the colloquia on the South Pacific and Africa, the debate was wide-ranging and the number of threats identified considerable: territorial (invasion, secession and annexation arising out of boundary disputes); political (coups, internal disturbances including subversion and destabilisation); social (drug trafficking, migration and demographic change); cultural (ethnicity and ideological penetration); economic (open and dependent economies); systemic (geopolitical situation, US hegemony in a variety of forms, and the structure of the international economic system); and environmental (proneness to natural disasters). However, no consensus on the significance or salience of these threats emerged and the summary conclusions of the colloquium did not attempt to establish one. The question as to their relative importance thus remained open, although the tone of the debate suggested less weight should be ascribed to territorial and political threats than to the others, particularly social, economic and systemic threats. The final recommendations of the colloquium reflected this, touching only briefly on traditional security issues (force levels and capabilities) while deliberating at length on appropriate policy-making responses in respect of economic and institutional development, coordinating foreign policies, and the national, regional and international mechanisms needed to give effect to them.[26]

The relevance of this wider agenda for *all* the Caribbean SIEDS was elaborated and endorsed in a conference held in Jamaica in early 1987 'to explore the future security of the small, independent states in the Caribbean region'.[27] This identified a number of threats and vulnerabilities arising from both the geopolitical and the national environment. Of greatest importance to the former was the United States. It was identified as having special security interests in the region and currently an obsessive preoccupation with it. Criticism was also levelled at the concept of the Caribbean basin which, to many, was inadmissible as a framework for policy since it linked the crisis in Central America to the very different experience of the English-speaking Caribbean. Finally, while note was taken of Soviet and Cuban interests in the region, they were not regarded as significant threats as neither were those from the Latin American states, the territorial disputes with Guatemala and Venezuela excepted. Indeed, vulnerabilities were generally recognised as more significant than threats *per se*. The focus was thus on the national environment and the constraints of small size, with consideration given to internal difficulties arising from weak institutional and parliamentary structures; rapidly rising populations; the imperative of structural adjustment; the erosion of national identity; and the recurrence of natural disasters. All of these were examined in depth and the weight of discussion on appropriate response was overwhelmingly directed toward fashioning effective strategies to deal with them. In the course of this the perspective inevitably shifted from east–west rivalries to the north–south divide as constituting the predominant concern of the region. Or as the final conference report put it: 'Until the end of the century, the primary threats to the peace, development and security of the small (Caribbean) states are likely to be internal and related to their dependence and underdevelopment'.[28]

The high measure of convergence obtaining on the salience of economic threats, however, should not be allowed to disguise divergences which were then appearing in the lower ranked military and political dimensions of threat. These were mapped at the time by Ivelaw Griffith who concluded that 'political histories, present political and economic circumstances, and the nature of Caribbean leadership do not permit the definition of a single regional security perception, or even multiple perceptions each marked by unanimity'.[29] Instead, what was emerging was a strong sub-system identification defining threats and response, particularly in the military dimension, in national or sub-regional terms. The OECS, for example, placed a greater premium on potential threats from internal subversion, secession and mercenary action than did the other SIEDS, while Guyana and Belize continued to worry about Venezuelan and Guatemalan claims. The Bahamas, Jamaica and Trinidad all had singular internal security preoccupations as also had Suriname. In short, within the region-wide consensus on socioeconomic vulnerabilities, distinct geostrategic divisions divided CARICOM from itself and prevented the determination of a common security response. This was not new. In June 1983 the Standing Committee of Ministers of Foreign Affairs had reviewed a paper prepared by the CARICOM Secretariat on 'A Scheme for Mutual Assistance' and had appointed a committee of officials to look into the matter further. This committee, after several postponements, met on a single occasion without achieving significant agreement. As of the end of 1992 history appeared to be repeating itself. Notwithstanding the decision of the CARICOM Heads of Government (meeting in scheduled session in July 1990 at the time of the attempted coup in Trinidad) to establish an inter-governmental committee to review existing arrangements on regional security little has transpired other than the occasional meetings of heads of armed forces and police commissioners. From this it may be inferred that military security, if it was indeed a regional priority, was not an urgent one, except when immediate and largely unforeseeable events dictated otherwise.

The Concerns of the 1990s

The foregoing suggests that in the 1990s Caribbean SIEDS will find it difficult to arrive at a common assessment of risk. On the one hand, vulnerabilities will be general with a proportionate effect on all. On the other hand, threats are more likely to be specific to a given situation with a disproportionate effect on some but not others. Nevertheless, six areas emerging from the experience of recent years can expect to command attention and resources: they are regime instability, economic difficulties, environmental hazard, drug abuse, extra-territorial jurisdiction and secession.[30]

Regime Instability. All the SIEDS currently claim to be parliamentary democracies. This form of government is the preferred political system and enjoys widespread legitimacy and almost universal support. All have held elections within the last five years to determine the composition of the legislature and/or executive and in every case such elections have been internationally recognised as free and fair. The key issue therefore lies not in the form of government but in the exercise and transfer of power by the political regime. The latter is not a major problem. Among Third World countries the Commonwealth Caribbean has been unique in the way incumbent governments have yielded to opposition victories at the polls, with only Grenada and Guyana at times excepted.[31] The main question thus relates to government abuse of power and, in particular, treatment of the opposition while in office. The question of size is important here. Governmental pervasiveness and exaggerated personalism is a feature of small states. When combined this can lead to intense partisanship and a lucrative political patronage which rewards governmental supporters handsomely and denies the opposition any role. In the worst cases the opposition can even be branded as 'disloyal' and subject to harassment and persecution. Extreme examples are rare but without much difficulty many lesser instances can be found throughout the Commonwealth Caribbean. These impose implicitly, and on occasion explicitly, low-level threats to democratic practice. By definition, the many forms these take cannot be predicted in advance, although consistent patterns of abuse in recent years in Antigua and Guyana have given, and in the former case still give, cause for concern.

Guyana, along with Suriname, is also the best example among the SIEDS of domestic regime instability through excessive militarisation. In Guyana four separate forces have represented state power: the Guyana Defense Force; the Guyana Police Force; the Guyana National Service; and the Guyana People's Militia. Between 1964, when the Burnham regime took office, and 1984, the year before his death, military and para-military forces grew by 829 per cent to 17,708 (a ratio of one military personnel for every 43 citizens).[32] The various services, however, are ill-equipped and the technology and configuration of the military is inappropriate to meet any sustained attack by Venezuela in the pursuit of its territorial claim. The purpose of the military is thus primarily internal and for many years it was oriented above all to maintaining the ruling party, the People's National Congress (PNC), in power. In the pursuit of this goal military officers have been systematic- ally politicised and the security services deployed to break strikes, intimidate opponents and rig elections. Overt repression, however, has been relatively muted and since the death of Burnham various measures have been taken to professionalise the armed forces and to distance them from direct involvement in politics.[33] The prospect of a coup in defence of the PNC and the Afro-Caribbean constituency it represents has thus diminished, although it cannot be ruled out entirely, particularly if there is widespread unrest in the wake of the recent victory by the opposition at the polls.

This has not proved to be the case in Suriname. The most recent intervention, on Christmas Eve 1990, was but the latest of a long line of coups and attempted coups (nine in all) stretching back to the initial action of 25 February 1980. Military direction and military participation in the government has become routine – institutionalised, in fact, under the provisions of the 1987 constitution which accorded the military a formal role in government and a virtual veto on constitutional change. Military domination also became centralised in the person of Lieutenant-Colonel Desi Bouterse. He saw to it that he was without serious rival, most notoriously through ordering the murder of 15 prominent opponents of the military regime on 8 December 1982 and sanctioning selective repression thereafter. In recent years justification for this policy, in which several hundred people have died or 'disappeared', has been provided by a continuing 'guerrilla' insurgency. This was initiated in 1986 under the leadership of a former soldier and Bouterse bodyguard, Ronnie Brunswijk. The political aims of his self-proclaimed Jungle Commando were never clear as neither is the strength of his forces nor his power of command over them. Military action has been confined largely to eastern Suriname, close to the border with French Guiana, and has occasioned serious ethnic animosities in so far as counter-insurgency operations by the largely creole Surinamese armed forces and their Amerindian allies have been directed mainly against the ethnically distinct Bush Negroes who provide the backbone of Brunswijk's support. Attempts at mediation in 1988 and 1989, involving the churches and the French prefect in French Guiana, secured an agreement to end the conflict but at various times it has proved unacceptable to Bouterse or to Brunswijk (or to his supporters who have initiated action on their own). The insurgency thus sputters on as isolated acts of violence and lawlessness in the interior and as rationale for the expanded role of the security forces in society as a whole.[34]

Note must also be taken of the recent terrorist action cum coup in Trinidad. Not because the country is particularly at risk but as an example of how an unpredictable action can suddenly emerge out of a complex mix of ethnic, religious and economic factors.[35] The 'coup' began on 27 July 1990, when 114 members of a fundamentalist black Muslim sect, the Jamaat-al-Muslimeen, stormed the parliament building and TV station in Port of Spain, taking as hostage around 40 people, including the Prime Minister and seven of his ministers. The violence of their action was unprecedented in Trinidad, with 23 people killed and nearly 250 injured in the assault and subsequent looting of the business district. The coup itself, however, was quickly contained by the army which immediately deployed in strength to surround the Jamaat and disperse the looters. The situation was eventually brought to an end after six days of negotiations when the rebel leader, Abu Bakr, a former policeman, secured an 'amnesty' for himself and his followers in exchange for the release of the hostages. Notwithstanding this outcome, on their surrender to the armed forces all were arrested and charged with a variety of offences. They were then held in custody until released on appeal in mid-1992 on the grounds that the 'amnesty' granted to them was indeed legal.

Finally, allegations of international subversion have been made from time to time. These have largely been directed at Cuba, Libya and left-wing groups throughout the region, although they have also been levelled at the United States by Grenada, Guyana and Jamaica. Nearly all are unproven, but they have led to the suspension of diplomatic relations or the withdrawal of diplomatic personnel, most notably in respect of Cuban diplomats assigned to Jamaica in 1980 and Grenada and Suriname in 1983. Libya is also currently under suspicion because of its known links to the Jamaat-al-Muslimeen in Trinidad and its continuing diplomatic presence and past association with Bouterse in Suriname.

Economic Difficulties. The present economic difficulties of the Caribbean SIEDS have their roots in the crisis of the early 1980s. This was particularly severe in Jamaica, Trinidad and Guyana. In all three countries development priorities established since independence were reversed as governments sought to implement programmes of structural adjustment in cooperation with the IMF and the World Bank. These specify, *inter alia*, removal of price controls and subsidies on basic items; regressive dismantling of protective tariff regimes; frequent devaluations to raise the price of imports and stimulate comparative advantage in exports; abolition of state trading monopolies and the sale of state-owned companies to the private sector; and reduction in the cost and size of the public service through forced redundancy and cuts in wages and salaries. The deliberate intent and effect of such measures is to reduce real income and to shift the burden of adjustment in favour of entrepreneurship and capital at the expense of labour and the socially disadvantaged. Since the latter are in the majority, a 'threat' of widespread political protest accompanies such policies. So also do economic and social threats, the potential of which are only just being acknowledged. For example, in recent years there has been the rapid growth of an 'informal' economic sector, thriving in the 'grey' area between legality and illegality, and living off services rendered in respect of money laundering, capital flight, exchange rate manipulation, governmental favour, corruption, and unethical business and professional practice. More directly, crime has been encouraged, through larceny, drug abuse and prostitution, as those without employment or much hope of it make a living in societies where there is no social security benefit net. None of the above has yet reached crisis proportions, but in so far as structural adjustment programmes fail to reach their goals, or prove to be unexpectedly protracted, or remain without a compensating welfare dimension, the threat of mounting social and economic disorder rises proportionately.

This is compounded by a growing fear of global marginalisation. Recent and anticipated changes in the international economic system are expected to impact negatively on the Caribbean. Among trends which can be readily identified are the globalisation of markets for goods, services, capital and technology which threaten the region's wage cost and location propinquity advantages in relation to the North American market; the strengthening of economic blocs in North America (the 1992 North American Free Trade Agreement) and western Europe (the single European market at the end of 1992) which threaten access to traditional markets for 'uncompetitive' agricultural export staples, manufactured goods, and services; the emergence of the Pacific rim as a 'pole of growth' and locus of new investment which threatens to marginalise the Caribbean regionally in relation to new dynamic business opportunities; the transformation of the centrally planned economies of eastern Europe into market economies which threatens trade and more worryingly aid diversion; and the failure of the international community collectively to deal with the problem of Third World debt, which in the case of the Caribbean SIEDS exposes the vulnerabilities of their small trade dependent economies and threatens debilitating service payments and consequent diminished growth. Set out like this the issues are alarming – sufficiently so, in fact, to prompt a warning from the Prime Minister of Trinidad and Tobago to the Tenth Conference of the CARICOM Heads of Government in July 1989 that, unless something was done to address the situation, 'the Caribbean could be in danger of becoming a backwater, separated from the main current of human advance into the twenty-first century . . .'.[36] In other words, the viability of the region as an independent entity in itself could be at stake; with the attendant loss of economic autonomy a real possibility as the individually impoverished states of the area become increasingly driven to function as mere off-shore platforms of the United States.

Environmental Hazard. The single greatest environmental threat in the Caribbean is the regular passage of hurricanes through the region. All the island SIEDS are at risk and in recent years hurricanes of exceptional severity have been recorded: in 1980 (Hurricane Allan), 1988 (Hurricane Gilbert) and 1989 (Hurricane Hugo). In all these cases loss of life has been minimised through effective monitoring and emergency service procedures, but loss of capital remains immense. In St Lucia, following Hurricane Allan, this was calculated as equivalent to 89 per cent of GNP; in Jamaica, following Hurricane Gilbert, at one billion US dollars (a sum in excess of annual foreign exchange earnings); and region-wide, following Hurricane Hugo, some four billion US dollars. Especially worrying are scientific reports that hurricanes may be increasing in frequency and intensity. If this is so, then many island SIEDS are ill-prepared to stand their effects since modern infrastructure, housing and agricultural practice has proven to be less resilient than traditional forms and techniques.

Other well-known natural threats in the Caribbean relate to periodic droughts (Antigua), volcanic eruption (St Vincent), and soil erosion (Barbados and Jamaica). A more recent threat arises from the prospective effect of global warming. Should this happen and associated sea level rises occur, then Guyana, in particular, is at risk since 90 per cent of its population and most of its agriculture is concentrated on a narrow coastal strip, much of which is below sea level. Suriname may also in part be affected. Indeed, the question of 'sustainable development' has recently been essayed as an important issue for all the Caribbean SIEDS. The example of Haiti, where environmental degradation is immense and in parts seemingly irreversible, serves as a grim warning of the essentially 'fragile' nature of Caribbean ecosystems and the need to husband resources accordingly.[37]

Finally, the use of the Caribbean as a major oil refining and trans-shipment centre poses threats to the marine environment through oil spillage, refinery discharge and tanker collision. Incidents of all three have been reported and in some instances extensive damage has resulted. It also has the potential to impact negatively on the tourist trade since many of the refineries and transshipment facilities are close to major tourist beaches.

Illegal Drugs. The drugs problem in the Caribbean is now regarded as the single most important threat to the security of the SIEDS. It has three primary manifestations: the SIEDS as suppliers; as way-stations on drug trafficking routes; and as targets for drug abuse and associated crime.

The only SIEDS cultivating drugs on any scale have been Belize and Jamaica. At its peak in 1984 the former was producing some 1,000 tonnes of marijuana a year; the latter at its peak in 1986 just below 2,000 tonnes a year. Nearly all was for export to the United States. Changes in the pattern of demand there, plus successful crop eradication programmes in both countries, have led to a considerable fall in production so that in 1988 Belize was estimated as producing only 120 tonnes and Jamaica 405 tonnes a year. This represented less than four per cent of total production from the main source countries (Mexico, Colombia and the United States),[38] which suggests that the Caribbean SIEDS in total (including Guyana and Trinidad) are essentially marginal producers facing mounting difficulties in maintaining production against increasingly successful methods of detection and eradication.

The real importance of the SIEDS lies not in the production but in the distribution of drugs. They act as valuable transshipment points for marijuana and cocaine produced in Brazil and Colombia. The most implicated of the SIEDS in the past has been the Bahamas. It has 700 islands, 2,000 cays and a surface area of 10,000 square miles. It faces a Florida coastline of 1,197 miles. The volume of small craft and light aircraft traffic make the islands and the coastline impossible to patrol effectively. It is therefore estimated that, despite continual seizures of drugs, some 75–90 per cent of the flow in recent years has passed undetected. The problem of detection is also confounded by continually changing methods and location. In the past light aircraft flying direct to the US were much favoured, involving the use of refuelling stops in Jamaica, the Caicos Islands and the Bahamas. While these still continue, a higher rate of detection has stimulated a switch to shipping, using either 'mother ships' discharging offshore or containers on established shipping routes. The latter is focused on Puerto Rico and has inexorably led to the involvement of the neighbouring Dependencies and SIEDS.[39] The drug network in the Caribbean is therefore spreading eastwards and southwards adding Barbados, Trinidad, Guyana and Suriname to the established networks centred on the Bahamas, Jamaica and Belize. The traffickers are also targeting new markets, especially in Europe where cocaine seizures doubled in 1990 as against 1989, so multiplying the problem and creating the need for co-ordination of detection (particularly at airports and open points of entry such as St Maarten in the Netherlands Antilles).

The growing problem of drug abuse in the SIEDS has only recently been acknowledged by their governments. Hitherto the main issue has been crime and corruption, especially the latter. Government ministers have been implicated or found guilty of drug trafficking in Antigua, the Bahamas, Belize, Jamaica, Suriname and Trinidad; as have an increasing number of officials, including senior security service personnel in the customs, immigration, armed forces and the police. The most serious recent incident concerns Antigua. In this instance the head of the Antigua Defence Force, Lieutenant-Colonel Clyde Walker, and the son of the Prime Minister, Vere Bird Junior, himself a minister, were dismissed in the wake of a judicial enquiry which established they had planned to use the Antigua Defence Force as cover for the establishment of a security training school for mercenaries and irregular forces; and jointly acted to supply weapons to the Colombian drug cartel using Antigua as a 'cut-out' and transit point.[40] Finally, negative images surrounding drug abuse and trafficking have begun to have an adverse impact on tourism, where there has been considerable publicity around the growing incidence of drug-related attacks on visitors to the islands, and on trade. The costs borne in the latter case can be very high. In Jamaica several major shipping lines have interrupted or suspended services as a result of 'exemplary' fines levied in the US following the discovery of drugs in containers, whilst the national airline, Air Jamaica, has been repeatedly targeted as a carrier and has been fined some US$ 37 million between 1989 and 1991 for illegal drugs discovered on its aircraft in the United States.

Extra-Territorial Jurisdiction. This is a fast-growing threat and arises from the security concerns of the United States. The most recent manifestations have been the measures taken in 1992 by President Bush and the US Congress to tighten the blockade on Cuba, isolating it commercially within the Caribbean and denying neighbouring SIEDS (and local subsidiaries of US companies) from developing economically profitable links with the country. To date, however, extra-territoriality has been invoked mainly with regard to the involvement of the Caribbean in drug trafficking and associated offshore activities of various sorts. In an attempt to combat the former directly the United States has greatly extended its juridical basis for intervention. The 1980 Marijuana on the High Seas Act gives US law-and-order agencies (particularly the coast guard) authority to intercept any vessel, anywhere in the world, if the intention is to take cargo to the US. Vessels in the Caribbean and the Gulf of Mexico are regularly boarded and searched on this basis. The extra-territorial principle was further strengthened in 1986 with the Anti-Drug Abuse Act which permits indictment in the US of foreigners who have been allegedly conspiring to import drugs to the US mainland. Under this provision General Noriega, the former President of Panama, has been imprisoned in Florida and Sir Lynden Pindling, a long-standing former Prime Minister of the Bahamas, placed under suspicion from 1986 to 1988. It has also alarmed Commonwealth Caribbean leaders who at the Heads of Government meeting in Antigua in July 1988 resolved to send a letter to President Reagan expressing 'deep concern' at 'attempts to extend domestic United States authority into the neighbouring countries of the

Region without regard for the sovereignty and independent legal systems of those countries'.[41]

Notwithstanding such protests, extra-territoriality has increased, particularly in respect of enhanced financial surveillance of the Caribbean's many offshore financial centres. These are to be found in Anguilla, Aruba, Antigua, the Bahamas, Barbados, Belize, the British Virgin Islands, the Cayman Islands, Dominica, Grenada, Montserrat, the Netherlands Antilles, St Lucia, St Vincent and the Turks and Caicos Islands in the form of banks, casinos, tax havens and company and shipping registers. Their number and their success have attracted, among others, the attention of the United States Inland Revenue Service and the Drug Enforcement Agency in an attempt to defeat tax evasion and combat drug trafficking. The latter, in particular, has become a major objective since it is clear that such facilities provide opportunities for money laundering running into billions of US dollars each year.[42] The US has sought to counter this in various ways. The British government has been persuaded to exercise closer financial supervision in its Dependent Territories, especially over Anguilla and Montserrat, and to impose on them disclosure treaties with the United States. The SIEDS have also been pressed to conclude exchange of information agreements with the US and, where they have resisted, as in the cases of Antigua and the Bahamas, considerable pressures have been brought to bear, for example automatic exclusion from certain benefits in the CBI. But US intervention has also gone further – embracing the conduct of 'sting' operations in the Bahamas without the knowledge or consent of the government; pressure on Caribbean governments to allow US agencies to select the local personnel for, and indeed to participate in the planning and operations of, Drug Enforcement Units; and exercise of the right of 'hot pursuit' of suspected drug traffickers in territorial waters. The sovereignty of Caribbean SIEDS has thus to some extent been compromised. It has also been deliberately set aside or put at risk in other offshore ventures such as freeports and export processing zones (where international corporations can be vested with control over security and labour relations) and offshore medical centres. In respect of the latter it must not be forgotten that one of the main reasons given by the Reagan administration to justify its invasion of Grenada was an alleged threat to several hundred US students attending the offshore medical school on the island.

Secession. The British colonial practice of separate administration and individual decolonisation of the islands of the Caribbean (as well as the phenomenon of insularism) has left a legacy of actual or potential secession in the region. The most publicised to date has been that of Anguilla from the Associated State of St Kitts–Nevis–Anguilla in 1967–69, which subsequently involved the use of 'invading' British forces to restore direct administration and the eventual return of the island to British colonial rule in 1981. Other islands, fearful of such a possibility, have sought to anticipate such difficulties, either through providing a measure of devolution – Antigua in respect of Barbuda and Trinidad in respect of Tobago – or the opportunity for constitutional separation should it prove necessary – Nevis in respect of St Kitts. The threat of secession has thereby been lessened, if not entirely removed from the agenda. Indeed, the last serious incidence of this was in December 1979 when a small group of Rastafarians seized control of Union Island in St Vincent. In this case authority was quickly restored by local forces with the assistance of a small detachment of the Barbados Defence Force (BDF).

THE CARIBBEAN RESPONSE

The response of the Caribbean SIEDS to the threat agenda outlined above has been concentrated for most part in two areas. One is a specific security response involving the development and deployment of military and para-military capabilities. The other is a complementary diplomatic practice designed to contain or on occasion resolve the threat in question. Only at the end of the 1980s has there been the recognition of a need for a broader response appropriate to new threats and a widening agenda.

Military and Para-Military Capabilities

The largest and best-equipped military forces are to be found in Guyana, Jamaica, Suriname and Trinidad. In each country there is a regular army in excess of 2,000 personnel (5,000 for Guyana), a small coast guard (except for Trinidad where it is 600 strong), and a small air support wing. The main function of each force (including Guyana) is internal security. In the cases of Jamaica and Trinidad, additional support is provided by an armed police force; and in Guyana and Suriname, by armed police, a militia and several intelligence services. The ratio of the armed forces to the population is low (Guyana excepted) and while military spending has increased in recent years it is characteristically modest (except for Suriname). The Bahamas, Belize, Barbados and Antigua also maintain armed forces separate from the police. In the Bahamas it comprises a coast guard some 700 strong and a small air wing; in Belize an army of approximately 700 with a small maritime and air transport wing; in Barbados a regular force of 300 divided between an army and a coast guard; and in Antigua an army of 90 men. The army in Belize and the coast guard in the Bahamas are oriented toward external threats, although inevitably there is an internal security dimension to their work. The military forces in Antigua and Barbados perform dual functions – internal security and assignment to the RSS. In the remaining SIEDS only para-military forces are available. They consist of military trained Special Service Units (SSUs) in the police in each island (including Barbados) and an expanding coast guard presence. The SSU typically consists of up to 80 men trained in internal security duties. The coast guard comprises an operational base and at least one fast patrol-boat in each country. The SSUs and the coast guard, although under national control, are integral parts of the RSS.[43]

The RSS remains the only example of routine military cooperation among the SIEDS. The core of the system is a Central Liaison Office in Barbados which provides a number of services for member states including planning, intelligence and training. Since 1985 it has staged an annual exercise in each member state in turn. Jamaica, and latterly Trinidad, have participated in these as have Britain and the United States. The RSS has accordingly gained military credibility, although there is political resistance to upgrading the existing MOU to the status of a formal treaty. A preference for a low-profile and essentially *ad hoc* response to threat thus remains.[44] At the same time the benefits of closer security cooperation are beginning to make themselves felt. This is not only among the RSS but also in the larger SIEDS. The recent 'coup' attempt in Trinidad has acted as a catalyst here, especially when it is recalled that units from the armed forces of Antigua, Barbados, Guyana and Jamaica were deployed for one month in Trinidad in supporting roles in the aftermath of the coup.

Support for enhanced military capabilities has also come from abroad. The PRG in Grenada, the Burnham regime in Guyana and the military in Suriname sought military aid from the socialist bloc in the early 1980s. This, however, has very much been the exception. Security assistance in the SIEDS as a whole has overwhelmingly been provided by the US, Britain and Canada.[45] The US has concentrated its programmes in Jamaica, Belize and the RSS. From 1980 through 1987 these countries received US$ 53.1 million in direct military assistance and US$ 645 million in security related development assistance.[46] These figures were unprecedented and marked a considerable expansion of US interests in security in the SIEDS which had hitherto been confined almost exclusively to Jamaica. However, in 1988 and subsequently US support has dropped steeply as the US assessment of an external threat to the Caribbean has diminished. This has had the effect of highlighting British and Canadian assistance which has greatly increased in recent years. Britain has concentrated on providing training, loan service personnel, and logistic and financial support, especially in Belize and for the RSS. Canada has emphasised training, especially of the various coast guards. Both have also provided police training programmes in the Caribbean Regional Police Training Centre and, in particular, to post-1983 Grenada. The military assistance programmes of all three countries have therefore been comprehensive and to a degree complementary.

Diplomacy as a Security Resource

Diplomacy has been utilised on a number of occasions to promote security. The most effective examples are those of Guyana and Belize in respect of preservation of their territorial integrity. Guyana has won the unconditional support of the Commonwealth, the UN and the NAM in the dispute with Venezuela which lays claim to some five-eighths of Guyana's territory. It has brought the matter before the UN and the NAM, seriously embarrassing Venezuela in the process, and has won support in the Organisation of American States (OAS) as a result of vigorous lobbying on its behalf by CARICOM. The consequence of this has been the gradual recognition by Venezuela that its claim is entertained by very few and that it can only be pursued with great difficulty. It has also recognised that confrontation and denunciation serve it less well than negotiation. Accordingly, the claim is now the subject of quiet diplomacy. By the agreement of both parties it has been referred to the UN Secretary-General to mediate. He, in turn, has appointed Alister McIntyre, the current Vice-Chancellor of the University of the West Indies, as his personal representative in this matter. A resolution of the dispute favourable to Guyana may therefore be in sight.

Much of the above applies also to Belize, the entirety of which is claimed by Guatemala. Its independence is recognised *de facto* by the Commonwealth, the UN, the NAM and the OAS. It too has sought to 'internationalise' the dispute by bringing it before organisations in which Guatemala is a member. However, Guatemala has not proved to be as susceptible to this tactic as has Venezuela. Neither has it proved to be as responsive to dialogue. Talks between both countries have broken down on a number of occasions and in each instance have been renewed only on the basis of a fresh mandate. Little progress has thus been made and the dispute remains at an impasse. Nevertheless, it must be apparent to Guatemala that annexation is no longer a tolerable option. Accordingly, a renewed search for a diplomatic solution within developing functional contacts can be anticipated.

Elsewhere, diplomacy as a specific security resource has been directed at two sets of actors. One is toward the extra-regional powers. Britain and Canada (and to a lesser extent the EC) have been lobbied to maintain a presence in the region and to impress upon the US that peace, security and development in the Caribbean is a continuing commitment and not a contingent one. The other is within the region itself. Here the record is mixed. Within CARICOM some progress has been made toward defining a security community, however partial it is and hedged about with qualification it may be. Outside this, movement has been slow, even negative. The refusal of all but Trinidad and the Bahamas to adhere to the Rio Treaty has already been noted. Another example is hesitancy over joining Venezuela and other Latin American states in promoting the Caribbean as a 'zone of peace' despite a measure of verbal commitment to it.[47] The issue here is clearly the fear of being party to a clash of interests between the US and Latin America. To date, the Caribbean SIEDS as a whole have regarded the former as paramount. The new security agenda that is emerging, however, places a greater premium on cooperation with other Caribbean basin states than hitherto, especially in respect of drug trafficking, environmental pollution and extra-territorial jurisdiction. A new identity of interests and an expanding security relationship with Latin America may therefore be in the making.

The 1980s have thus provided a security practice for all the Caribbean SIEDS where before there was little experience and in some cases virtually none. This has given rise to most of the SIEDS acquiring a military capability, but not a disproportionate one; to expansion of regional military cooperation, but one that stops well short of formal treaty arrangements; and to the continued engagement of extra-regional powers in security provision, particularly Britain and Canada. Experience also points to diplomacy as a resource, both in a regional and a global context. Indeed, this is the most promising area in which to build future security provision. This is explicitly recognised, if not developed, in the recently published *Report of the West Indian Commission*. Here suggestions are advanced for pooling resources and coordinating policy guidelines in response to a range of threats and emergency situations; for establishing a regional security service in the form of an officer corps (in the armed forces and the police) who can expect to move from force to force; and for creative thinking within the region which goes beyond the Caribbean in finding a global solution to the vulnerabilities of small states in general.[48] The experience of the

1980s demonstrates that none of this will be easy to realise. Nevertheless, there are some grounds for hope that, with the proper encouragement, a momentum impelling regional solutions to problems of security could be set in train and beyond this the international system itself could be engaged in developing security regimes appropriate to the special needs of the SIEDS.

NOTES

1. T.D. Anderson, *Geopolitics of the Caribbean: Ministates in a Wider World* (New York, 1984), 2.
2. J. Braveboy-Wagner, *The Caribbean in World Affairs: The Foreign Policies of the English-Speaking States* (Boulder, 1989), 25.
3. The literature on US strategic interests in the Caribbean is extensive. The most useful sources consulted were L. Schoultz, *National Security and United States Policy toward Latin America* (Princeton, 1987); D. Ronfeldt, *Geopolitics, Security and U.S. Strategy in the Caribbean Basin* (Santa Monica, 1983); and H. Garcia Muniz, *La Estrategia de Estados Unidos y la Militarization del Caribe* (Rio Piedras, Puerto Rico, 1988).
4. For details of bases throughout the Caribbean see H. Garcia Muniz, *Decolonization, Demilitarization and Denuclearization in the Caribbean*, Florida International University Latin American and Caribbean Center Dialogue No. 131 (Miami, 1989).
5. For details see P. Sutton, 'The Caribbean as a focus for strategic and resource rivalry' in P. Calvert (ed.), *The Central American Security System: North–South or East–West?* (Cambridge, 1988), 18–44.
6. See M.C. Desch, 'Turning the Caribbean Flank: Sea-lane vulnerability during a European war', *Survival*, Nov.–Dec. 1987, 528–51; and Schoultz, *National Security and United States Policy toward Latin America*, 191–222.
7. US National Bipartisan Commission on Central America, *Report of the National Bipartisan Commission on Central America* (Washington DC, 1984), 93.
8. Address to the Joint Session of Congress, *Vital Speeches of the Day*, Vol.XLIX, No.15, 15 May 1983.
9. See in particular J. Greene and B. Scowcroft, *Western Interests and U.S. Policy Options in the Caribbean Basin*, Report of The Atlantic Council's Working Group on the Caribbean Basin (Boston, 1984).
10. See H.M. Erisman, 'The Caricom States and US Foreign Policy: The Danger of Central Americanization', *Journal of Interamerican Studies and World Affairs*, 31, 3 (1989), 141–82.
11. For details see J.E. Meason, 'War At Sea: Drug Interdiction in the Caribbean', *Journal of Defense and Diplomacy* (June 1988), 7–13; and A.P. Maingot, 'Laundering the Gains of the Drug Trade: Miami and Caribbean Tax Havens', *Journal of Interamerican Studies and World Affairs*, 30, 2&3 (1988), 166–87.
12. This is the general theme of P. Sutton (ed.), *Europe and the Caribbean* (London, 1991).
13. For details see Major-General E. Fursdon, 'The British, the Caribbean and Belize', *Journal of Defense and Diplomacy* (June 1988), 39–41; and A.J. Payne, 'The Belize Triangle: Relations with Britain, Guatemala and the United States', *Journal of Interamerican Studies and World Affairs*, 32, 1 (1990), 119–35.
14. See, in particular, P. Meel, 'Money Talks, Morals Vex: The Netherlands and the Decolonization of Suriname, 1975–90', *European Review of Latin American and Caribbean Studies*, 48 (1990), 75–98; and G. Oostindie and R. Hofte, 'The Netherlands and the Dutch Caribbean: Dilemmas of Decolonisation' in Sutton, *Europe and the Caribbean*, 71–98.

15. See R. Menu, 'La France, Puissance Caraibe', *Defense Nationale* (Aout–Septembre 1988), 99–108.
16. See, in particular, S. Baranyi and E. Dosman, 'Canada and the Security of the Commonwealth Caribbean' in A.T. Bryan, J.E. Greene and T.M. Shaw (eds.), *Peace, Development and Security in the Caribbean: Perspectives to the Year 2000* (London, 1990), 102–25.
17. L. Searwar, 'Foreign Policy Decision-Making in the Commonwealth Caribbean', *Caribbean Affairs*, 1, 1 (1988), 63.
18. See, in particular, A. Serbin and A. Bryan (eds.), *Vecinos Indiferentes: El Caribe de habla inglesa y America Latina* (Caracas, 1990).
19. The most informative account of Cuban interest in the Caribbean basin at this time is J.I. Dominguez, 'Cuba's Relations with Caribbean and Central American Countries' in R. Reading and A. Adelman (eds.), *Confrontation in the Caribbean Basin: International Perspectives on Security, Sovereignty and Survival* (Pittsburgh, 1984), 165–203.
20. See A. Serbin (ed.), *Venezuela y las Relaciones Internacionales en la Cuenca del Caribe* (Caracas, 1987).
21. *Caribbean Contact*, June 1979, 10–11.
22. See P. Dunn and B. Watson (eds.), *American Intervention in Grenada: The Implications of Operation 'Urgent Fury'* (Boulder, 1985); and M. Adkin, *Urgent Fury* (London, 1989).
23. Speech before the Royal Commonwealth Society, London, 9 Dec. 1983.
24. In an interview with G. Brana-Shute, 'An Eastern Caribbean Centrist', *Caribbean Review*, 4, 4 (1985), 28.
25. See United States House of Representatives, *The English-Speaking Caribbean: Current Conditions and Implications for US Policy*, Report by the Congressional Research Service of the Proceedings of a Workshop held December 11 1984, Hearings, Subcommittee on Western Hemisphere Affairs, Committee on Foreign Affairs, 99th Congress, 1st Session, 13 Sept. 1985.
26. 'Commonwealth Colloquium on the Special Needs of Small States: Caribbean Region', Unpublished Main Report, plus Conclusions and Recommendations (Nassau, Bahamas, 7–9 Feb. 1985).
27. See L. Searwar, *Peace, Development and Security in the Caribbean Basin: Perspectives to the Year 2000* (Ottawa, 1987). The conference papers were subsequently published in Bryan et al., *Peace, Development and Security in the Caribbean*.
28. Searwar, *Peace, Development and Security*, 21.
29. Military threats were terrorism, civil war, US intervention, Cuban intervention, mercenary action – all ranked nil or low; political threats were factionalism, secession, US destabilisation, Cuban destabilisation, Venezuelan hegemony – the first two ranked high and the other three low; and economic threats were drugs, foreign debt, economic system failure, brain drain – all ranked high or very high. See I.L. Griffith, 'Image as Reality: The Security Perceptions of English Caribbean Elites', Paper presented to the Fourteenth Annual Conference of the Caribbean Studies Association, Barbados, 23–26 May 1989.
30. The subjects are similar to a recent listing by A.N.R. Robinson, Prime Minister of Trinidad and Tobago: 'The threat to the security of the Commonwealth Caribbean does not emanate from external military intervention. The real threat arises from the internal sources of social instability, the migration of skills and expertise, the debilitating effects of unaided structural adjustment and diversification programmes, natural disasters, the pollution and spoilation of the environment, and the plague of illegal drug trafficking'. Speech on 13 April 1989, as reported in *Caribbean Insight*, 12, 5 (1989), 5.
31. This theme is developed in P. Sutton, 'Constancy, Change and Accommodation: The Distinct Tradition of the Commonwealth Caribbean' in J. Mayall and A.J. Payne (eds.), *The Fallacies of Hope: The Post-colonial Record of the Commonwealth Third World* (Manchester and New York, 1991), 106–28.
32. G.K. Danns, 'The Role of the Military in the National Security of Guyana' in A.H.

Young and D. Phillips (eds.), *Militarization in the Non-Hispanic Caribbean* (Boulder, 1986), 113.

33. For an evaluation of the post-Burnham military in Guyana, see I. Griffith, 'The Military and the Politics of Change in Guyana', *Journal of Interamerican Studies and World Affairs*, 33, 2 (1991), 141–73.

34. The record of the military in Suriname is dissected by P. Meel, 'The March of Militarisation in Suriname' in A.J. Payne and P.K. Sutton (eds.), *Modern Caribbean Politics* (Baltimore, 1993), 125–46.

35. The background to and details of the coup are given in S. Ryan, *The Muslimeen Grab for Power: Race, Religion and Revolution in Trinidad and Tobago* (Port of Spain, 1991); and a special issue of *Caribbean Quarterly*, 37, 2 & 3 (1991).

36. Cited in The West Indian Commission (Chairman: Sir S. Ramphal), *Let All Ideas Contend* (Bridgetown, Barbados, 1990), 6.

37. See C. Kimber, 'Changing Caribbean Ecosystems', Paper presented to the Conference on Alternatives for the 1990s Caribbean, University of London, 9–11 Jan. 1991. On the specific problems of the small islands of the eastern Caribbean, see the study by The Caribbean Conservation Association and The Island Resources Foundation, *Environmental Agenda For The 1990s: A Synthesis of the Eastern Caribbean Country Environmental Profile Series* (Barbados and US Virgin Islands, 1991).

38. Figures from A.B. Wrobleski, 'Global Narcotics Cooperation and Presidential Certification', *Current Policy No. 1165*, United States Department of State, Bureau of Public Affairs (Washington DC, 1989).

39. See the informative special reports 'Cocaine War in the Caribbean' carried in The *San Juan Star* (Puerto Rico), 28–31 Aug. 1988.

40. For details see L. Blom-Cooper, *Guns for Antigua: Report of the Commission of Inquiry into the Circumstances Surrounding the Shipment of Arms from Israel to Antigua and Transshipment on 24 April 1989 En Route to Colombia* (London, 1990).

41. *Caribbean Insight*, 11, 8 (1988), 2. See also D. Nina, 'Extraterritorial Jurisdiction: Implications of US Drug-Control Policies for the Caribbean Basin', Paper presented to the Caribbean Societies Seminar, University of London, 16 Oct. 1990.

42. The figures are officially estimated by US sources at 5–15 billion US dollars. See R. Sanders, 'Narcotics, Corruption and Development in the Caribbean: The Problems of the Smaller Islands', Paper presented to the Symposium on Narcotics, Centre for Caribbean Studies, University of Warwick, 10–11 July 1989.

43. Figures taken from the International Institute for Strategic Studies, *The Military Balance 1989–1990* (London, 1989), and interviews in Washington DC in May 1989 and London in March 1990.

44. This policy was confirmed in a review of the RSS undertaken in 1988 and presented to the OECS Heads of Government in November 1988. Interview: London, March 1990.

45. US military assistance to Guyana was suspended in the early 1980s and none has yet been provided to Suriname. Arms in both countries have been acquired from a variety of sources, including Brazil.

46. The figures for direct military assistance are (US$ mil.): Jamaica – 24.6; Belize – 2.2; RSS – 26.3. Calculated from US Department of Defense, *Foreign Military Construction Sales and Military Assistance Facts, as of September 30, 1989* (Washington DC, 1989). The totals for security related assistance (Economic Support Funds) are (US$ mil.): Jamaica – 409.8; Belize – 21.3; and RSS (1981–86 only and including special assistance to Grenada) – 213.9.

47. The concept is explored at length in A. Serbin, *El Caribe: Zona De Paz?* (Caracas, 1989).

48. The West Indian Commission, *Time For Action* (Bridgetown, Barbados, 1992), 471–2.

The Failure of the Abu Bakr Coup: The Plural Society, Cultural Traditions and Political Development in Trinidad

BISHNU RAGOONATH

At about 6.30 on the evening of Friday 27 July 1990, Yasin Abu Bakr, the leader of the Jamaat Al Muslimeen, announced on Trinidad and Tobago television that the government was overthrown. The population of Trinidad and Tobago (hereafter referred to as Trinidad) looked on with disbelief, for such insurrection seemed neither probable nor possible in easy-going, fete-loving Trinidad. But the impossible had happened. Harsh austerity measures and a reduction of social programmes, designed to satisfy World Bank and IMF conditionalities, had caused the National Alliance for Reconstruction (NAR) government to lose popular support. Capitalising on the alienation of the public generated by the government's economic and social policies, Abu Bakr believed that the masses would support his attempted coup. However, this belief could not have been further from reality for two reasons. Firstly, Trinidad's political culture and level of political development ensured that the citizenry would not take up arms against the government. Secondly, and more importantly, even if there had been support for the overthrow of the government, the fact that Trinidad is a multi-ethnic society, comprised of several races and religions, meant that mass support for any religious sect leading the attempted overthrow would not easily be attained. Thus, when Abu Bakr called upon the masses, they divided according to race and religion and refused to lend support to the attempted coup. The plural character of Trinidadian society proved to be the crucial factor which ensured the failure of the coup. Accordingly, this article will locate the coup's failure principally in the elements of ethnic and cultural pluralism in Trinidadian politics. Before doing so, we first provide a brief introduction to the country's multi-ethnic society.

Bishnu Ragoonath is a Lecturer in Government at the University of the West Indies, St Augustine, Trinidad.

RACE, CLASS, RELIGION AND CULTURE IN TRINIDAD'S POLITICS

Any attempt to deal with the politics of Trinidad must start with the issue of race. The population of Trinidad is split amongst several ethnic or racial groups, the major ones being Afro-Trinidadians (hereafter referred to as Blacks) and Indo-Trinidadians (hereafter referred to as Indians). These two ethnic groups are equally balanced and together account for approximately 84 per cent of the population.[1] The remainder of the population is split between those of mixed ancestry and several small groups of descendants of Europeans, Chinese, and Syrian/Lebanese, among others. Race, normally defined as the distinguishing of persons based on the colour of their skin or texture of their hair, does condition how people act and participate in Trinidadian society. Consequently, Trinidad is often described as a plural society. The plural society theory, as postulated by Furnival[2] and M.G. Smith,[3] is characterised by the notion of different races living side by side but restricting their interactions to the market place. Such a society is not integrated. Thus, in the Trinidad case, participation in the various sectors of the economy is determined by race: oil and public sector workers are predominantly Black; sugar workers are mainly Indians; and the French-Creoles dominate the private sector. Similarly, race also conditions political behaviour in Trinidad. Political parties can be distinguished by the race of the leader, which influences the racial composition of their supporters. For example, over the period 1956–1986 the People's National Movement (PNM) can be described as a Black party. It had a Black leader and the majority of its followers were Blacks. Similarly, the majority of Indians supported a party with an Indian leader: in the pre-1976 period the People's Democratic Party (PDP), which later evolved into the Democratic Labour Party (DLP), and from 1976 the United Labour Front (ULF).[4]

With race as a key conditioning factor in economic and political behaviour in Trinidad, the plural society thesis has some validity. However, it must be noted that strict separation of the races, as postulated in the thesis, is not present in Trinidad. There are many instances of inter-mixing. To illustrate, first with respect to political behaviour, the PNM, though a Black party, generally has had the support of the Muslim Indians. Moreover, several political parties have claimed a multi-racial base. For example, the Organization of National Reconstruction (ONR) made substantial inroads into 'traditional' PNM and ULF strongholds at the 1981 elections, albeit without actually winning a seat. What is more, in 1985 a coalition of the predominantly Indian ULF, the predominantly Black parties of the Democratic Action Congress and the Tapia House Movement, and the multi-racial ONR joined together to form the National Alliance for Reconstruction (NAR), which went on to defeat the PNM in the 1986 general election. With respect to the economic integration of the races, although it is true that the French-Creoles dominate the private sector, Indians and Blacks do control about 30 per cent of that sector. Similarly, from a cultural perspective, persons of all races participate together and in harmony in major festivals, religious activities, and all major sports. In short, the plural society thesis is not fully applicable to Trinidadian society.

Alongside race, class factors also influence political behaviour in Trinidad. Indeed, there is inextricable linkage between race and class. For instance, in the past, according to both Weberian and Marxist class analyses, the French-Creoles comprised the upper class, controlling the means of production. Moreover, since they were in possession of wealth, their children were afforded educational opportunities which bolstered their class positions. Blacks and Indians, as the owners of labour, were confined to the lower class. However, within the more recent past, although remaining largely suppliers of labour, the educational achievements and income of Blacks and Indians have enabled many to join and dominate the middle class, with some even entering the upper echelons of society. With respect to the political affiliations of the members of these classes, there are no clearly demarcated divisions, although it has been suggested that, prior to 1986, the upper class, regardless of race or religion, supported parties, such as the Party of Political Progressive Groups (POPPG) in 1956 and the ONR in 1981, in opposition to the PNM.[5] The PNM was supported by middle and lower class Blacks. Similarly, the lower and middle class Indians supported the PDP, the DLP and then the ULF prior to 1986. Class influences thus impacted heavily upon Trinidad and Tobago's party politics.

So too does religion. Born in a Black Anglican home and christened Lennox Phillips, Yasin Abu Bakr renounced both his religion and name in the 1970s and converted to Islam. He then went on to lead the Jamaat al Muslimeen, one of the two 'Black Muslim' groups in Trinidad.[6] The presence of 'Black Muslims' in Trinidad was virtually unknown prior to 1970. It was only following the Black Power uprising of that year that some Blacks, acknowledging their heritage as Islamic, converted to Islam.[7] By 1990, 'Black Muslims' accounted for just over five per cent of the followers of Islam in Trinidad. Indians continue to dominate the

Muslim population. Even so, it accounts in total for only a little over eight per cent of the nation's population.[8] With respect to other religious denominations, European Christian beliefs predominate, if only because of the country's colonial past. The Spanish colonists brought the Roman Catholic Church while the English established the Anglican Church. Together these churches today account for just under 50 per cent of the religious affiliations of the population.[9] With the majority of Indians being Hindus, that group accounts for about 25 per cent of the population. The remainder is spread over a multitude of other Christian sects.[10]

As indicated, religion, like race and class, influences political support in Trinidadian politics. Selwyn Ryan noted that in the formative general election of 1956, Hindus voted for the People's Democratic Party (PDP), Catholics for the POPPG and followers of the other religions, which included the Muslims, voted for the PNM.[11] This pattern was more or less maintained during the period 1961–1983, with the only real change being the transfer of Catholic support to the PNM. During this time the Muslims remained unswerving in their support for the PNM.

Notwithstanding the various race, class and religious divisions and distinctions within Trinidadian society, all sectors and strata of the population live in what may be termed 'peaceful co-existence'. These various influences also give rise to a unique blend which is the 'Trinidadian culture'. From the perspective of politics, this is operationalised as a 'civic culture' whereby the citizenry is active in politics to the extent that preferences vis-à-vis government are expressed, but is not so much involved as to refuse to accept the decisions of the legitimate political authority.[12] Accordingly, although citizens complain, they generally refrain from resorting to violence against the democratically elected government. There is a real commitment to the principles of democracy with free and fair elections. In fact, as one commentator has argued, 'nobody denies that Trinidad and Tobago, as a country has problems . . . except that the national psyche insists that the solving of the problems should be done with strict adherence to the principle of rule of law and with the meticulous practice of parliamentary democracy'.[13] To this extent, Trinidadians have become accustomed to the protection of their freedom and rights, many of which were taken for granted prior to July 1990, so much so that revolution was preached on the streets, and even in front of the Parliament building, without persecution. Abu Bakr himself did so on many occasions between 1985 and 1990. Political freedoms and liberties were guaranteed in Trinidad, it seemed, at least until 27 July 1990.

With race, class, religion and culture entrenched as factors influencing politics in Trinidad and Tobago, the question that now needs to be answered is : how did these factors affect the outcome of the attempted coup in 1990? But, before attempting to posit an answer, we first trace the developments which led Imam Yasin Abu Bakr to stage the coup.

BACKGROUND TO THE COUP

We could no longer stand by while our country reach the abyss of no return [*sic*]. Amidst all the poverty and the destitution where people can't find jobs, where there is no work, where children are reduced to crime in order to live, where there is [*sic*] no jobs in the hospitals, the Prime Minister this week, the last Prime Minister, the ex-Prime Minister broke the camel's back when he said that half a million dollars was going to be allocated for a stone monument for Gene Miles. We could no longer take that kind of action from our leaders.

So said Abu Bakr, explaining on television the reason for his 'overthrow' of the government of Trinidad and Tobago on the evening of 27 July 1990. Further justifying his actions in a later statement, he noted that the government had failed to resolve the social and economic problems facing the nation. Using the example of the poor state of the health sector, he argued that the government had been negligent and uncaring of the social needs of the masses. With reference to the economy, unemployment had reached its highest level since independence. (In 1988, the official unemployment figure was 22 per cent.) In addition, the NAR government had lost its 'legitimacy' when, in 1988, the party had expelled Basdeo Panday, the leader of the former ULF element, along with several other Indian leaders.[14] These expulsions had, in turn, led to the withdrawal of a significant proportion of Indian support, without which the NAR was only a shadow of the multi-ethnic party which had won the 1986 elections. In other words, Abu Bakr, an ex-policeman, claimed to have initiated the coup in order to protect the integrity of the nation, to return power to a legitimate government, to end corruption, and to restore some semblance of values and standards within the society.

However, one can legitimately ask whether or not such noble goals were the only motives for the attempted overthrow of the government. Did Abu Bakr have another hidden agenda? Although claiming that he intended to bring an end to corruption, unemployment and poverty, these objectives seemed to change when he realised that he was losing control of events. In a later broadcast, he made specific reference to the failure of the courts to deliver judgment in a matter which he had brought against the state. The coup therefore had a dual purpose, that of returning some sense of integrity and dignity to the nation and to the impoverished masses, and serving some of Abu Bakr's and the Jamaat's personal objectives. Both considerations need to be further explored, starting with the personal agenda.

In 1969, the PNM government allocated a plot of land in Mucurapo, west Port of Spain, to the Islamic Missionaries Guild (IMG). This land, however, was owned by the Port of Spain City Corporation and not the state. Consequently, no legal transfer of the property was ever made. Early in the 1980s, Abu Bakr and the Jamaat, a sub-sect of the IMG, took the land and developed it as the base of the Muslimeen. However, the City Corporation maintained its claim to the land, thereby starting the dispute which culminated in the attempted coup. In 1984, in its attempt to fight off the City Corporation's claim to the land, the Jamaat Al Muslimeen started construction of a Mosque on the property. This immediately increased the delicacy of the situation, for any attempt to seize the land would have been likely to entail the wrath of the Muslim community. The City Corporation invited the Jamaat to regularise its occupancy of the property, but Abu Bakr bluntly refused the offer, with the result that the City Corporation subsequently took the matter to the courts. In a judgment delivered in late December 1984, the court ordered Abu Bakr and the Jamaat to demolish the uncompleted structure, an instruction which was again refused. Abu Bakr was charged with contempt of court and sentenced to 21 days in prison. The court again ordered the demolition of all illegal structures on the premises.

Following the latter court order, the police went to the Jamaat with a warrant for Abu Bakr's arrest. According to the police, Abu Bakr surrounded himself with women and children, making it impossible for the police to detain him without causing undue harm to the other persons present. For their action, or rather lack of action in executing the warrant, the police were commended by the government, but not by other sections of the population.[15] Indeed, the Law Society of Trinidad and Tobago expressed 'grave concern' and 'utter dismay and astonishment' over the failure to enforce the law.[16] Some eight days after these events, in early February 1985, Abu Bakr was finally imprisoned. Yet even as he served his sentence, construction on the Mosque proceeded apace. Two months later it was formally opened, the ceremonies being well attended by Muslims from several other Jamaats and sects in the country. Their attendance served as an indictment of the state and appeared to Abu Bakr to confirm the Muslim community's support for the Jamaat. On the basis of this support, he initiated the construction of several other buildings on the site. In the meantime, alleging illegal activities at the Jamaat, the police kept up their campaign against the Muslimeen. In raids carried out during 1985 and 1986, guns, ammunition, stolen cars, cocaine, marijuana, tear gas and even fugitives from the law were found at the Jamaat. Consequently, in October 1986, a police post was set up adjacent to the Jamaat, but was removed by the NAR government when it took power in December. The police nevertheless continued to monitor the Jamaat, making occasional raids.

The climax was not long in coming. Early in 1990, the police reported intensified activities at the Mucurapo compound. In April the government ordered the police and army to set up a camp on the grounds of the Jamaat. The official reason for this action was to put a halt to further illegal construction; already there were ten completed buildings in the compound, with several others at various stages of construction. In response to the police and army's actions, Abu Bakr claimed that his constitutional rights were being violated and took the government to court. The court subsequently threw out his claim, on the grounds that the case could not be considered a constitutional matter, but should have been filed instead as a private civil matter. Abu Bakr denounced this decision, claiming that the judicial system no longer protected the rights of the citizenry. More importantly, the issue of the right to ownership of the property at Mucurapo still remained unresolved. The coup was therefore initiated in good part to facilitate a final solution to this ownership issue, or rather to make official and formal the Jamaat's claim to the property at No. 1 Mucurapo Road.

Beyond this relatively narrow consideration, however, Abu Bakr also associated his attempted coup with the need to halt and reverse rising decadence, and to restore the sense of pride and self-worth of the citizenry, all of whom were suffering as a result of the economic policies of the NAR government. The NAR had come to power in 1986 in the midst of a deep economic recession. In immediate and acute financial difficulty, it sought and received assistance from the IMF and the World Bank, but such assistance came only with conditionalities. Above all, the government was required to reduce its expenditures. It did so by withholding civil servants' Cost of Living Allowances in 1987 and by cutting salaries by ten per cent in 1988. It also reduced its expenditure on social programmes, including health, thereby affecting, in the main, the lower classes who could not afford such services privately, especially in the light of the rising cost of living and growing unemployment. As a result, and in an attempt to force the government to revise its social and economic policies, protest action was initiated.

This took varying forms, ranging from simple marches in 1987[17] to a 'Day of Resistance' in March 1989. It may be instructive to note that the latter was the first general strike in the country since 1937, the trade union movement claiming that it brought the country to a virtual standstill.[18] The government, nevertheless, stuck to its economic programme, so much so that in 1990 a new Value Added Tax was introduced. Consequently, several trade unionists and opposition politicians, along with other social leaders, Abu Bakr included, came together and called upon the government to review its strategy. They argued that, with decreasing social services, increasing poverty, and a pro-business fiscal programme, the masses were being alienated.[19] To strengthen their call, the 'Summit of Peoples Organizations' (SOPO) was formed in February 1990 and SOPO, with its 'mass-based' support, immediately assumed the form of a social movement demanding relief for the masses.[20] In response to its demands, several government ministers acknowledged that their policies were not really meeting the needs of the masses, but still argued that relief was on the way as the economy was being turned around. This answer failed to appease SOPO's leaders, especially Abu Bakr, who apparently decided that since the government was not about to change its programmes voluntarily, then it should be removed.

Although Abu Bakr blamed the social and economic problems of the society on the NAR administration, it must be acknowledged that several of these problems existed prior to the NAR's assumption of office in 1986. As early as his return from Canada in the late 1970s, Abu Bakr had become the benefactor to several underprivileged youths. Later, as we have seen, he went on to form the Jamaat, by means of which he was in a better position to provide food and shelter to needy persons. Indeed, by 1986 when the NAR took power, there were already over 200 persons living at the Jamaat. Abu Bakr also collected food from amongst the Muslim community and distributed it to the poor and destitute, mainly around the Port of Spain and Laventille areas. Laventille has always been an urban slum, with high levels of poverty and unemployment and its problems certainly cannot be attributed to the NAR government's policies. Nevertheless, Abu Bakr blamed the NAR for the poverty, destitution and other societal ills which were rampant in that area and in the country as a whole by the late 1980s. Moreover, the government, he claimed, was unable to halt the spiralling decline and he felt he could no longer stand by and watch 'the country reach the abyss of no return'. He thus initiated the coup in an attempt to replace the government with one that would be more sensitive to the people's needs.

It is worth noting at this point that Abu Bakr had managed to build up a considerable measure of support for himself and his causes. To elaborate: by providing food and shelter to the poor and the underprivileged in the Black communities around Port of Spain and Laventille, he had won the support of the Black lower/working class. His appeal to this group increased following his participation in the labour struggle, which was concentrated on actions initiated by the Black-dominated Public Services Association (PSA).[21] In the end, it was from this segment, the Black population, that he got the majority of his support. As regards the Muslim community, the property issue and the battle against the police had generated unity. Although the Muslim community was and still is multi-segmental, Abu Bakr had undoubtedly made significant progress in lessening the distance between the various segments, especially with respect to the race issue.

The Muslim community in Trinidad has traditionally been split, with 'Black Muslims' having little contact with the 'Indian Muslims' before 1985, and the 'Indian Muslims' themselves divided between 'conservatives' and 'radicals'.[22] Furthermore, both the 'conservatives' and the 'radicals' were comprised of several sects and Jamaats. Following the actions of the City Corporation and the government, the 'radicals' were first joined with the 'Black Muslims', calling upon the government to withdraw and cease all actions against the Jamaat and Abu Bakr. Such unity was further promoted by the attendance of Indian Muslims, including prominent personalities within the society and government, at Islamic conferences and programmes which the Jamaat Al Muslimeen organised or hosted, the last of which was the Muslim 'Day of Solidarity' in June 1990. Based on the brotherhood of Islam, it was therefore believed that the entire Islamic community supported Abu Bakr. Such a belief was apparently vindicated, and the issue of unity sealed, when Abu Bakr took Fatima Juman, the daughter of a prominent 'Indian Muslim' family as his 'third wife'. As always, though, the true test of the tenacity of both Muslim and Black support could only come when Abu Bakr finally made his coup attempt.

THE COUP ITSELF

Abu Bakr's plan to overthrow the government depended upon the calculated action of just over 100 'soldiers', and the 'un-orchestrated' actions of the masses. A small group (approximately 42 men) was deployed to destroy the police headquarters, silence the NBS radio station and then move and take over the parliament, whilst a second group, 74 men under the leadership of Abu Bakr himself, went to take over the television station and eliminate the other radio station.[23] Both groups had some success in their primary objectives, seizing the Prime Minister, A.N.R. Robinson, and most of his cabinet in parliament, only to be subsequently trapped in the buildings which they had taken. The success of the coup then lay primarily in the hands of the masses, who, although not bearing arms against the state, were expected to stage a popular uprising.[24] Using Abu Bakr's announcement that there should be no looting as the signal, the supporters of the coup launched an attack on Port of Spain, swarming down upon the city but only to start a looting and burning spree. On the night of 27 July, some 95 businesses were looted and 47 premises razed in Port of Spain alone. In the following days, even with the country under 'a state of emergency' and an 18-hour curfew, the looters and firebugs returned and ravaged many more business enterprises. In all, the losses by the business sector in Port of Spain have been conservatively estimated at approximately TT$300 million. What is more, looting and arson were also experienced along the east–west corridor in north Trinidad. For instance, in San Juan, a small commercial centre about four miles from the city, all the businesses and warehouses were completely looted. The insurrection was not therefore limited to the attempted overthrow of the government, but also included an assault on the business sector.

Shortly after Abu Bakr announced that the government had been overthrown and that the Robinson-led cabinet was 'under arrest', the military moved into action. Troops took up positions in and around Port of Spain, concentrating their focus on the parliamentary building known as the Red House and the television station. They took control of the NBS radio station which, although set on fire by the Jamaat members, was still transmitting. Battalions were also deployed to Piarco to secure the only international airport in the country. In the meantime, defence force personnel sought and transferred several ministers and the Acting President, who were 'not arrested', to Camp Ogden – the army base in the city. Camp Ogden thus became the base of operations from which the army and government attempted to regain control of the situation. In moving to reassert control, the army was able to break into the television transmission emanating from the TTT studios twice during the first night, thereby allowing two government ministers to reassure the nation that the government had not fallen. The next morning television transmission was stopped completely, leaving Abu Bakr with no means of communication to the wider public.

Also during the course of the night of 27 July negotiations were initiated. These facilitated the release of several of the hostages early the next morning, although not the majority of the parliamentarians. As a result, with occasional gunfire and even mortar fire directed towards the seized buildings, the army continued to build up pressure on the insurgents during the course of the crisis. On two occasions, due to the intensified firing upon the Red House, the insurgents apparently believed that the army was setting the stage to storm the building.[25] In these moments the captors lined up all the male NAR parliamentarians and ordered that they be shot should the lights go off. In addition to instilling a degree of fear and apprehension within the ranks of the Jamaat, the military offensive also had another important effect: it caused Abu Bakr to rescind his claim that the government had been overthrown. The reality was that a caretaker government had evolved from amongst the 'free Government Ministers'; no support was coming from SOPO or other pressure groups and political parties; and, most importantly, the display of military might was more than enough to overpower his forces. Accordingly, on Sunday 29 July, speaking to the British Broadcasting Corporation (BBC), Abu Bakr said that what had happened in Trinidad was nothing more than a 'family quarrel'. He thus pleaded that the negotiations should be allowed to continue to resolve the 'quarrel'. Moveover, he insisted that there was no need for external intervention to resolve the crisis. In short, Abu Bakr's attempt to overthrow the government had effectively failed, but with several persons still being held hostage, he had some bargaining power left with which to negotiate both with the forces outside and the hostages.

Early on 30 July 1990, a 'Heads Of Agreement' document highlighting five issues was drawn up and agreed by the 'arrested' members of the government. Included was confirmation of the resignation of Robinson and his replacement by his deputy Winston Dookeran, who had earlier been released from the Red House. There were also 'heads' relating to the composition of the interim government, which was to follow the format demanded by Abu Bakr; the holding of elections within 90 days; and the granting of amnesty to the Jamaat members. Selwyn Richardson, the Minister of Justice and National Security, also drew up a letter recommending the amnesty. It is claimed that he also pledged that they would be allowed to return to their Mucurapo headquarters. However, although these arrangements were agreed by the Jamaat and the members of the government held in the Parliament building, that did not mean that they were supported by the military and cabinet on the outside. Indeed, Robinson was completely unable to make contact with those in authority outside the Red House. The impasse was only broken when, during the course of the day, media personnel from the

Australian Broadcasting Corporation (ABC) and the BBC telephoned the Red House and were able to speak directly to the Prime Minister. Robinson informed them of the agreement and asked for their assistance in making contact with officials in the government and army. Still without response by nightfall, both Robinson and Richardson related their plight to Tony Fraser, a highly respected freelance journalist in Trinidad. Fraser immediately called the radio station and repeated 'on air' the information he had received from Robinson. Officials 'on the outside' still did not contact their Prime Minister. A similar scenario developed the following day, when Robinson, who had been shot and was suffering from glaucoma, was expected to be released 'on humanitarian grounds'. However, the army and the 'outside' cabinet seemed apprehensive about accepting his release and again the media (both local and international) had to be called upon to force those in command to secure the release on Tuesday 31 July. With both the Prime Minister and Deputy Prime Minister outside, it was then only a matter of time before the other hostages were released.

The question that remained was: what would be included in the package for the release of the hostages? Claiming that 'no deals with this extremist group' had been made and that their surrender was 'unconditional', Dookeran announced that 114 members of the Jamaat Al Muslimeen had been taken prisoner and would be charged. The Jamaat members thought otherwise: they believed that in surrendering their arms and releasing all remaining hostages on 1 August 1990, they would at least have amnesty. They thought that they were only being taken to Teteron Bay, the Army's headquarters, as a precaution and for their own personal safety and that eventually they would be released with full amnesty. This did not happen. Each arrested Jamaat member was charged with 22 offences ranging from treason to murder to illegal possession of arms and ammunition. Probably Abu Bakr realised that this was to be his fate when he walked out of TTT House on 1 August 1990. For the next two years lawyers representing the Jamaat and the state wrangled with each other over the validity of the alleged amnesty. Initially, on calling upon Abu Bakr to surrender, the Jamaat's attorney and leading human rights lawyer, Ramesh Lawrence Maharaj, had appeared to indicate that he believed an amnesty signed under duress was null and void.[26] Yet in June 1992 Justice Clement Brooks ruled in the High Court in favour of the Jamaat and the Muslimeen were freed. The state has since appealed against that decision.

EXPLANATIONS FOR THE FAILURE OF THE COUP

The success of Abu Bakr's attempted coup depended upon a popular uprising which never came. It was thus merely a matter of time for the strategies operationalised by the military to take effect and put the coup down. But the question arises as to why the masses failed to produce a popular uprising. The answer to this question resides in the issues of race, religion, class and the political culture of the Trinidadian people.

Trinidadians boast that their political culture, although relatively young, is steeped in the principles of peaceful democracy and built upon the foundation of a people with a peace-loving disposition. The jovial, almost besotted, carnivalistic mentality of Trinidadians ensures that no situation escapes the opportunity to be made into some 'bachannal'. Thus, following the attempted coup, when the state of emergency was imposed, bars and pubs engaged in brisk business. Moreover, during the curfew hours 'curfew parties' were held, whereby for the duration of the curfew citizens would 'fete' without interruption, since they could not leave. Put another way, tenacity and seriousness are not amongst the virtues of the Trinidadian. Such a disposition guarantees that Trinidadians will never involve themselves in any real violence, and makes it very unlikely that they will bear arms against a legitimate, democratically elected government. Of course, this is not to suggest that Trinidadians do not rebel or revolt. In fact, since the time of slavery, there has been a record of rebellions and revolutions in Trinidad. To this end, Ryan has identified a list of revolutionaries,[27] all of whom preceded Abu Bakr. But, unlike the Abu Bakr coup, although several of these revolutionaries sought to remove the ruling regime from power, their mode of attack was launched only with prior popular support. Moreover, in many instances open force or violence was used only when all other options failed.

In this regard, the 1970 Black Power uprisings are instructive. Although having its origin in a march organised in solidarity with Black students who were being discriminated against at North American universities, Black Power in Trinidad in 1970 was more of a social movement which had as its primary goal equality of opportunity for all, regardless of race or colour. With this goal in mind, the movement was able to win the support of the young urban Blacks, many of whom were deprived of employment opportunities because of their race and colour. To this end, a protest which started off with 20 odd university students was able to attract up to 20,000 persons within a matter of two weeks.[28]

It is important to note too that, although this social movement represented a genuine eruption in Trinidadian society, its activities were kept on a non-violent level. In other words, the activities of the movement were largely confined to protest marches and rallies. There were several acts of violence and arson subsequent to some of the Black Power rallies, but these were perpetrated by followers of a small group operating under the banner of the National Union of Freedom Fighters (NUFF). The Black Power movement, its leaders and supporters were not involved in the violence, nor did they attempt to overthrow the government with force. In fact, given its numerical strength, which included not only young Blacks, but also market vendors, trade unionists and even politicians, if the movement had wanted to remove the ruling regime from power, its chances of success would have been quite good. However, the basic disposition of the Trinidadian, combined with the democratic tradition of the country, ensured that Black Power remained a peaceful movement.

It is in this respect that Abu Bakr was guilty of not knowing 'his' people.[29] Had he understood how Trinidadians thought, he would have known, as Major Williams of the Defence Force acknowledged, that there is a tradition of non-violence in Trinidad. The people 'fraid guns and violence', and will not participate in an armed revolt, regardless of how harsh their economic and social conditions. Hence, when he expected them to act 'maturely' and engage in a popular uprising he was let down. For instead of rallying behind the coup whilst the police headquarters burned, the people went to 'watch the fire'. And later, appreciating what had ensued and realising that the police were in disarray, hordes of people descended upon the city, again not to rally around Abu Bakr but rather to engage in a massive orgy of looting.[30] The 'suffering masses' preferred first to seek their personal well-being and satisfy their materialistic needs, rather than involve themselves in any armed uprising, and then, when such needs were fulfilled, to engage themselves in 'partying and feting' rather than supporting any coup. This is what ensured the failure of the coup. In emphasising this point, and in a statement explaining on behalf of the rebels who had seized the Red House that things had not turned out the way they expected, Kwesi Atiba said: 'We expected the people on the streets to take some kind of action, . . . some did and some didn't.'[31] Ryan's 1991 survey supported this argument and revealed that no less than 75 per cent of the sample disapproved of Abu Bakr's forceful method of seeking to remove the government.[32]

The failure of the masses to stage a popular uprising against the government can also be explained by religious perception and belief.

Even allowing for the 'work' which the Jamaat had done amongst the wider society, it had never won the approval of the other religious denominations. Consequently, non-Muslim religious leaders quickly distanced themselves and their followers from the activities initiated by Abu Bakr, claiming that their followers (non-Muslims) had remained loyal to the state. Such a perspective was summed up by Sat Maharaj, the Secretary-General of the Maha Sabha. He claimed that during the crisis the Hindus remained unaffected by the civil disobedience that was taking place in Port of Spain. They 'continued to carry out their daily task of tending to their crops and animals in the fields. They had and wanted nothing to do with the coup'.[33] Similar responses were heard from the various leaders of the Christian community in Trinidad.

As for the Islamic community, it too sought to distance itself from Abu Bakr and his followers. The former 'conservative' Indian Muslim sects, namely the Anjuman Sunnat Jamaat Association (ASJA), Trinidad Muslim League (TML) and the Tackveeyatul Islamic Association (TIA), claimed that they had never supported the Jamaat Al Muslimeen. Moreover, both the TML and ASJA went on to assert that the actions of Abu Bakr and the Jamaat Al Muslimeen were contrary to Islamic teachings.[34] But while the 'conservative' Islamic sects could distance themselves from Abu Bakr, the 'radicals' could not so easily do so. Ever since the first 'attack' by the City Corporation to reclaim the lands of the Jamaat Al Muslimeen in 1983, Abu Bakr had sought and received the support of several 'radical' Indian Jamaats and organisations, such as the Islamic Trust of Trinidad, the Islamic Missionaries Guild, the Islamic Peoples' Morement, the Mujahadeen of Islam and even the University of the West Indies Islamic Society among others. Moreover, by 1990, these 'radical' sects had united with 'Black Muslim' Jamaats under the banner of the United Islamic Brotherhood, later renamed the United Islamic Organizations (UIO). The 'radical' Indian Muslim sects could not simply disclaim their association to the Jamaat Al Muslimeen. However, following the events of 27 July, the UIO, although not condemning the coup attempt, stated that they did not support the taking of hostages.[35] In a more elaborate statement, the IMG deplored the activities of the coup makers and expressed their sympathy to those who were injured and for the loss of life during the attempted coup. In sum, no religious denomination supported the attempted coup, and the Inter-Religious Organization (IRO) was able unanimously to condemn the whole affair.[36]

Such religious condemnation may also, however, be viewed from a racial perspective. In Trinidad, race is closely related to religion. To elaborate, the majority of Indians are Hindus, while the rest of that ethnic group subscribe to either Islamic or Christian teachings. Regardless of their religious persuasions, Indians, in general, did not support Abu Bakr. Indeed, in a survey of Indians between the ages of 18 and 34, it was found that only 21 per cent felt that he was right to attempt to overthrow the government.[37] With respect to the Blacks, they are spread over a range of Christian churches. The Roman Catholic Church, which accounts for slightly over 30 per cent of the nation's population, is comprised of a wide cross-section of persons of various ethnic backgrounds. However, the Catholic leadership in Trinidad, including both the Archbishop and Bishop, is under the control of the 'French-Creoles' or the 'Trinidad-Whites'. The position of the Roman Catholic Church would reflect the views of its leaders and it could not have supported a Black radical Muslim group. Ryan's survey thus found that 79 per cent of the Catholic community felt it was wrong for Abu Bakr to attempt to overthrow the government.[38] The Anglican Church similarly condemned the coup. This position was made most clear because some of the leaders of this denominational group were somewhat compromised. Through their participation in SOPO, Canon Knolly Clarke, a senior cleric, and David Abdullah, the son of the Bishop, were close associates of Abu Bakr. However, SOPO, by maintaining a deafening silence during the crisis, facilitated the Anglican Church's desire to distance itself from the attempted coup. Again, Ryan's survey revealed that 77 per cent of Anglicans opposed the attempted coup.[39]

From a straightforward race perspective, the entire non-Black population, regardless of class or religion, condemned Abu Bakr and refused to participate in a popular uprising. As for the Black community, with the exception of a small minority, the majority also refused to lend support to the coup. While accepting that many non-Blacks looted in the aftermath of the announcement of the coup, the fact does remain, however, that the only areas which suffered were those in close proximity to predominantly Black residential areas. Areas with predominantly Indian populations or mixed communities experienced little or no looting. Moreover, in police raids in the post-crisis period, looted items were retrieved mainly from Black communities. As already indicated, this should not be used to suggest that the entire or even a significant proportion of the Black population participated or supported Abu Bakr. Even if all the looters were Black, and they were not, they amounted to a very small percentage of the Black population in Trinidad. Nonetheless, it remains the case that participation on a race basis in the activities between 27 July and 1 August 1990 was skewed in favour of Afro-Trinidadians compared to peoples of other races. More generally, though, too few people of whatever race or religion supported the attempted coup and that is what caused its failure.

CONCLUSION

The Jamaat claims its attempted coup as a victory. This partly reflects the fact that, for the moment, the 'rebel members' have all been freed with a valid amnesty, but, more importantly, derives from the claim that the political changes which have occurred since 27 July 1990 have given credibility to its attack on the government. Specifically, the regime upon which the attack was launched is no longer in power. In general elections held in December 1991, the Robinson-led NAR suffered a landslide defeat, retaining only two of the 33 parliamentary seats it had won in 1986. On his release from prison, Abu Bakr could thus claim that the objective of his coup had been achieved and that the Jamaat was victorious.

This is disingenuous. To begin with, the defeat of the NAR had nothing to do with the Jamaat Al Muslimeen and the coup. True enough, the opposition campaign platforms focused on the same national issues which Abu Bakr had used to justify his attempted coup, but they cast them in the context of elections in a more orthodox and acceptable fashion. Put differently, using the franchise, the electorate was given the opportunity to decide, in a formal, traditional manner, who would govern the country for the next five years. Thus, the electoral victories of the People's National Movement (PNM) and the United National Congress (UNC) rested purely on the decision of the electorate. To this end, neither the Jamaat Al Muslimeen nor the attempted coup played any part in the electorate's decision. In fact, little mention of the events of 1990 was made on the campaign trail. Furthermore, the removal of the NAR regime from office was only the means to an end for Abu Bakr: it was not an end in itself. Although the Muslimeen sought to remove the government of the day, it believed that in so doing the policies which were being implemented by that regime would be halted and even reversed. Such a position was made clear by Abu Bakr himself, when, at the height of the attempted coup, he announced that under 'his government' the 'Value Added Tax would be immediately abolished'. Again, in point of fact, the accession of the PNM into government has not meant the withdrawal of the various 'oppressive' NAR policies. VAT has not been removed,[40] while a bill to extend the student cess[41] for the 1992–93 academic year was recently passed in parliament. The structural adjustment programme dictated by the World Bank and the International Monetary Fund is also continuing apace, and is arguably being extended in respect of 'trade liberalisation', with the removal of the negative list by the end of June 1992.

With the policies and programmes which led to the attack on the government in 1990 still therefore in place, the question which arises is: will there be another attempt to overthrow the legitimate government of Trinidad and Tobago? In response, Abu Bakr has said merely that, should the circumstances warrant another attack on the government of the day, there is nothing to prevent it. This does not necessarily imply that Abu Bakr and the Jamaat Al Muslimeen will launch another attack on the Trinidad government. Nevertheless, as the Speaker of the Trinidad parliament noted in early 1984, 'no state can consider itself secure unless it benefited from substantial economic development'.[42] The stringent conditions imposed in recent years by the IMF and other lenders have tended to destabilise recipient governments and, to this extent, Trinidad, like many other developing countries which are debtors to the IMF and World Bank, is susceptible to violent attacks on the government.[43]

Turning to the question of what measures can be put in place to minimise the threat of future uprisings and attempted coups in the Commonwealth Caribbean region, there is a need, as has already been suggested, for greater economic development. It has been proposed that the 'best way to protect a Third World region from coups is to develop the institutions and sense of community necessary to make the coup unacceptable as a means of resolving political disputes'.[44] To be sure, popular support for coups and attacks on legitimate governments will not be attained once a government holds office legitimately. In the Trinidad case, with the break-up of the NAR in 1988, it was suggested that the NAR government had lost its legitimate authority to continue in office. While this argument has some credibility, it must be remembered that, even after the expulsion of the ULF element, the NAR still held an overwhelming majority in the parliament and deserved to be viewed as the legitimate government. The popular uprising, which Abu Bakr expected to develop in order to remove this 'illegitimate' government from office, failed to materialise and it took the electorate, using the power of the vote, to succeed where Abu Bakr failed. In short, the perceived legitimacy of the government, along with the fact that the people can effectively participate in Trinidadian politics, guaranteed minimal support for Abu Bakr and his coup, but at the same time ensured that one of the goals of the coup, the removal of the NAR regime from office, was in the end achieved.

But alongside the need to facilitate mass participation there must also be the greater acceptance of a 'civic culture'. Such a culture would ensure participation that is politically, socially and culturally acceptable to the wider society. The development of such a culture is, however, dependent upon the creation and maintenance of civilian institutions, which in turn facilitate the emergence of an integrated society with a national identity. Thus, notwithstanding the plural nature of Trinidadian society, the constitution, the parliament, the independent judiciary and other such institutions are held in high regard by all, regardless of race, religion, class or culture. These allegiances suggest that some degree of national identity exists in Trinidad, thereby rendering support for the attempted coup unacceptable. To this end, therefore, the maintenance of viable civilian institutions would go a long way towards restricting support to malcontents wishing to destabilise a ruling regime, be it in Trinidad or any other Caribbean territory.

But even this is insufficient to remove the threat of coups in the Commonwealth Caribbean. There is a need for a proper, loyal defence force/system within the region as a whole and even within the various states. Put differently, 'mercenaries' plotting an attack on governments in the Caribbean region will only be deterred by raw firepower. In this regard, it is important to stress that Abu Bakr's attack on the government was launched in the belief that the military would support the overthrow of the regime. However, the Trinidad and Tobago Defence Force, whose members are predominantly Black, maintained its loyalty to the state and acted heroically in putting down the coup. Its firepower ultimately overwhelmed the 'rebels'. To this end, the mere presence of the Defence Force in Trinidad should serve as a deterrent to future plotters of similar attacks against the state. Moreover, there also exists in the Commonwealth Caribbean a Regional Security System, which possesses the ability to deter, if not counter, attacks against the states of the region.[45] It may be instructive too to note that units from this system were utilised to secure various installations in Trinidad immediately after the coup was put down.

For all the capacity of Caribbean governments to promote political development, or even the role of the military in serving as an effective deterrent against attempted coups, there is still no way of precluding the plotting and even operationalising of future attempts to overthrow a regime in power. To this extent, governments and peoples in the region must be constantly wary of the possibility of some 'madcap' quest to take over the government. More importantly, however, in conceding such a possibility, governments must seek to facilitate the development of an environment and a society which will restrict popular support for any such plot or attempted coup. Governments must seek to address the issues of the legitimacy of their regime, the ability of the citizenry to participate meaningfully in decision-making, and the equitable distribution of rewards within society. Only when these matters have been effectively resolved can attempted coups be easily put down.

NOTES

1. See Central Statistical Office (CSO), *1989 Annual Statistical Digest* (Port of Spain, 1990).
2. See J.S. Furnival, *Colonial Policy and Practice* (London, 1948).
3. See M.G. Smith, *The Plural Society in the British West Indies* (Los Angeles, 1965).
4. B. Ragoonath, 'Race and Class in Caribbean Politics', *Plural Societies*, 18, 1 (1988), 92–3.
5. S. Ryan, 'Race, Religion, Class and Voting Behaviour In Trinidad and Tobago: 1956-1983', mimeo, Port of Spain, 1984.
6. The term 'Black Muslim' is used to distinguish the Afro-Trinidadian Muslims from the Indo-Trinidadian Muslims.
7. J. La Guerre, 'The 1990 Violent Disturbance in Trinidad and Tobago: Some Perceptions', *Caribbean Quarterly*, 37, 2&3 (1991), 55.
8. CSO, *1989 Annual Statistical Digest*.
9. Roman Catholics account for approximately 33 per cent and the Anglicans approximately 15 per cent of the population according to official statistics. See CSO, *1989 Digest*.
10. CSO, *1989 Digest*.
11. Ryan, 'Race, Religion, Class and Voting Behaviour'.
12. G. Almond & S. Verba, *The Civic Culture* (Princeton, 1963).
13. H. Addo, 'Crisis of Shock: Insurrection in Trinidad and Tobago, 1990', *Caribbean Quarterly*, 37, 2&3 (1991), 2.
14. R.R. Premdas, 'Review of Muslimeen Grab for Power', *Caribbean Review of Books*, 2 (November 1991).
15. For a more detailed account of these events, see S. Ryan, 'The Trigger Pulled in the Name of Almighty Allah', *Caribbean Quarterly*, 37, 2&3 (1991), 16–18.
16. See letter in *Trinidad Express*, 1 Feb. 1985, 8.
17. Abu Bakr, displaying solidarity with the masses, joined in these marches and was twice arrested in 1987.
18. D. Abdullah, 'Jamaat Al Muslimeen Insurrection in Trinidad and Tobago, 1990', *Caribbean Quarterly*, 37, 2&3 (1991), 84.
19. See B. Ragoonath, 'On West Indian Politics', in B. Ragoonath (ed.), *Tribute to a Scholar: Appreciating CLR James* (Mona, Jamaica, 1990).
20. Although the leaders of several trade unions and political parties along with some religious leaders comprised SOPO, this in no way guaranteed that the people whom these leaders represented supported SOPO. Nevertheless, the leaders claimed that they had mass support.
21. In a 1989 survey, Professor Selwyn Ryan, the Director of the Institute of Social and Economic Studies at the St Augustine campus of the University of the West Indies, found that over 67 per cent of public service employees were Black. This is significant, if only because the proportion of Blacks in the national population amounts to just above 40 per cent.
22. For an account of the divisions within the Muslim community in Trinidad, see S. Ryan, *The Muslimeen Grab For Power* (Port of Spain, 1991), Ch. 4.
23. A detailed account of the movements of the various groups of Abu Bakr's 'soldiers' is given in V.E.T. Furlonge-Kelly, *The Silent Victory* (Port of Spain, 1991), 35–43.
24. S. Ryan, 'The Trigger Pulled', 26.

25. See Sworn Affidavit of Mrs Jennifer Johnson in *Trinidad Guardian*, 15 Feb. 1992, 6.
26. Maharaj, on hearing of the attack on the government, fled to Grenada. He claimed that he did not want to be party to the crime which his clients were in the process of committing. Accordingly, it was from Grenada that he issued his call to Abu Bakr to surrender.
27. Ryan, *Muslimeen Grab for Power*, 11.
28. *Trinidad Guardian*, 7 March 1970.
29. In a survey conducted by Ryan in June 1991, it was found that 65 per cent of the sample believed that Abu Bakr was either a charlatan, a crook, mad or misguided. See Ryan, *Muslimeen Grab for Power*, 226, Table 6.
30. See C. Searle, 'The Muslimeen Insurrection in Trinidad', *Race and Class*, 33, 2 (1991), 29. See also Furlonge-Kelly, *The Silent Victory*, 70.
31. See M. Cuffie, 'Spokesman: We Expected People On Streets to Take Action', *Trinidad Guardian*, 4 Aug. 1990, 8.
32. See Ryan, *Muslimeen Grab for Power*, 225, Table 1.
33. The Maha Sabha is the largest Hindu organisation in the country, representing over 75 per cent of all Hindus.
34. See 'Statement from Dr M.A. Aziz (Religious Head of the TML),' *Trinidad Guardian*, 20 Aug. 1990. See also 'Statement from Haji Zainool Khan (1st Vice President of ASJA),' *Sunday Guardian*, 12 Aug. 1990.
35. See *Trinidad Express*, 23 Aug. 1990, 3.
36. See *Trinidad Express*, 20 Aug. 1990, 12.
37. Ryan, *Muslimeen Grab for Power*, 229–30, Tables 15 and 16.
38. Ryan, *Muslimeen Grab for Power*, 230, Table 18.
39. Ryan, *Muslimeen Grab for Power*, 230, Table 18.
40. It may be noted that some over-the-counter medicines have, however, been zero-rated since the PNM took office.
41. The cess is a tax paid by all Trinidadian students attending the University of the West Indies. The tax was first introduced in 1988. The PNM, while in opposition, had. claimed that this tax restricted the availability of education to all, and had promised to discontinue all policies which made education available only to those who could afford it.
42. This point was argued by Hon. Matthew Ramcharan, the then Speaker of the Trinidad and Tobago House of Representatives, at the 30th Commonwealth Parliamentary Conference in 1984. See 'The Security of Small States', *The Parliamentarian*, LXV, 4 (1984), 266.
43. Ramcharan, 'Security of Small States', 271.
44. S. David, *Defending Third World Regions From Coup d'Etat* (Lanham, 1985), 10.
45. See 'The Role of the Regional Security System in the Eastern Caribbean', *Bulletin of Eastern Caribbean Affairs*, 11, 6 (1986).

An Inside-Out Insurgency: The Tukuyana Amazones of Suriname

GARY BRANA-SHUTE

Two Indian warriors, garbed in loin cloths and feathers and armed with formidable spears, flank and guard the national shield of the Republic of Suriname. Following the 1980 coup and subsequent revolution, these Indian stalwarts were replaced by two Afro-Surinamese soldiers wearing camouflage outfits and sporting Uzi machine guns and hand-grenades. The public outcry was such that the Indians were soon returned to protect the symbolic public patrimony. However, such apparent respect is also accompanied in common parlance by cliches such as 'one is as drunk as an Indian' or 'as stupid'. American Indians, primarily Arawak and Carib, occupy an ambiguous and contradictory position within the highly fragmented, polyethnic society of Suriname.[1] It is argued here that Carib culture and behaviour, particularly their resistance of the past three years, can only be measured and understood in relation to their situation *vis-à-vis* other ethnic groups in Suriname, in other words by reference to the Carib 'place' within the nation-state context. Focus will be on the mobilisation of Carib ethnicity through an armed nativistic movement designed to resecure resources and prestige in a neo-colonial society that has ignored and belittled them.[2]

A TROUBLED DECADE

The 1980s was a troubled decade for the former colony of the Netherlands, opening and closing as it did with military *coups d'état*. The 1980 coup overthrew a fragile parliamentary democracy based on consociational agreements of proportionality and access to resources by the three largest ethnic groups in Suriname – Afro-Surinamese (hereafter called Creoles), East Indians, and Javanese – each of which was represented by its own political party. The military and its civilian clients ruled the country via a bizarre succession of regimes and methods until 1987 when elections were finally held.[3] The three traditional ethnic

Gary Brana-Shute is Deputy Director of Latin American and Caribbean Studies at the Foreign Service Institute of the US Department of State, Washington, DC.

parties responded to this democratic opening by confederating into 'The Front for Democracy and Development' to contest the election and, in what constituted a public mandate for a return to civilian control of government, won 41 of the 51 National Assembly seats. Constitutionally, the president became head of state and commander-in-chief and was supported by a legislature and independent judiciary. None of this corresponded to reality, however, as the military, through its military police and commando units, continued to rule indirectly and manipulate frightened civilian politicians. The Front was a weak government, chronically unable to rule under the stress constantly applied by the military and their handmaiden insurgencies in the interior. The government stumbled along until the December 1990 coup, by which time it was so morally and intellectually bankrupt that it could barely whisper a sound of protest.

Whereas elections in 1987 had been characterised by an atmosphere of carnival and 'jump-up', a hope that the victorious Front would bring salvation from military rule and get the country moving again, the most recent elections of May 1991 were sombre, demonstrating the public's frustration with the inability of the civilian politicians to take advantage of the massive mandate they had acquired three years earlier. Nothing had changed: a promised removal of a constitutional clause permitting military intervention was still on the books and, ironically, the military through its own civilian political party – the National Democratic Party (NDP) – had actually grown in strength during the period it had served as (the military-appointed) caretaker government from the 1990 coup to the 1991 elections. This period provided ample time to loot the treasury and promote NDP interests.[4] Also relevant to the popular mood at the time was a sense of paranoia beneath the usual jovial Surinamese spirit: this had been spawned by the emergence of four jungle insurgencies in the interior of the country and the growth of urban terrorism in the form of unexplained murders and drive-by shootings.[5]

In fact, the elections, which were secret and fair, sprang surprises on everyone. Of the total of 51 seats in the National Assembly, the New Front old guard won 30 (down from 41 in 1987). The NDP, well funded as expected, secured second place with 12 seats (up from three in 1987). The Democratic Alternative '91 (DA '91), first dismissed as neophytes and upstarts, landed nine seats in its first election run by appealing to the widespread feeling of dissatisfaction and yearning for something new among the country's professional and middle classes. A New Front government, although weaker than before, was thus installed and operative by early September 1991.[6]

Meanwhile, Suriname's thick jungle interior had been beset by several 'on-and-off again' insurgencies, including three sponsored by the military itself. Warring groups of Maroons (Afro-Surinamers descended from the rebel slaves of the 17th and 18th centuries) and American Indians effectively shut down access to the bush and kept the central government under continual pressure. Beginning in mid-1986, a Maroon guerrilla movement, known as the Jungle Commando and led by former army sergeant Ronnie Brunswijk, rose up against Colonel Bouterse, then the sole power in the country. Although the Jungle Commando did not have the full support of the five Maroon tribes – especially the elders – it mustered a loose-knit group of young insurgents, attacked provincial towns, choked off the major highways to east Suriname, occupied one-third of the country, and temporarily crippled the bauxite-based economy.[7] The peak of the Jungle Commando's territorial acquisition came in late 1989 with the occupation of Moengo, a bauxite processing centre in east Suriname.[8]

At the same time, but coincidentally, a group of Carib American Indians, who reside in tribal territories in between Maroon lands to the west and the Maroni River border with French Guiana, opened hostilities with the Maroons.[9] Heavily armed and taking the name Tukuyana Amazones, the Carib faction sought to speak for all American Indians in Suriname. Organised and armed by the military, the Tukuyana launched attacks against Maroon positions in east and west Suriname, and raided Arawak American Indians who had attempted to remain neutral and distant from the surrounding frays. In addition to rekindling latent hostilities between American Indians and Maroons (primarily over land and hunting rights), the military successfully engineered ethnic mitosis by playing on tensions between rival factions of American Indians themselves.

Evidence of military-Tukuyana complicity was blatant. In early 1990 a contingent of heavily armed Tukuyana was welcomed at the National Palace by Colonel Bouterse. At a press conference the Tukuyana leader, Thomas, and his lieutenant, Matto, both wearing headdresses and ceremonial costumes, announced a declaration of war against the civilian police force (which had always been anti-military but whose officer corps had been increasingly co-opted by the army leadership) and any 'uncooperative' journalists who might venture into what was called 'Tukuyana territory'. They also called for complete autonomy within Suriname and during 1990–92 went on to rule their portion of this fragmented country as warlord bandits, extracting tribute from all non-combatants.

CARIB POLITICAL ECONOMY

Presently in Suriname there are some 5,000 Caribs occupying about 20 permanently settled villages which vary in size from 75 to nearly 1,000 inhabitants.[10] Their traditional means of livelihood – shifting cultivation, hunting, fishing, and gathering – have become increasingly supplemented by wage labour activities, such as working in the capital, Paramaribo, labouring on government-owned palm oil plantations, fishing and fish marketing in Nieuw Nickerie and Paramaribo, and working freelance or for corporations in the timber industry. Caribs are neither primitive nor isolated people within Suriname. Although they are rural dwellers who often have to make a long and arduous journey to reach markets and central places, Caribs have had access to elementary schools, the cash economy, and, before the Tukuyana Amazones, the police and the judicial, welfare and taxation systems of the state too. Diesel generators, at least when fuel was available or they were in repair, provided episodic electrical power. Roman Catholic missionaries have also been active since the mid-19th century. Nevertheless, Caribs, despite their perceived adaptation to nature, are poor even by Surinamese standards and earn perhaps US$350 per year for each nuclear family, which is the basic building block of Carib social life.[11]

To the casual observer Carib life can appear exceedingly dull. It has been described by Kloos as 'a quiet affair of rather solitary men, women and children. Without caring much for the inhabitants of the village the Caribs go fishing, hunting and collecting . . . Social life at the village level hardly exists'.[12] This view, which is deliberately overstated, is difficult to reconcile with the historical accounts of great Carib war chieftains leading fierce braves into battle against other American Indians or the later European interlopers. For the young Carib man today, tattooed with a stylised war eagle on his chest and with a red bandanna tied around his head, the Tukuyana Amazones offer a truly fantastic restoration of past glories and redemption of a way of life that existed in the murky, quasi-reality of myth.

The period since World War II was characterised by a wholesale state penetration of Carib institutions: missionary work increased, schools were founded and medical services and clinics were opened. Surinamese law superseded traditional modes of conflict resolution, the Dutch and Creole languages were spoken more widely, and urban politicians began to show more of an interest in harvesting Carib votes. Young Caribs increasingly went to high school in Paramaribo and returned to their villages determined to make improvements having been not a little bit humiliated in the city for being a *'dun ingi'* (Creole for 'stupid Indian'). In addition, traditional village headmen were recognised by and appointed as 'chiefs' by the central government and consequently provided with a salary as well as a statutory position.[13]

Early sources on the Carib painted the picture of strong and entrenched leadership displayed by a sort of *cacique* who mobilised village and larger groups for warfare in the role of supreme commander. These observations were made by martially oriented, hierarchically attuned Europeans and do not provide an internal view of Carib leadership, or lack of it. Contemporary evidence for extraordinarily warlike tribes such as the Yanomami Indians of Brazil indicates that, even for groups in a state of chronic combat, leadership roles are but poorly developed and not that firmly institutionalised. Shamans, as religious practitioners, curers, and intermediaries with the spirit world, always exerted great influence in the group but did not occupy a leadership role *per se*. Speculatively, peace treaties signed with Europeans in the late 17th century could have diminished what incipient *cacique* leadership roles there were by nullifying warfare and hence the need for such a (temporary/situational/institutionalised?) command and control position.

Contemporary descriptions of Carib leadership patterns stress personal operational qualities such as the ability to gain cooperation and consensus among followers, who themselves voluntarily bestow allegiance on the wise, persuasive and successful organiser. No amount of ordering, protesting, haranguing, bullying or threatening on the part of a Carib leader will achieve his goals or dissuade the group from theirs. Hence, in modern times, we are left with the notion of a leader as somebody who has no real, operational power but possesses rather a loose and amorphous influence in so far as he cannot restrict, define, order or denounce the behaviour of his 'followers'. As a consequence, there is in Carib society a great deal of social and political space wherein Carib individuals can select numerous behavioural options and alternatives. It is precisely this space that has allowed the emergence of, and is being exploited by, the Tukuyana Amazones who, in turn, have undermined what little traditional leadership remains in Carib society.

The role of the contemporary Carib leader, selected by the village and appointed by the central government, is to link village-level society to the nation state. They are liaison officers between the inhabitants and government – provided with uniforms and salaries, but no power, either over the villages or in Paramaribo. Leaders, called Captains in Suriname, thus perform minor administrative duties: cooperating during the census, undertaking routine paperwork, bringing problems to the attention of district and national authorities, collaborating with the local police and cooperating with the electoral commission during elections.

With the advent of the Tukuyana Amazones movement, an insurgency organised and coordinated in a hierarchical command and control fashion, the traditional leaders, now cut off from any civilian government support, have found themselves reduced to figureheads, unsure of their position with older Caribs and ignored by younger Carib Tukuyana Amazones. With decision-making and the definition of power in Paramaribo confused and dangerous, powerful local leaders can easily come into being. This seems to be the case among the Carib. However, it has not been the old traditional leaders who have expanded their power, but rather the young, military-backed warlords, such as Thomas and Matto, who have in effect transformed the traditional fabric of Carib life in the name of liberation. Interestingly, this transformation harks back to the early colonial period of Carib *caciques*, mobilising and directing their braves for warfare.

THE TUKUYANA AMAZONES

Tukuyana hostilities broke out in late 1989 when an armed band of Caribs took several civilian hostages in west Suriname in what seemed to be a protest against an imminent peace treaty to be signed with the anti-military Maroon movement known as Jungle Commando and headed by Ronnie Brunswijk.[14] In a flurry of assaults the Tukuyana sacked the Coppename River ferry boat killing one person, hijacked two small aircraft at west Suriname jungle airstrips, mounted a road block near the international airport and attacked a rice barge on a river which ran through 'Tukuyana territory'. Through its spokesman, Thomas, from the village of Bigi Poika, the group demanded direct talks with Bouterse. As a consequence, in early 1990, a group of some 50 Tukuyana warriors wearing combat fatigues and carrying weaponry, including grenade launchers, similar to that possessed by the national army, were welcomed by Bouterse at the palace in Paramaribo. This formidable group was led by Thomas and his lieutenant, Matto, both attired in Carib robes, beads, feathered headdresses and very dark sunglasses. Bouterse and his Tukuyana guests agreed that the Caribs' protests and actions were legitimate so long as the Jungle Commando had not yet signed a peace treaty and was in command of its arms.

Members of the National Assembly and representatives from various human rights groups have also testified that the army trained and armed

Tukuyana Amazones rebels throughout west Suriname and in an enclave along the coast adjacent to French Guiana. It was estimated that by early 1990 there were some 75 to 100 heavily armed Tukuyana whose activities were allegedly coordinated by a lieutenant of the Surinamese army. By mid-1991 their numbers had reached nearly 300. Relations between Caribs and Maroons have traditionally been strained, despite the fact that both ethnic groups reside in the jungle interior and are at the bottom of Suriname's neo-colonial social hierarchy. In effect, the national army made use of this tension, organising the Caribs into an anti-Maroon rebel militia and preparing them in training exercises at its Ayoko Caserne (fort) in the interior behind the international airport. The result was that, in late 1989 and 1990, several bouts of fighting broke out between Tukuyana units and supporters of the Maroon Jungle Commando.

Small scale, but still damaging, operations executed by Tukuyana groups of some 20 to 25 men armed with Uzis, FN FALs and AK-47s, continued throughout 1990. They included attacks on civilian police posts and the eventual expulsion of a civilian police presence in Tukuyana Amazones territory, harassment of the large state-owned mechanised rice plantation at Wageningen, the seizure of the Coppename River ferry resulting in the country literally being cut in half, several kidnappings, and demands for pay-offs from timber cutters operating along the Coppename River leading to the collapse of the lucrative timber industry in west Suriname. At the same time, mindful of public relations and the necessity to organise itself into an urban cell, the military structure of the Tukuyana Amazones developed a parallel civilian representative arm. In late 1989, an eight-member Carib commission headed by Nocdus Jubitana was identified and entered into fruitless negotiations with the civilian government. Likewise, the Tukuyana Amazones opened their own human rights organisation called Alfobigi '86, claiming that Caribs were being victimised and oppressed by Maroon Jungle Commandos.[15]

The national army's complicity in sponsoring the Tukuyana Amazones was extended in 1990 when army units smashed an internal Tukuyana revolt against Thomas and Matto's leadership. Some 14 dissenters were killed in the conflict while another 11 fled to Guyana, only to be handed back to the Surinamese army by Guyanese officials. Eight of the men disappeared and have not been seen or heard of since. Attempts to investigate their alleged murder were obstructed, with civilian police prevented from entering Tukuyana territory to investigate. The Surinamese army did nothing to assist the police in gaining access to the illegally controlled portion of the country. It is arguable too that, because of military intimidation, the police themselves did not have much appetite to investigate cases such as this. As regards the nature of the internal conflict, it has been suggested that the Tukuyana dissenters opposed the growing influence that Bouterse was having over Thomas and Matto and, consequently, over the entire Tukuyana Amazones movement.

Expanding the scope of their operations, armed Tukuyana militias subsequently took to banditry and plunder, turning west Suriname into a no-man's land. Rumours of Tukuyana complicity in drug trafficking, undertaken from airstrips deep in Carib territory, also emerged in early 1990 and increased in authenticity during 1991. The narcotics trafficking opportunities, as well as access to and the monopoly of rich resources in the interior, such as gold, timber and land concessions, indicate that the national army and their Tukuyana Amazones have an enduring commitment to an alliance. Near Apoera, for example, not far from the Tibiti River in Tukuyana Amazones-controlled territory, there have been built up, according to Dutch police officials, laboratories for the refinement of coca paste, stockpiles of cocaine-producing chemicals and supplies of refined cocaine awaiting shipment to the European market. Several airstrips, the largest near Tijger Kreek along the road from the international airport to Apoera, have been carved out of the jungle and accept several flights per week from Colombia. Simply put, then, the entire area to the south-west of Paramaribo is Tukuyana Amazones/ Surinamese military-controlled and devoted to narcotics processing and transshipping.[16]

This had obvious implications for the conduct of the elections held in May 1991. Concern about the fairness of the balloting in the violence-torn interior was immediately raised by opposition parties and international observers. The three rural districts of Marowijne, Sipaliwini and Brokopondo, where elements of Tukuyana Amazones, Jungle Commando, Angulla, Mandela and units of the National Army were operating with impunity, were allocated ten of the 51 National Assembly seats. Since radio and television reception is poor to non-existent in the major part of this area, the only way to campaign was through visits from party representatives themselves. In Tukuyana Amazones-controlled territory in Marowijne (around the villages of Galibi, Pierrekondre and Langamankondre) and in Brokopondo/ Sipaliwini (around Donderkamp, Corneliskondre, Bigi Poika, Matta, Apoera, and Kwamala Semutu), representatives of the two opposition anti-military parties, the New Front and DA '91, were not permitted entry and hence were denied the right to campaign. They were forcibly turned back by armed insurgent patrols. Police units, of course, had not been allowed in the areas for several years.

Tukuyana Amazones collaboration with the military was therefore palpable. Interior rivers, the Coppename, Wayambo and Arawara, were patrolled by heavily armed young Tukuyanas in camouflage uniforms and sailing in aluminium skiffs still bearing the decal of the Suriname National Army.[17] On one occasion, serving as an election monitor, I was stopped about 15 miles behind the international airport at a roadblock manned by two insurgents armed with heavy Bren guns and FN FALs. I was interrogated and robbed and was held at gunpoint until Commander Matto was summoned. He told me to follow him to the village of Matta where, in an abandoned school house, he questioned me further. He wrote my answers in a school-boy's lined paper examination booklet and told me to clear out of Tukuyana Amazones territory by nightfall. The room in which I was questioned was piled high with an arsenal of weapons of every conceivable kind: ancient M-1 carbines, Uzis, Bren guns, German assault rifles, rocket-propelled grenade launchers and several small-bore mortars. Belts and boxes of ammunition and untidy piles of hand grenades lay scattered about. Despite their uniforms, there did not seem to be a quartermaster among them. And, on a small blackboard, carefully outlined and scrawled, was a flow-chart indicating tasks, by person, unit and location (for example, river patrol areas, availability of boats, motors and fuel) and by date, day and time. The most remarkable feature of this military organisation was that it was not inherently Carib; outsiders were teaching and directing them how to do it. Those outsiders, of course, were advisors from the Surinamese National Army. The *cacique*, albeit rationalised with a flow-chart and supported by modern weaponry, was back.

As indicated, in the elections of May 1991, no representatives were allowed to campaign in any of the Carib, Tukuyana-controlled territories. Every single Carib village polling station voted overwhelmingly for the NDP, the civilian arm of the military. Perhaps this exercise can explain to us just how much and how little elections can do in the restoration of democracy. The balloting on election day in Donderkamp on the Wayambo River, which I personally witnessed as an official, was done freely, fairly, and secretly.[18] The OAS observer instructed the Captain that NDP banners and posters had to be removed from the polling station and he cordially complied. Virtually all the Caribs were wearing NDP T-shirts, including the nurse at the government clinic. Several Tukuyanas whom I recognised from the day before appeared wearing NDP baseball caps. One hundred and sixty-seven Carib men and women, all with national identity cards and voter registrations, secretly marked their ballots and deposited them in a slotted metal milk urn. At the count at the end of the day the tabulated ballots yielded 165 votes for the NDP and two voided ballots. In neighbouring Corneliskondre, the score was 34 for the NDP, six null and void. This consistency in voting behaviour throughout Carib villages and constituencies provided the NDP with two of the ten seats at stake in the three interior districts. Had the NDP relied only on the considerably larger Maroon populations in these districts – who are by and large anti-military and hence anti-NDP – they would have won no seats. In fact, Maroon voters showed a variety of voter preferences by selecting from a menu of civilian parties; not so the Caribs.

CARIB CONSCIOUSNESS IN SURINAME

The roots of this remarkable Carib resistance movement, despite the damaging and insidious involvement of the Surinamese military and narco-traffickers, can be found more or less directly in the late 1940s when a Carib man from Bigi Poika (the western command village for the contemporary Tukuyana) named R. J. Kiban began a weekly radio talk show in the Carib language on news and matters of concern to Caribs, including national politics.[19] He also wrote a small book on Carib music and dance and encouraged the publication of American Indian stories in one of Paramaribo's newspapers. Critical of central government for doing nothing for American Indians, in 1962 he organised a group of about 75 Caribs and Arawaks into the VIP (the Verenigde Indiaans Partij, or United Indian Party), and ran in the 1963 elections, securing over 1,500 votes out of an American Indian pool of about 2,000 voters. Not enough to win him a seat, the number of ballots nevertheless indicated that, true to Surinamese custom, American Indians also would 'vote their own'.[20] In 1967 the VIP decided not to go it alone any more but to join with a Creole, Roman Catholic labour party with a progressive reputation. Other major parties, seeing that the American Indians, particularly the Caribs, were a potential source of votes, fielded candidates in Carib areas and made robust campaign promises. Invited to Paramaribo to be feted and courted, Carib leaders noticed that the more numerous interior-dwelling Maroons were put up in hotels while they were warehoused in a large dance-hall, reflecting their ranking at the bottom of Suriname's neo-colonial status hierarchy.

Throughout the 1970s, the American Indian vote continued to be courted by, and went to, the largest of the Creole political parties, even though little in the way of traditional patronage or development-related assistance was given in return. What did develop was Carib cultural awareness. Nardo Aluman, a young Carib from the Galibi area on the Maroni River (and educated in Paramaribo), organised a pan-Suriname Carib awareness group, lobbied the Ministry of Education and Culture for research and documentation funds, prepared a Carib language-Dutch dictionary and made Carib cultural presentations at theatres and halls in Paramaribo and at international conferences.[21] Add to this the fact that the late 1970s were an economic disaster for all Surinamers as millions of dollars of Dutch aid money was squandered on huge macro-development projects such as locating, accessing and exploiting bauxite reserves in west Suriname. Virtually nothing was spent by comparison on infrastructure, grassroots development, social programmes or the interior – not even for co-op funded outboard motors, a common request of Carib fishermen. Frustrated, increasingly marginalised and powerless, the Caribs were thus ripe for revolutionary plucking in the mid-1980s when the military needed to shop for domestic allies. The politics all came together in the Tukuyana Amazones.

CONCLUSION

What then do the Caribs, and the Tukuyana Amazones, want and what are their chances of getting it? The Caribs will point out, with historical legitimacy, that they (along with other American Indians) were the first inhabitants of Suriname and hence possess what we can call usufructual privilege to the land and resources of the country. Not only does this include access to the wealth of their traditional territories but it also encourages the widespread feeling among virtually all Caribs that they have a *moral* right to aid, resources, territory, recognition and anything else that the state has to offer. Traditionally, certainly up to the 1950s, Caribs saw themselves as 'passive receivers of desired goods and services, instead of active participants who seize opportunities offered to aid themselves'.[22] This situation has changed since the emergence of the Tukuyana Amazones movement but in a way which leaves open the question of whether the Caribs have redefined themselves or some other ethnic group has done it for them, thereby rendering them once again passive agents unable to control their own destinies. Who then is using whom?

It is too simple to say that the Surinamese national army, totally and in a one-sided fashion, is using and manipulating the Caribs via the Tukuyana Amazones insurgency. The situation in Suriname's rainforest interior is chaotic and has been so for the past decade, ever since the civilian government first collapsed after the coup of 1980 and, in effect, abrogated its centralised power to the military and their henchmen. In short, the centre of the state has virtually collapsed and the periphery has emerged as more powerful and independent. The emergence of the Jungle Commando under Ronnie Brunswijk was the first evidence of this and, as has been seen, several other rival Maroon groups and the Tukuyanas themselves soon followed. Yet all these groups have had their own agenda, whether they were military-sponsored or not. For virtually all of its history the interior of Suriname has been ignored by state politicians in the capital – unless they wanted something and then they would literally flood out, chase out, lock out or buy out the indigenous populations.[23] This has all changed now as young Caribs (and Maroons) locate their future not in neo-colonial patronage – beads, trinkets and tribute – from Paramaribo, but in active and independent involvement in the modern national market economy (including the production and transshipment of narcotics). If this takes the compliance of and cooperation with the Surinamese military (which has its own agenda, that of survival and continued economic privilege), then so be it: they will advance the interests of the military while at the same time advancing their own.

What, then, do they want, these Tukuyana Amazones and their sympathisers? An anecdote will tell. Caribs are familiar with the fate of American Indians in the USA and several asked me, over rum and cigarettes, to tell them 'stories' about my 'Carib countrymen'. Stories were told of Cheyennes and Sioux, Iroquois and Seminoles, Apaches and Hopi, of battles and glories and horses and maize and tepees and any tales I could muster. My Tukuyana hosts listened and at the end said: 'You see, if you lay there and do nothing, everybody will kick you around. You have to fight back'.[24] In other words, they want cultural glory, pride and a resurgence of their heritage. But they also want gold, timber, and land concessions, development funds and programmes, participation in the narcotics rackets, incorporation on their own terms into the national and international market economy, access to state power in Paramaribo, autonomy within Suriname's highly culturally fragmented society, and that age-old rivalry of young Caribs wanting to wrest power from the old heads in order to lead their people back to the future during this nativistic revival. Nor has the wider historical meaning of 1992 been lost on the Tukuyana. In a revealing letter sent to President Venetiaan in late 1991 congratulating him on his electoral victory, the Tukuyana Council of Eight noted that 'it will be 500 years ago that the suffering of the native people in the Americas started, and . . . it is time that in an honourable way an end be made to this suffering'. The Council also embarked upon a campaign to distribute documents, materials, and information about the Tukuyana to the general public in the hope of soliciting their sympathy and support. All of this may happen. For the moment, after nearly two years of intermittent negotiations, a peace treaty was signed between the government of Suriname and all guerrilla groups operating in the interior on 5 August 1992. The groups included the Tukuyana, the Jungle Commando, the Mandela, the Angulla and the Koffimaka. The peace accord included the following provisions: all parties, including the military, will be covered by a general and comprehensive amnesty for abuses of human rights, murders and misdeeds undertaken since the Jungle Commando insurgency broke out in early 1985. Provision will be made for the entitlement of land ownership for Carib Indians, Arawak Indians and all Maroons in respect of land located within their traditional tribal areas of habitation. All illegal weapons will be collected and destroyed under the supervision of the Organization of American States and Ronnie Brunswijk further insinuated after the treaty signing that his troops would be incorporated into the Surinamese police force as a sort of rural guard. All insurgent groups would also return stolen property to individuals and companies from whom they had extorted it. The destroyed infrastructure of the interior would be rebuilt and a large portion of the Dutch development monies soon to be put back on stream would be devoted to developing the interior. The treaty was signed by President Venetiaan for the Republic of Suriname, Thomas Sabajo for the Tukuyana and Ronnie Brunswijk for the Jungle Commando.

Brunswijk and Sabajo strongly endorsed amnesty for the military for all crimes and abuses from the onset of the military dictatorship in 1980, including the infamous murders of 1982. This unsolicited move strongly suggests Jungle Commando, Tukuyana and military complicity in setting up the peace treaty. The elected civilian government thus faces an uncertain future. The government will soon have to devalue its currency, privatise inefficient state enterprises, reduce its bloated bureaucracy, find a new way to dispense patronage to rival ethnic groups, curtail narcotics trafficking and the laundering of narco-dollars, and bring Suriname back into the democrat fold of nations. To say the least, the peace treaty of August 1992 does not provide much glue to hold this effort together. The prognosis, for Suriname and for the Caribs themselves, is not good for, as the local proverb goes, 'when you eat with the devil you better have a long fork'.

NOTES

1. Suriname has a population of some 400,000 divided into the following groups: East Indian (35 per cent), Afro-Creoles (30 per cent), Javanese-Indonesians (15 per cent), Maroons or Bush Negroes (ten per cent), American Indians (seven per cent), and the rest made up primarily of Chinese, Lebanese and persons of European descent. See G. Brana-Shute (ed.), *Resistance and Rebellion in Suriname: Old and New* (Williamsburg, VA, 1990).

2. I use nativistic in the loosest of ways: simply that a group wishes to recreate a time of ethnic glory, pride and eminence and seeks to do so through a revitalisation of its traditional culture. See A.F.C. Wallace, 'Revitalization Movements', *American Anthropologist*, 58, 3 (1965), and P. Worsley, *The Trumpet Shall Sound* (London, 1957).

   Carib is not only the name of the American Indian ethnic group under specific discussion in this article, but is also the name given to the larger and more inclusive language group to which belong some 20 distinct Carib-speaking ethnic groups. The Carib-speaking Carib of Suriname (as opposed to the Carib-speaking Trio, Waiyana and Akurio) occupy three geographical enclaves, yet maintain a remarkable coherence of language, culture and social organisation. These enclaves are the marshy, coastal savanna of north-east Suriname adjacent to French Guiana; the riverine, rainforest environment along the mid-Maroni river border with French Guiana; and the rainforest and savanna niche in west-central Suriname. See E.B. Basso (ed.), *Carib-Speaking Indians: Culture, Society and Language* (Tucson, 1977) for a thorough overview of Carib-speaking groups, and P. Kloos, *The Maroni River Caribs of Surinam* (Assen, 1971) for a splendid ethnography of the Maroni River Caribs. Arawak-speakers are linguistically and culturally distinct American Indians.

   To a certain, although more brutal, extent, American Indians elsewhere, such as the Aymara, Miskiti, Maya and Mohawk, have experienced the same social misery and deprivation as the Carib. See NACLA, 'The First Nations 1492–1992', *Report on the Americas*, 25, 3 (1991).

3. Suriname's history from 1980 to 1987 has been as confusing as it has been treacherous. The literature in English is sparse but of generally good quality. See particularly G. Brana-Shute, 'Back to the Barracks? Five Years Revo in Suriname', *Journal of Interamerican Studies and World Affairs*, 28, 1 (1986); E. Dew, *The Difficult Flowering of Suriname* (The Hague, 1978); S. MacDonald, 'Insurrection and Redemocratization in Suriname? The Ascendancy of the Third Path', *Journal of Interamerican Studies and World Affairs*, 30, 1 (1988); H.E. Chin and H. Buddingh', *Suriname: Politics, Economics and Society* (London, 1987); and B. Sedoc-Dahlberg (ed.), *The Dutch Caribbean: Prospects for Democracy* (New York, 1990).

4. Actually the period of NDP rule lasted past May and until early September 1991 when a President and Vice-President were finally elected. It was the deliberate policy of the NDP to spread around as much money as possible, even though the country was nearly bankrupt.

   Knowing that it would not win the 1991 election (although it did in fact do well), the NDP wanted the voters to remember its six months of rule as the 'good old days'. It thus left the elected New Front government with an empty treasury when assuming office in September 1991. Most NDPers think that the New Front is so weak and in such an unenviable position that new elections will be held before they are constitutionally scheduled (1996) and that the NDP will be swept into power by memories of clientelist nostalgia. See G. Brana-Shute, 'Suriname Tries Again', *Hemisphere*, 3, 2 (1991).

5. Several human rights reports have examined and documented these charges. See Organization of American States (OAS), *Annual Report of the Inter-American Commission on Human Rights, 1990–1991* (Washington DC, 1991); Americas Watch, *Suriname: Human Rights Conditions on the Eve of the Election* (New York, 1991);

and US Department of State, *Country Reports on Human Rights Practices for 1990* (Washington DC, 1991).

6. See Brana-Shute, 'Suriname Tries Again', for a description and analysis of the 1991 elections. The author served as an OAS election observer in Suriname for four months and spent a good deal of time in the interior, in part with Carib Indians and their Tukuyana Amazones insurgents on the Wayambo River in the villages of Donderkamp and Cornelis Kondre. On other occasions the author visited the Tukuyana Amazones strongholds of Matta and Bigi Poika, headquarters of Commanders Thomas and Matto, as well as Carib villages along the Maroni River.

7. For a discussion of the Brunswijk Jungle Commando, see Brana-Shute, *Resistance and Rebellion*, and 'Politics and Revolution', *Caribbean Affairs*, 4, 2 (1991).

8. The capture of Moengo also led to Brunswijk's first conventional defeat by the Suriname National Army when his irregulars were driven from the town. He had broken the first rule of guerrilla warfare: do not hold territory, keep moving.

9. Two other anti-Jungle Commando insurgencies were created by the military at this same time. Young Maroons from the Saramakka tribe took the name Angullas and, modestly armed, terrorised neutrals and pro-Jungle Commando civilians alike. The Mandela Commandos, also military-sponsored, undertook similar activities in Matawai Maroon tribal territory. They wore uniforms, were better armed and appeared more centrally organised than the Angullas who operated more in the fashion of a 'gang'. Neither of these groups will be treated here, although I was told by a Mandela commando that 'Mandelas and Tukuyana work together'.

10. These villages include Langamankondre, Christiaankondre, Erowarte, Tapuku, Pierrekondre, Bigiston, Calbo, Redidoti, Pierrekondre (2), Bernharddorp, Maho, Columbia, Cabendadorp, Matta, Bigi Poika, Kalebaskreek, Sabana, Josedorp, Corneliskondre and Donderkamp.

11. Suriname's currency, the guilder, is hopelessly inflated and using it here to provide an average per household income figure for urban/rural/jungle dwellers would not make much sense. Suffice it to say that for the Caribs of west Suriname a litre of beer costs US$7.50, a litre of rum US$22.50, a package of cigarettes US$6.50, a pound of rice US$1.00 and a litre of kerosene US$1.50.

12. See Kloos, *The Maroni River Caribs*.

13. For a discussion of Carib social organisation, economic institutions, religion and political structures, see *inter alia* Kloos, *The Maroni River Caribs*; Basso, *Carib-Speaking Indians*; F. Jara and E. Magana-Torres, 'Astronomy of the Coastal Caribs of Suriname', *L'Homme: Revue Francaise d'Anthropologie*, 23, 1 (1983); and P. Riviere, 'Aspects of Carib Political Economy', *Anthropologica*, 59/62 (1983).

14. This peace treaty was the so-called Kourou Accord, named after the town in French Guiana where it was agreed in principle. The accord called for a ceasefire between the Suriname military and the Jungle Commando but did not require the Jungle Commando to turn in its weapons. The ceasefire held throughout most of 1992. See Brana-Shute, 'Small Country, Smaller Revolution: Surprising Suriname', *Caribbean Review*, 15, 2 (1987); 'Suriname: Politics and Militarism', *Hemisphere*, 1, 2 (1989); *Resistance and Rebellion*; and 'Politics and Revolution'.

15. Alfobigi '86 was a case of shameless hypocrisy. It was meant to rival, as a Carib propaganda arm, the responsible national human rights organisation Mooiwana '86 which has been concerned primarily with national army abuses of Maroons. By late 1991, Alfobigi '86 was basically defunct as its leader, George Pierre, had fled for his life to the Netherlands, claiming that he was threatened by other Carib compatriots.

16. See the excellent reportage in *NRC Handelsblad*, 27 July 1991, 1 and 3 and *Washington Post*, 4 Nov. 1991, 1 and 15.

17. The author's role as an OAS election monitor took him to Donderkamp, District Brokopondo, for some nine days, along with a seven-member civilian election monitoring board and two police officers who were allowed in with the OAS observer but told to get out and stay out after election formalities were completed.

18. Donderkamp is a large village of about 575 inhabitants, not all of whom reside there

permanently or year round. There are about 25 Tukuyana Amazones from Donderkamp and the commander and sub-commander were assigned to keep an eye on
me. To reach Donderkamp – the airstrip had been shut down by the Tukuyana – one
had to drive two and a half hours from Paramaribo to Boskamp on the Coppename
River. There then followed an eight-hour river trip in an open 20-foot canoe powered
by outboard motor. The village is approached by a rickety wharf and a winding trail
from the river about half a mile long. There are several small European-style houses
along the trail for the school teacher, the clinic nurse and police officers (although the
latter are no longer present). The Catholic church has fallen into disrepair and is no
longer used or visited by a priest. Past these houses lie the soccer field, meeting house
and a three-room elementary school. Beyond the veneer of the state and the nuclear
family settlements are the homes of the Caribs themselves. Houses are made of
rough-cut timber planks and palm thatch, and roofed with thatch, and are universally
built on sandy patches of ground that punctuate the otherwise general rainforest
foliage.

19. This era was marked by the emergence of political nationalism amongst the other
    ethnic groups in Suriname as well and preceded the 1954 'Statuut' granting Suriname
    domestic autonomy within the Kingdom of the Netherlands. Universal suffrage was
    granted in 1948. See Dew, *The Difficult Flowering*.

20. Kloos covers this extensively in *The Maroni River Caribs*, 224–5, and also reports
    that there seems to have been formed as early as 1949 a political club or interest
    group called 'Caribs Wake Up'. They did not, however, contest any elections.

21. The author met Aluman at a cultural festival in Trinidad in 1976 when, along with
    Creole poet laureate Robin Ravales, he represented Suriname's traditional cultures.

22. Kloos, *The Maroni River Caribs*, 267.

23. This is not hyperbole. In the 1960s thousands of Saramakka Maroons were flooded
    out of their village when a hydro-electric power dam was built.

24. In Sranan Tongo, the Afro-Creole now used by almost all Caribs, it was rendered:
    'Joe no sie, if joe didon wan den tra wan o scopoe joe. Joe moesoe foe feti baka'.

Drugs and Security in the Commonwealth Caribbean

IVELAW L. GRIFFITH

Dramatic domestic and international changes in both the developed and the developing worlds over the past few years have been progressively altering the security agenda throughout the world. One subject that is rising progressively to the top of the security agenda in the Caribbean is drugs. The drugs question is a legitimate security issue because drug operations present dangers to the physical and psychological safety of citizens, and to the governability of states, in the Caribbean and elsewhere. As will be seen below, drug operations have military, political, and economic security ramifications.

The links between drugs and security are examined here in the context of the redefinition of the term 'security'. This redefinition goes beyond the 'high politics' characterisation of security, which emphasises its military dimension, especially in relation to the international arena. It extends the conceptual boundaries of the term to economic and ecological questions, stressing links between security and development. This conceptualisation of security also posits that internal security questions are not only important in their own right, but that they complicate, and sometimes aggravate, external problems. Moreover, the distinction between internal issues and external ones is often blurred.[1]

The main narcotics problems in the Caribbean relate to drug production, abuse and transshipment, and to money laundering. These problems constitute the single most critical security problem in the region. Lynden Pindling, Prime Minister of the Bahamas from independence in 1973 until August 1992, made the following observation more than a decade ago: 'I have no doubt . . . that it's the greatest single threat to the social, economic fabric . . . Unchecked it will destroy us . . . the money available is just too great.'[2] The Prime Minister of Barbados, Lloyd Erskine Sandiford, deemed the drugs issue 'perhaps the single most serious problem for the region in the next decade'.

Ivelaw L. Griffith is an assistant professor of political science at Lehman College, The City University of New York.

Michael Manley, Prime Minister of Jamaica until March 1992 when he resigned his office because of failing health, called illicit drugs a 'scourge' and described the drug network as 'probably the most highly organized and successfully interfaced collection of interlocking cartels of criminal purpose in human history'.[3] The report of the West Indian Commission, published in 1992, similarly warned: 'Nothing poses greater threats to civil society in CARICOM countries than the drug problem; and nothing exemplifies the powerlessness of regional governments more. That is the magnitude of the damage that drug abuse and drug trafficking hold for our Community.'[4]

The perception of drugs as dangerous exists not only in the Caribbean, but in Europe, Latin America, the United States and elsewhere. Indeed, the entire international community expressed this concern at the specially convened session of the United Nations General Assembly in 1990:

> [T]he magnitude of the rising trend in the illicit demand, production, supply, trafficking, and distribution of narcotic drugs and psychotropic substances [is] a grave and persistent threat to the health and well-being of mankind, the stability of nations, the political, economic, social, and cultural structures of all societies, and the lives and dignity of millions of human beings, most especially our young people . . . [5]

Appreciating how drug production, abuse, trafficking and money laundering present actual and potential threats to the security of Caribbean nations requires an initial indication of the drugs involved and an understanding of the manner in which the various narcotics operations are conducted. We can then proceed to examine their security implications, in political, military and economic terms. As was indicated above, Caribbean governments are conscious of the threats involved, and have attempted various individual and collective responses that warrant attention. The final section of this article will therefore look at some of the domestic and regional countermeasures adopted in the battle against drugs.

NARCOTICS AND NARCOTICS OPERATIONS

The Danger Drugs

The use and misuse of drugs like alcohol and tobacco have long been problematic for countries in the Caribbean. Yet these are not the drugs that have given rise to problems with security implications. The 'danger drugs' are mainly cocaine, marijuana, heroin and their derivatives, such as crack.

Cocaine is the most potent stimulant of natural origin. It is extracted from the coca plant, *Erythroxylon coca*, which has been grown in South America's Andean region since prehistoric times. Pure cocaine was isolated first in the 1880s. It was used later in eye, nose, throat and other surgery because of its ability to anaesthetise tissue and simultaneously constrict blood vessels and limit bleeding. Illicit cocaine is usually distributed as a white crystalline powder, often diluted by a variety of other ingredients, including inositol, mannitol and lactose. It is the adulteration of the drug that increases its volume, thereby increasing its profitability. The substance is peddled under numerous names, among them 'coke', 'flake', 'snow', 'toot', 'superblow', and 'crack'.

Crack delivers ten times the impact of powdered cocaine, with of course the same proportion of danger. It is made by mixing cocaine with bicarbonate of soda and water, boiling to a paste, and allowing the mixture to harden. The mixture makes a crackling sound while being boiled, hence the name of the product. Powdered cocaine takes three to four minutes to enter the blood-stream and reach the brain, but crack does so in seconds. And because it can be easily concocted and is cheap, crack use has developed to explosive proportions in many American, Caribbean and European cities.[6]

Cocaine is a stimulant with powerful psychotropic impact. The intensity of its effect depends on the rate of entry into the blood-stream. Intravenous injection or smoking produces an almost immediate experience. Inhalation of cocaine fumes, via the smoking of crack for instance, produces a fast onset effect. However, the 'high' is over very quickly. Indeed, with a 1–2 hour duration, cocaine has the shortest 'high' of all dangerous drugs. By comparison, opium, morphine, heroin and codeine have a 3–6 hour duration; benzodiazepines, methaqualone, glutethimide and many other depressants have a 4–8 hour duration; marijuana and hashish have a 2–4 hour duration. LSD and mescaline have a duration of 8–12 hours, and the 'high' of Angel Dust, PCP, and TCP lasts for several days.[7]

Because of cocaine's short 'high' and the intensity of its pleasurable effect, there is an extraordinary dependency factor. Addicts need to resort to larger doses at shorter intervals and addiction has serious physiological and psychic consequences. There is often a toxic psychosis similar to paranoid schizophrenia, reflected by anxiety, restlessness and extreme irritability. Tactile hallucinations develop in some cases, to the point where addicts injure themselves in attempting to remove imaginary insects from beneath their skin. Others feel persecuted and fear that people are watching and following them. Excessive doses of cocaine can also be fatal. Death can result from seizures, respiratory failure, strokes, and cerebral haemorrhage.[8]

Marijuana is a tobacco-like substance produced by drying the leaves and flowering tops of the Indian hemp plant. Its potency varies depending on the source and selectivity of the plants used. For example, while varieties of Indian hemp in the United States have a THC (tetrahydrocannabinol) concentration of less than 0.3 per cent, those in Jamaica, Colombia and Mexico have between 0.5 and seven per cent. Sinsemilla (from Spanish *Sin Semilla*, without seed), prepared from the unpollinated female cannabis plant, has been known to have as much as 20 per cent THC.[9] Marijuana is known as 'pot', 'ganja', 'joint', 'herb', 'Acapulco Gold', 'reefer', 'grass', and 'sinsemilla', among other names.

Marijuana is generally smoked or chewed. It has been used for both medical and non-medical purposes for over 3,000 years. It was used in China long before the birth of Jesus Christ, for treatment of hypertension and glaucoma. Marijuana also has been used in India for centuries. Indeed, it was Indian migration to the Caribbean in the nineteenth century that led to its introduction in the western hemisphere. Abuse of this drug can lead to euphoria, disorientation, and increased appetite. It also relaxes many inhibitions. Abuse rarely results in death, but overdose effects include fatigue, paranoia, and possible psychosis.

Unlike cocaine and marijuana, heroin is a semisynthetic narcotic, derived from morphine, which itself is obtained from the opium poppy, *Papaver Somnifernum*. It was first synthesised in 1874 and the German company, Bayer, started producing it commercially as a pain remedy in 1898. Pure heroin is a white, bitter tasting powder, but illicit heroin varies in colour and form. The colour variation – from white to dark brown – results from impurities of the manufacturing process or from additives. Pure heroin is rarely peddled on the street. The street heroin often has a mere five per cent of the pure matter, with dilutents such as sugar, powdered milk, or quinine, in ratios ranging from 9:1 to as much as 99:1. Known also as 'horse', 'smack', 'dope', 'snow', as well as by other names, heroin is administered through injection, sniffing or smoking.

The AIDS epidemic in the United States has caused many heroin users to alter their pattern of administering the drug. Heroin addicts in the United States, and most likely elsewhere, are rapidly abandoning injections and resorting to sniffing. Heroin has a high physical as well as psychological dependency factor. The effects of its use are drowsiness, respiratory depression, constricted pupils and nausea. Heroin overdose can be fatal. But even if death does not result, there can be shallow breathing, convulsions and comas.

Production and Abuse

Only marijuana is produced in the Commonwealth Caribbean. It is not cultivated throughout the region and cultivation varies from place to place. Belize, Guyana, Jamaica and Trinidad and Tobago are among the places with the highest levels of marijuana production. For instance, in March 1992 joint police–army operations in Guyana discovered 60,000 pounds of marijuana in the Mahaica River area, and ten fields, with an estimated 160,000 marijuana plants, along the Maduni Creek. Two months later, similar operations uncovered 799,700 pounds of marijuana, this time in the Berbice river, in eastern Guyana. That find had a street value of more than G$1 billion.[10]

Among the four states named above, Belize and Jamaica stand out for their levels of production and export of the drug. In both countries, marijuana has been the largest cash crop, producing an estimated US$350 million annually in Belize, and about US$2 billion in Jamaica.[11] The Bahamas, which features prominently in drug transshipment, has traditionally been neither a drug-producing nor a drug-refining country. However, the production alarm was sounded in 1991 following the discovery and destruction of 40,000 cannabis seedlings and 1,000 medium-sized plants, and the seizure of 22 kilos of prepared marijuana.

Marijuana is cultivated mostly in the north and west of Belize in small plots of about one acre or less. Significant cultivation began in the 1960s, mainly for the United States market. By the early 1980s Belize was the fourth largest supplier to the United States, behind Colombia, Mexico, and Jamaica. But production has since plummeted from that peak, largely due to countermeasures taken by the Belize government, often under pressure from the United States. The Belize government began aerial spraying in 1982, with the help of Mexico and the United States. Prime Minister George Price found it politically expedient to discontinue the spraying in 1984, given the impending general elections and the fact that the spraying operations generated a storm of protest from environmentalists and farmers. Belize specialists believe that the loss of the 1985 elections by the People's United Party (PUP) was due partly to the anger generated by farmers. However, spraying was resumed in 1986 by the wish of the new government. The victorious Prime Minister, Manuel Esquivel, defined the drug problem as a serious national security threat, justifying an 'all-out war'. In fact, he perceived the drug trade as a greater threat to the country's sovereignty and democracy than the long-standing territorial claims of Guatemala.[12]

Eradication measures have drastically reduced marijuana production. Most marijuana that is discovered is destroyed immediately, either by aerial eradication or by hand where it is in close proximity to residences or legitimate crops. The US Department of State proudly reported in 1991 that 'after three years of intensive eradication efforts and the maintenance of an effective suppression program supported by the USG [United States Government], Belize is now only a marginal producer of marijuana'.[13] Personnel from the Belize Defense Force (BDF) now fly in aircraft belonging to the State Department's Bureau of International Narcotics Matters (INM) as part of the eradication programme. Some drug experts believe that Belize may be near the maximum achievable level of suppressible marijuana production. Indeed, it is estimated that only 54 hectares were cultivated in 1991, compared with 67 hectares in 1990, and 132 hectares in 1988. However, in spite of the overall reduction, there is some concern about the cultivation of the *indica* variety of cannabis, which is much shorter than the six-foot tall indigenous plants.

Jamaica's subtropical climate makes the entire island ideal for cannabis cultivation. 'Ganja', as marijuana is popularly known in the island, grows year-round and traditionally is harvested in two main annual seasons, of five- to six-month cycles. However, the *indica* variety mentioned above matures in three to four months, making four harvests possible. Large-scale cultivation, of five- to fifty-acre plots, was once common, but because of eradication measures, most cultivation is now done in plots of one acre or less, with yields of about 1,485 pounds per hectare. Cultivation was once highly concentrated in the wet lands of western and central Jamaica, but production countermeasures have resulted in shifts to remote highland areas, including the Blue Mountains in the eastern part of the country. Most of the cultivation is now on inaccessible mountainsides, ridges or valleys.[14]

Marijuana production in Jamaica rose continuously until eradication measures, introduced in response to United States pressure and with its assistance, began to reduce cultivation. The campaign, called Operation Buccaneer, is still undertaken annually. One dramatic success saw a drop in production from an estimated 405 metric tons in 1988 to 190 metric tons in 1989. Yet shifts in cultivation patterns, a change in variety, and reduced resources for aerial spraying led to a dramatic rebound in the 1990s. Although Operation Buccaneer eradicated about 1,000 hectares of marijuana in 1990, cultivation actually expanded from 280 hectares in 1989 to 1,220 hectares in 1990.[15] Aerial spraying of cannabis in Jamaica is more controversial than in Belize because marijuana is an even larger source of income there, one estimate for the

1980s placing the number of farmers cultivating the crop at 6,000. Indeed, in the late 1980s, it is said to have contributed between US$1 and US$2 billion to the island's foreign exchange earnings, in excess of all other exports combined, including bauxite, sugar and tourism.[16]

The narcotics used illegally in the Commonwealth Caribbean are mainly marijuana and cocaine. Like production, drug use differs from place to place. The greater concern is found in Jamaica, the Bahamas, Barbados, Guyana, Trinidad and Tobago, and in parts of the eastern Caribbean. While marijuana is abused in many places, it has had a long history of accepted socio-religious use, dating to the introduction of indentured workers from India following the abolition of slavery by the British in 1834. The nature of this socio-religious use has changed over the years since 1834. It is now primarily associated with Africa-oriented socio-religious groups called Rastas, and thus is found in places with large numbers of Rastas, including Jamaica, Guyana, Trinidad and Tobago, Barbados, and Grenada. One writer explained: 'Part of the Rastafari faith condoned the use of *ganja* . . . [T]hey smoke, eat, or drink *ganja*. Rastas argue that there is a Biblical justification for *ganja* use and cite the following passages: Genesis 1:12, 3:18; Exodus 10:12; and Psalms 104:14. To the Rastas, *ganja* is not a drug, but a herb. Drugs are alcohol, tobacco, and pork.'[17]

Cocaine abuse in the Caribbean is primarily a spill-over from the illicit cocaine trade. This problem is found mainly in the principal transit states: Bahamas, Jamaica, Belize, Trinidad and Tobago and, to a lesser extent, in Guyana. In the case of the Bahamas, one United States agency reported: 'The Bahamas suffers from a serious drug abuse and addiction problem brought about by the ready availability of drugs as they transit the country. Cocaine is the drug of choice for addicts.'[18] Belize continues to suffer from an increase in the availability of cocaine. Indeed, one official source noted that cocaine and crack use has increased since 1990, contributing to an increase in crime and violence. This increase was clearly demonstrated during the September 1991 Belize Games when 44 out of 180 winning athletes tested positive for illegal drug use.[19] Data from elsewhere also suggest the extent of the cocaine problem: cocaine seizures in Guyana rose from 400 grams in 1987 to 3,575 grams in 1988; the registration of addicts seeking rehabilitation in Barbados rose from seven in 1986 to 115 in 1988; hospital admission of cocaine and marijuana addicts in Trinidad and Tobago rose from 376 in 1983 to 1,041 in 1989; and there was a dramatic increase in the number of 'crack bases' in Jamaica.[20]

Carl Stone concluded from a study in 1990 that the pattern of cocaine finds in Jamaica suggests that the country has become a cocaine and crack market for both residents and tourists. He considered the use of these drugs, combined with the long tradition of marijuana use, as creating an increasingly serious drug abuse problem in Jamaica. Yet the Stone survey, conducted from August to October 1990, revealed that Jamaican public opinion has a favourable view of ganja, alcohol and cigarettes, and reserves most of its concern for cocaine use. Drugs are used increasingly by the youth in urban areas such as Kingston, St Andrew and Spanish Town and in tourist centres such as Ocho Rios, Negril and Montego Bay.

Stone found that crack and cocaine are used most by people in the country's highest and lowest socioeconomic groups. He also detected that ganja, once used mainly by the lower class and the Rastas, had become part of the lifestyle of the 'fast moving uptown yuppies'. Stone also indicated a sharp contrast between the frequency of cocaine and crack use, and that of marijuana. Among users of the former drugs there was a greater concentration of daily and weekly users, reflecting the compulsive nature of cocaine use. For cocaine, there was a two per cent occasional use; a 21 per cent monthly use; a 37 per cent weekly use; and a 40 per cent daily use. For marijuana, the results were: occasional use, 38 per cent; monthly, 14 per cent; weekly, 27 per cent; and daily, 21 per cent.[21]

Quite importantly for Stone, the survey showed 'a close relationship between the use of various drugs to a degree that one can define a syndrome of multiple drug use as a central feature of Jamaica's drug culture'.[22] He considered this finding a contradiction of analysts who argued previously that ganja use in Jamaica was resistant to the use of 'hard drugs'. According to him, the previous approach was flawed in looking at the use of the varying drugs as separate and distinct phenomena. He thus concluded: 'Jamaican society at all class and societal levels is highly disposed to consume drugs which relax tensions, suppress worries and problems, manage stress in their lives, and give them a feeling of overcoming their problems and being on top of the world.'[23] This may well be true too for many other places in the Caribbean.

Transshipment

In addition to trading their own marijuana in the United States, some Caribbean countries are important transshipment centres for South American narcotics bound for Europe and North America. For more than two decades the Bahamas, Belize and Jamaica dominated this business, but recently Barbados, Guyana, Trinidad and Tobago, the eastern Caribbean countries and the Cayman Islands and other British

TABLE 1

BAHAMAS DRUG SEIZURES (POUNDS), ARRESTS, AND CONVICTIONS

ACTIVITY	1983	1984	1985	1986	1987	1988	1989	1990	1991	TOTALS
Cocaine Seizures	3,354	3,701	14,469	6,687	23,126	20,620	12,088	5,569	9,921	99,535
Marijuana Seizures	705,554	180,468	83,413	12,583	171,408	19,587	1,015	5,249	661	1,179,938
Number of Arrests	NA	1,501 [1,130]	1,580 [1,218]	1,530 [1,212]	1,596 [1,172]	1,277 [1,040]	1,255 [1,043]	1,443 [1,241]	1,200 [NA]	11,382 [NA]
Percentage Convicted	NA	NA	NA	66	69	71	67	NA	NA	NA

Notes:
NA – Not available
[ ] – Number of Bahamians arrested.
Sources: Government of the Bahamas Ministry of National Security, *Summary Report on the Traffic in Narcotic Drugs Affecting the Bahamas in 1990,* 28 March 1991; US Department of State, *International Narcotics Control Strategy Board,* Washington, DC, March 1992.

dependencies have featured more prominently in the trafficking.[24] On 4 July 1992, for instance, a joint police–army interdiction in Barbados confiscated over 2,000 pounds of marijuana, worth B$6 million, and arrested two Barbadians and one Canadian with arms and ammunition. Later that same month, the Trinidad and Tobago police seized 26.5 kilos of cocaine, worth about TT$35 million, at Cali Bay, Tobago, following transshipment from Venezuela. Two months later, on 11 September 1992, a Barbadian national was caught trying to smuggle 20 pounds of cocaine, worth US$12 million, out of Guyana.[25]

The geography of the Bahamian archipelago makes it an excellent candidate for drug transshipment, given its 700 islands and cays, and strategic location on the airline flight path between Colombia and South Florida. While most of the Bahamian islands could be used for smuggling, the trade has been concentrated over the years in a few strategic places: Bimini; the Exumas; Andros; Grand Bahama; Abaco; Berry Islands; Cat Islands; Ragged Island; Mayaguana; Eleuthera; Long Island; San Salvador; and Inagua. Bimini, for example, is a mere 50 miles from the United States mainland.[26] One writer makes an uncomplimentary, but valid, point about the country: 'In a way, geography had always been the Bahamas' main commodity, and they had always marketed it with great skill.'[27] This, of course, is true of other countries in the region.

Typically, aircraft depart from the north coast of Colombia, arriving in the Bahamas five hours later. The cargo is dropped to awaiting vessels for the final leg, a United States port of entry. The Bahamas has also become (in)famous for the marijuana and hashish traffic, from South America as well as Jamaica. In fact, when the Bahamas first became a transshipment centre, the drug involved was mainly marijuana, with a few consignments of hashish.[28] The 1983–84 drug inquiry found evidence of drug trafficking as far back as 1968, when Jack Devoe and Robert Bireck undertook a 'fly-drop' mission with 250–300 pounds of marijuana from Jamaica to Bimini. One of the earliest cocaine seizures was made in 1974: 247 pounds of pure cocaine, with a 1974 street value of US$2 billion, at an airport in George Town, Exuma. That same year, the Bahamas police discovered a store of marijuana off Grand Bahama Island. It was over six feet high and more than two miles long.[29]

One measure of the amount of trafficking in the Bahamas is the extent of drug seizures and related arrests. Table 1 suggests that the Bahamas is a major part of the illicit network. American citizens are always the largest group of foreigners arrested, followed by a combination of Jamaicans, Colombians and Haitians. For example, more than 50 per cent of the 202 foreigners arrested in 1990 were American. The next largest group were Haitians and Jamaicans. However, there is also trafficking by nationals of places far away from the Bahamas. In one case, in August 1990, a Nigerian woman was given a seven-year sentence by the Bahamas Supreme Court, following her arrest for attempting to smuggle 4.1 pounds of heroin and 1.25 pounds of cocaine out of the country.[30]

Bahamian National Security authorities noted a steep decline in cocaine seizures from 26 June 1989 to 14 November 1990: a mere 3,479 pounds. But there was a dramatic upsurge in seizures in the month from 14 November to 14 December 1990: 3,617 pounds of cocaine seized in three air delivery interceptions. In 1991, Bahamas officials were convinced that use of the country as a transit centre for marijuana moving from Colombia and Jamaica to Florida by air and sea had virtually ended. However, following a reevaluation in 1992, they concluded that the major seizures of cocaine in Bahamian and adjacent international waters during late 1990 and early 1991 indicated that the traffic from Colombia had returned to pre-August 1989 levels.[31]

The geography and topography of Belize also make that country ideal for drug smuggling. There are large jungle-like areas, sparse settlements, and about 140 isolated airstrips that facilitate short stops on the flight from South to North America. Moreover, there is virtually no radar coverage beyond a 30-mile radius of the international airport at Belize City. The 1992 *International Narcotics Control Strategy Report* produced by the US State Department noted: 'Belize is now a marginal producer of marijuana. [However,] its growing importance as a transshipment point for South American cocaine is now the most important narcotics-related challenge confronting Belize.'[32] Evidence of the increased trafficking was reflected in the increased number of drug seizures, the many crashed and seized aircraft, and the increased availability of cocaine and crack in Belize. Trafficking arrests for 1987, 1988 and 1989, for example, numbered 1,540. In 1989 alone, 539 people were arrested.

Jamaica has long been a linchpin in the drug trade, given its long coastline, proximity to the United States, many ports, harbours and beaches, and its closeness to the Yucatan and Windward Passages. Table 2 gives an idea of the scope of the Jamaican smuggling problem. There is both air and maritime trafficking. For the maritime traffic, use is made of pleasure boats with storage compartments to ferry small quantities of drugs. Bigger loads are put aboard commercial cargo and fishing vessels. Both large and small amounts of drugs are also smuggled by air and arrests of couriers at the two international airports are almost daily occurrences.

TABLE 2
JAMAICA DRUG SEIZURES (POUNDS) AND ARRESTS

ACTIVITY	1986	1987	1988	1989	1990	1991	TOTALS
Cocaine Seizures	1,213	18,960	22	287	1,676	132	22,290
Marijuana Seizures	——	473,989	1,168	83,775	63,933	94,799	717,664
Foreigners Arrested	782	567	625	638	524	674	3,810
Jamaicans Arrested	3,341	3,400	3,100	2,956	4,908	4,353	22,058
Total Number of Arrests	4,123	3,967	3,725	3,594	5,432	5,027	25,868

Sources: US Department of State, *International Narcotics Control Strategy Report*, Washington, DC, March 1990; March 1991; March 1992.

Between 1984 and 1989 there were five major drug seizures by United States Customs on board Air Jamaica flights, involving 15,000 pounds of marijuana alone. After a significant drop in both marijuana and cocaine seizures, there were dramatic increases for both substances in 1989. Two astronomical finds in 1989 contributed to the increase:

• On 1 April 1989 United States Customs found 4,173 pounds of marijuana on an Air Jamaica A-300 AirBus in Miami. The drugs were packed in 88 boxes labelled 'wearing apparel' and consigned to Joseph and Schiller, Inc of Miami. The 'garment' consignment was from Threadways Garments of Jamaica.

• On 8 April 1989 a seizure of 5,000 pounds of marijuana was made in Gramercy, Louisiana, on board *MV Kotor*, which was there to deliver a shipment of Jamaican bauxite. The smuggling was discovered after violent clashes by two rival drug gangs over ownership of the marijuana.[33]

Money Laundering

Money laundering is really the conversion of profits from illegal activities, in this case drug activities, into financial assets which appear to have legitimate origins. There are several different techniques and methods of doing this. One way was outlined by William Rosenblatt, Assistant Commissioner of the United States Customs Service. According to Rosenblatt, money laundering has three stages: placement, layering and integration.

Placement refers to the physical disposal of bulk cash, either by commingling it with revenues from legitimate businesses, or by converting currency into deposits in banks, securities companies, or other financial intermediaries. Layering involves transferring the money among various accounts through several complex transactions designed to disguise the trail of illicit takings. Integration, the last stage, requires shifting the laundered funds to legitimate organisations with no apparent links to the drug trade.[34] It is estimated that about US$300 billion in drug revenues are laundered annually.

Commonwealth Caribbean countries involved in this aspect of the drug business are the Bahamas, the Cayman Islands, Montserrat, and the Turks and Caicos Islands. Antigua-Barbuda, Dominica, Grenada, St Lucia, St Vincent and the Grenadines and Trinidad and Tobago are designated as 'sleepers' by the US State Department, countries that have 'the potential to become more important financial centers and havens for exploitation by money launderers, as the game of global musical chairs by narcotics money launderers continues'.[35] The INM considers these countries to have the appropriate qualifications for money laundering: bank secrecy, willingness to cooperate and limited, usually poorly trained, enforcement resources. During 1991 there were, for example, several allegations of money laundering in Grenada where the number of off-shore banks had grown from three in early 1990 to 118 by late 1991.[36]

Most of the money laundering allegations centre around the British dependencies in the Caribbean. A study undertaken in 1989 by Rodney Gallagher of the international accounting firm Coopers and Lybrand revealed some telling reasons for this. According to the Gallagher Report, over 525 international banks and trust companies have offices in just one of these territories, the Cayman Islands. With 26,000 people, 10,000 of whom are foreigners, the Cayman Islands accommodate 46 of the world's 50 largest banks, including Dai Ichi Kangyo and Fuji, Japan's two largest banks; Bank America; Barclays of the United Kingdom; the Swiss Bank Corporation; and Royal Bank of Canada. Registration data for 1987 showed 18,264 companies registered in the areas of international investment, sales trading, shipping, insurance, real estate and related areas. This amounted to a ratio of one international bank for every 49 residents. Banking sector assets in 1987 stood at US$250 billion.

There are many benefits of doing business in the Caymans and other dependencies. The Cayman Islands, for example, have no income, corporate or withholding tax, and no international double taxation treaties. Companies that operate mainly outside the Caymans can register there as non-resident companies or incorporate as exempt companies, with the ability to issue bearer shares to non-residents and thus avoid disclosure of beneficial owners. In addition, bank secrecy is guaranteed under the 1976 Preservation of Confidential Relations Act. The offshore financial industry itself is critical to the economic security of the Caymans, having grown to US$360 billion during the past decade. It provides one-third of the jobs in the Caymans and about the same proportion of their GDP.[37]

Anguilla, another British dependency, with 91 square kilometres and a 1990 population of 8,500, was home to 2,400 registered companies in 1988, including 38 banks and 80 insurance companies. The inducements are freedom to move capital without exchange controls, no domestic taxes, minimum disclosure requirements and the availability of professional services. The British Virgin Islands (BVI) does have a tax regime, although a light one. They had 13,000 companies registered in 1988. Although they now have only six major banks, money launderers use their services extensively. However, BVI and United States authorities have been able to obtain vital bank records and freeze drug-related money. In 1991, for example, over US$3 million was transferred to the United States for forfeiture and sharing between the United States and the BVI. Of the British dependencies, it is only really the Turks and Caicos Islands which do not have a developed financial services sector.[38]

The narcotics production, abuse, trafficking and money laundering operations described above clearly all have security implications. In the light of the conceptualisation of security being applied here, it is important now to move on to examine the three main security dimensions involved: the political, the military and the economic.

SECURITY IMPLICATIONS

Political Security

One of the most critical aspects of political security relates to the corruption of government officials. Drug corruption not only undermines the credibility of governments, but it also impairs the ability of government agencies to protect the public interest. It can even warp the ability of politicians and bureaucrats to define the national interest adequately. It can also of course lead to the development of cynicism within the general society and to an increase in the level of public tolerance for corruption, both of which are dangerous. As such, corruption subverts the political security of the nations concerned.

Corruption has been unearthed in the Bahamas, Jamaica, Trinidad and Tobago, St Lucia, the Turks and Caicos Islands, and elsewhere. Even more dangerous than general government corruption is the corrupting of law enforcement officials in police and defence forces, immigration and customs services, and internal revenue agencies. For example, in August 1988 I had an extensive interview with Cuthbert Phillips, then Police Commissioner of St Lucia, on eastern Caribbean security concerns. The drug problem consumed much of our attention and Phillips waxed eloquent in declaiming against the drug barons and those who aided them.[39] Less than a month later he was dismissed for being implicated in drug-related corruption and inefficiency in the Royal St Lucia Police Force. He was also later imprisoned, following a manslaughter conviction.

In some cases, law enforcement officials go beyond facilitating smuggling; they themselves become couriers. One of many such cases recently involved the arrest in May 1990 of a Barbadian immigration officer at London's Heathrow International Airport with a large quantity of cocaine he had brought from Barbados. And in March 1992

Sergeant Roger Newman of the Royal Bahamas Police Force (RBPF) was charged with possession and intent to supply six kilos of cocaine. Interestingly enough, Sergeant Newman worked with the Bahamas special drug court where he often acted as a prosecutor in drug cases.[40]

Some of the region's most notorious corruption cases were in the Bahamas. Continuous allegations about high-level drug-related corruption involving the Prime Minister and other government officials prompted an official enquiry in 1983. In its 1984 report, the Commission of Inquiry noted that widespread transshipment of drugs through the Bahamas had adversely affected almost all strata of society. Several top officials were indicted. Five government ministers either resigned or were dismissed. The Commission noted several questionable practices by the Prime Minister, and drew attention to the fact that between 1977 and 1984 his expenditures and assets far exceeded his official income. For example, his bank deposits were US$3.5 million in excess of his salary for that period. Nevertheless, there was no firm evidence of his being on a drug payroll as alleged. In general, the Commission reported:

> We were also alarmed by the extent to which persons in the public service have been corrupted by the illegal trade. We have given our reasons later in this report for concluding that corruption existed at the upper and lower levels of the Royal Bahamas Police Force and we have concluded that certain Immigration and Customs officers accepted bribes. We were particularly concerned to discover that those corrupting influences made their presence felt at the levels of Permanent Secretary and Minister . . . In our opinion, the whole nation must accept some responsibility. Apathy and a weak public opinion have led to the present unhappy and undesirable state of affairs in the nation.[41]

Only three months after the publication of the report of the Bahamas inquiry, the Chief Minister and the Commerce and Development Minister of the Turks and Caicos Islands, Norman Saunders and Stafford Missick respectively, were among several people arrested in Miami on drug-related charges. The March 1985 arrests followed three months of investigations by the United States Drug Enforcement Administration (DEA), in cooperation with the British government and Turks and Caicos law enforcement agencies. The charges included conspiracy to import narcotics into the United States, conspiracy to violate the United States Travel Act, and the conduct of interstate and foreign travel to aid racketeering enterprises. During the trial, the DEA alleged that Saunders had accepted US$30,000 from its undercover agents to guarantee safe stop-over refuelling on flights from Colombia to the United States. Moreover, the prosecution showed a video tape, filmed before the arrests, where Saunders was shown receiving US$20,000 from a DEA agent. The money was allegedly to protect drug shipments passing through South Caicos Island, *en route* to the United States. All the defendants were convicted in July 1985 on the conspiracy charges, although Saunders was acquitted of the more serious charge of conspiring to import cocaine into the United States. Missick was convicted of the additional charge of cocaine importation. Saunders and Missick were sentenced to eight and ten years respectively and each was fined US$50,000.[42]

In April 1992, Assistant Commissioner Rodwell Murray of the Trinidad and Tobago Police Service made public an allegation he had made in 1991 to top National Security Ministry officials in Port of Spain: that there was a drug trafficking cartel operating within the police force. Drug corruption had surfaced before in Trinidad. In 1987 the Scott Commission report resulted in the suspension of 51 police officers and the eventual resignation of Commissioner Randolph Burroughs, who was indicted but later acquitted. In 1991, the report of the La Tinta Commission into an aborted drug operation during which one policeman had been killed led to the suspension of 16 policemen. Because of the increasing scale of drug trading in Trinidad and Tobago and the seniority of the police official making the allegations, the Prime Minister, Patrick Manning, invited Britain's Scotland Yard to investigate the claim.[43]

There is another important political security dimension to narcotics operations. While there is no imminent threat of the 'Colombianisation' of the Caribbean in terms of violence waged by the drug barons against government officials and institutions, the openness and vulnerability of Caribbean societies are such that drug barons can easily subvert their sovereignty and governability. Indeed, some analysts contend that the Air Jamaica drug discovery in April 1989, coming just one week after Prime Minister Manley had declared a war on drugs, resulted from a deliberate act, and was meant as a direct challenge to the Jamaican government.[44]

On this score a former Caribbean diplomat made the very pertinent observation: 'A handful of well-trained narcotic soldiers or mercenaries could make a lightning trip to a country, wreak destruction, and fly out before a defense could be mounted by states friendly to the small island.'[45] Shridath Ramphal, former Commonwealth Secretary-General and chairman of the West Indian Commission, once put it even more poignantly: 'It only takes twelve men in a boat to put some of these governments out of business.' This was precisely one of the points made to me by the former St Lucian Commissioner of Police in our interview in 1988. Officials within and outside the British Virgin Islands also harboured this very concern in January 1989 after a group of Colombian traffickers had been arrested. It would be even greater where there are grounds for suspicion of significant collusion of government officials, especially in law-enforcement agencies, with the traffickers.

Military Security

The corruption of law-enforcement officials noted above also has distinct implications for military security: it compromises the agents of national security, with the consequence that (a) their capacity for effective action is undermined, and (b) individuals and groups become inclined to resort to vigilante tactics because of that diminished capacity. Moreover, drugs have precipitated a sharp increase in crime generally and gang warfare in particular. Jamaica has suffered the brunt of this increase. One writer explained: 'Jamaica over the past few years has experienced, through an upsurge in violent crime, the effects of a combination of drugs and money in the form of the naked display of power through the use of arms.'[46]

Perhaps even more worrying, the drug business is linked in some places with a dangerous ancillary operation: gun running. In one case, a ten-ton shipment of arms, with an estimated value of J$8 million, arrived in Jamaica in December 1988. It was to be air-lifted later to Colombia. The shipment, from Heckler and Koch of West Germany, included 1,000 G3A3 automatic assault rifles, 250 HK21 machine guns, ten 60 millimetre commando mortars, and 600 rounds of high explosive 60 millimetre mortar shells. The planned operation involved West Germans, Englishmen, Panamanians, Colombians and Jamaicans. Interrogation of the conspirators revealed that the arms were destined for a leftist insurgent group called the Revolutionary Armed Forces of Colombia (FARC). The operation was underwritten by the Colombian cocaine dealers who finance FARC. The arms had been paid for out of a special drug shipment made earlier to Europe.

The affair ended in early January 1989 when the arms were placed on a Colombian military aircraft and sent to Bogota. The foreigners were extradited and the Jamaicans held on a variety of charges. Nor was that the first or only reported incident of gun running in the region. Scott MacDonald, author of *Dancing on a Volcano*, documented the involvement of 'Mickey' Tolliver, an American pilot, in a similar operation in July 1986. It began in Haiti where he picked up a DC-3 aircraft with weapons and ammunition. He then flew to Costa Rica and thence to Colombia where he took a consignment of 4,000 pounds of marijuana and 400–500 kilos of cocaine. Tolliver said he then flew to the Bahamas where he watched Bahamian police unload the guns and drugs.

This 'narcoterrorist' aspect of drug operations was even more dramatically exposed in the Antigua-Barbudan case, which therefore warrants extended discussion. On 15 December 1989 the Colombian police killed Rodriguez Gacha and his son Freddy, both of the Medellin drug cartel. One of the raids made on several of Gacha's properties uncovered hundreds of Israeli-made Galil rifles and supporting ammunition. The disclosure by Israel that the weapons were part of a larger sale to the Antigua-Barbuda government for the Antigua-Barbuda Defense Force (ABDF) led to a Colombian diplomatic protest being made to Antigua-Barbuda in early April 1990. The protest prompted Antigua-Barbuda to retain United States attorney Lawrence Barcella to investigate the matter and, shortly afterwards, to institute an extensive public inquiry by a one-man Commission of Inquiry.

The inquiry, by British jurist Louis Blom-Cooper, uncovered an extraordinary scheme involving Israelis, Antiguans, Panamanians and Colombians. Yair Klein, a retired Israeli army colonel, and Pinchas Schachar, a retired brigadier-general, then a representative of Israel Military Industries (IMI), were told by Maurice Sarfati, another Israeli, that the Antigua-Barbuda government was interested in acquiring weapons and ammunition. Sarfati presented forged documents showing (a) that he was an authorised Antiguan government representative, and (b) that an arms purchase had been authorised by Vere Bird Jr, Antigua's 'National Security Minister', and the head of the ABDF, Colonel Clyde Walker. Consequently, the relevant End-User Certificate, the official weapons requisition by an arms purchaser, was forwarded to Israel.[47] Incidentally, but not irrelevantly, Vere Bird Jr is the son of Prime Minister Vere Bird Sr. It also should be noted that Sarfati had indeed been a government representative at one time, but in this case the documents were forged. Moreover, there was no person in the Antiguan government designated 'Minister of National Security'.

Investigations into the affair by the United States Senate revealed that the initial order was for 500 weapons and 200,000 rounds of ammunition, valued at US$353,700. The final order total was US$324,205. A down payment of $US95,000 was made and between 14 November 1988 and 13 February 1989, 13 financial transactions, ranging between US$44,000 and US$100,000, were made on the deal. The banks used were Banco Aleman-Panameno; Philadelphia International Bank; Manufacturer Hanover Trust; Bank Hapoalim of Israel; and American

Security Bank of Washington, DC.[48] The weapons were placed aboard a Danish ship, *MV Else TH*, which sailed from Haifa, Israel on 29 March 1989, bound for Central and South America, via Antigua. The Antiguan consignment was transshipped at Port Antigua to the *MV Seapoint*, a Panamanian ship. The *Seapoint* then took the arms to Colombia to the real consignee, the Medellin drug cartel. The Antiguans implicated were Vere Bird Jr, Minister of Public Works and Communications, Lieutenant Colonel Clyde Walker, ABDF Commander, Vernon Edwards, Managing Director of a shipping and brokerage agency, and Glenton Armstrong and Sean Leitch, customs officers.

Sarfati, the leading Israeli figure, had first gone to Antigua in April 1983. He cultivated a friendship with Vere Bird Jr, then an attorney in private practice, who was subsequently instrumental in the granting of official approval for one of Sarfati's pet schemes, a melon cultivation project. The Bird–Sarfati friendship produced many advantages for Sarfati between 1983 and 1990: appointment in October 1984 by Vere Bird Jr as Special Adviser on Civil Aviation; appointment in May 1985 as Special Envoy in the Ministry of External Affairs, Economic Development, and Tourism; an OPIC ([US] Overseas Private Investment Corporation) loan of US$700,000 in 1985; a supplemental loan from OPIC for US$600,000 in 1986; appointment in February 1986 as Managing Director of Antigua-Barbuda Airways, with a token annual salary of US$100, but a US$70,000 expense account; and receipt in 1987 of a series of promissory notes by the Antiguan government, amounting to US$4 million.[49]

Vere Bird Jr, of course, also benefited from the links. For example, his law firm, Bird and Bird, handled the legal interests of Sarfati's corporate holdings – Roydan Ltd, and Antigua Promoters Ltd. In addition, Sarfati guaranteed a loan to Bird, amounting to US$92,000, in November 1988. Blom-Cooper observed: 'It seems to me a matter of some significance that at the time the conspiracy was negotiated, Mr. Vere Bird, Jr. was in financial difficulties and was beholden to the bankrupt Mr. Sarfati. Not only did he need money, but he also needed to help Mr. Sarfati earn money.'[50] The Commissioner then made an even more damaging observation: 'I entertain no doubt Mr. Vere Bird, Jr. was paid by, or at least with, money emanating from Senor Rodriguez Gacha, for the services rendered to the arms transshipment.'[51]

This transshipment was, however, only part of a larger scheme which was initiated in September 1988 to create a mercenary training establishment, using the ABDF as an organisational cover. According to the brochure produced by Spearhead Ltd, the project's corporate entity, the aim was to establish a central civilian security school to train 'corporate security experts, ranging from the executive level to the operational level, and bring them to the highest professional capacity in order to confront and defuse any possible threat'. A central part of the enterprise was to be a 'speciality shop' to sell small arms, among other things. The planners were catering for a special clientele, including 'local private and official entities'; international banks; international oil and industrial companies; and 'international private business people'. Blom-Cooper asserted: 'To any one with the slightest knowledge of armed forces it was obvious that the training school proffered by Spearhead Ltd was intended, among other things, to train mercenaries in assault techniques and assassination.'[52] The implications of such a scheme for questions of military security are too obvious to require emphasis.

Economic Security

Much of the drug corruption in the Caribbean has a feature common to drug corruption elsewhere: greed. However, some of it relates to the relative economic deprivation in parts of the region where, according to the Caribbean Development Bank, unemployment in 1989 was 19 per cent in Jamaica, 23 per cent in Trinidad and Tobago, and 26 per cent in Guyana. GDP growth has also generally been low of late. Indeed, in Barbados, Guyana and Trinidad and Tobago, the economy actually declined in 1990. Moreover, the Commonwealth Caribbean has a huge public debt – US$10.2 billion in 1990. In addition, high inflation drives up prices, even of basic commodities. Under these circumstances one can appreciate that some people who engage in drug production and trafficking are driven by basic economic needs. Even for those without such motives, like public officials, it is often difficult to resist the temptation to earn 'easy money' to supplement low incomes.

The drug trade takes a heavy toll on the already weak Caribbean economies. One aspect relates to the charges and fines levied against the owners of carriers on which drugs are found. For example, a US$1.2 million fine was imposed by the United States Customs on the Guyana Airways Corportion (GAC) in January 1992 after a GAC flight had arrived in New York with close to 100 pounds of marijuana.[53] The toll has been heaviest for Jamaica, with several noteworthy instances:

• In 1986, two Air Jamaica planes were impounded in Miami and New York and a US$657,000 fine was levied.
• Also in 1986, the now defunct Eastern Airlines was fined

TABLE 3

BAHAMAS DEFENSE FORCE EXPENDITURE, 1989 AND 1990 ($ BAHAMAS)

BUDGET ITEM	1989 OVERALL	1989 D.R.	% D.R.	1990 OVERALL	1990 D.R.	% D.R.
Transportation within the Bahamas	7,580	3,790	50	5,514	2,757	50
Gas (Cooking)	7,271	3,635	50	7,003	3,502	50
Insurance - Equipment	174,238	139,390	80	742,865	594,292	80
Spare Parts - Marine Equipment	608,452	486,761	85	391,208	332,527	85
Spare Parts - Air Equipment	18,210	15,478	85	78,446	66,679	85
Provisions (Food)	678,504	610,652	90	621,378	559,240	90
Fuels	1,165,226	1,048,702	95	1,119,753	1,063,766	95
Household & Cleaning Supplies	78,394	39,197	50	76,440	38,220	50
Clothing Supplies	373,640	224,184	60	311,328	186,797	60
Military Supplies	79,102	67,236	85	48,032	40,827	85
Sea Craft (Upkeep)	156,318	125,054	80	585,640	468,512	80
Air Craft (Upkeep)	215,170	172,136	80	45,530	36,424	80
Subsistence within the Bahamas	7,967	3,983	50	4,823	2,416	50
Personal Emoluments	12,203,050	10,372,592	85	14,496,569	12,322,084	85
TOTAL	15,773,122	13,312,790	84	18,534,529	15,718,043	85

Note: D.R. – Drug related.
Source: Government of the Bahamas, Ministry of National Security, *Summary Report on the Traffic in Narcotic Drugs Affecting the Bahamas*, Nassau, The Bahamas, March 1990; March 1991.

US$900,000 after marijuana was found on a cargo flight. Three weeks later it was fined US$1.6 million for the same infraction. Cargo flights from Jamaica were then suspended.

• In 1987, Evergreen, a Korean-owned line, paid US$135 million in fines to the United States Customs.

• In 1988, Sea-Land Services paid a similar US$85 million fine.

• In 1989, the United States Customs imposed another US$96 million charge against Sea-Land Services, following the discovery of 12,000 pounds of marijuana shipped from Jamaica. Sea-Land subsequently withdrew its services from Jamaica.

• In April 1989, an Air Jamaica plane was impounded in Miami and a US$28.8 million fine was imposed.

• Two boats belonging to the Jamaica Banana Cooperative Association were impounded for most of Spring 1989, unable to pay the heavy fines imposed following the discovery of marijuana aboard them.[54]

Both state and commercial enterprises have, therefore, felt the crunch. The fines have been devastating for Air Jamaica, contributing to its 1988–89 losses of US$14 million, 20 per cent more than the previous year. All in all, between 1989 and 1991 Air Jamaica was fined about US$37 million for illegal drugs found on its planes entering the United States. The fines were, however, reduced to US$3 million, with agreement that the remaining money be used to upgrade security at the country's international airports. The security measures introduced to curb the trafficking are also financially burdensome. For instance, all container cargo is now subject to a 100 per cent search, resulting in about 85 per cent shipping delays. Moreover, it costs about J$3,000 to strip and search each container. The overall costs of this operation to businesses in any single year are astronomical, considering that Jamaica operates between 850,000 and one million containers annually.[55] Obviously, these costs are passed on to the consumer.

The campaigns to eliminate production and curb the trafficking of drugs also require Caribbean states to devote considerable portions of their already scarce financial resources to drug problems. A look at Table 3, for example, reveals that in recent years most of the Bahamas Defense Force expenditure has been devoted to drug operations. In 1990 it was 85 per cent.

Because of economic and institutional limitations, Caribbean countries are forced to rely significantly on foreign economic and technical assistance at both the bilateral and the multilateral levels.[56] At the bilateral level, United States assistance is important to many countries. However, drug operations have often jeopardised assistance to some countries. Under the 1986 United States Anti-Drug Abuse Act (PL 99-570), the President is allowed to impose trade sanctions, including duties, loss of tariff benefits, a 50 per cent withholding of bilateral aid, and suspension of air services against 'offending countries'. In the western hemisphere these include the Bahamas, Belize, Bolivia, Brazil, Colombia, Ecuador, Jamaica, Mexico, Panama and Peru. The Congress can reverse presidential action to grant aid or impose sanctions by passing a joint resolution within 45 days of the President's determination on the matter, due on 1 March of each year.[57] Ever since the passage of PL 99-570 the Commonwealth Caribbean countries concerned have managed to receive certification. Congress, however, did not always agree with the President's assessment and certification efforts. In both 1988 and 1989, for instance, Congress attempted to overturn the certification for the Bahamas.[58] What is troubling about the drugs-aid link is that the United States pressures countries into specific kinds of cooperation, using the aid suspension as a threat.

Moreover, the economic security implications of the drug operations discussed above reflect only part of the economic security matrix. Tourism, a key sector in many Caribbean economies, has been adversely affected in many places. While the drugs-tourism linkage needs more studying, there is evidence that drugs affect tourism adversely both because of the negative press which scares potential tourists away and the high incidence of drug-related crime in some places. In addition, drug use contributes to the loss of employment man-hours due to addiction, rehabilitation, and incarceration. It also affects the shaping of attitudes and norms in societies that are highly vulnerable to American materialist values.

COUNTERMEASURES

As might be expected, countermeasures have been taken by Caribbean governments at the domestic, regional and international levels. The importance attached to the regional and international efforts reflects the recognition that the countries of the region do not possess the capabilities to deal adequately with the problems on their own. But perhaps, more importantly, it also reflects acceptance by states in the Caribbean and, indeed, throughout the world, that the international scope of the problem demands international responses. It is also important to note that responses come not only from governments and international governmental agencies, but also from non-governmental organisations aware that the collective will and the resources of all are required.

Countermeasures have included campaigns to eradicate cultivation and reduce production of drugs, to rehabilitate addicts and to educate the public on the dangers of drug use. Interdiction and law enforcement have been boosted, and several countries have found it necessary to introduce draconian laws to deal with aspects of the drugs problem. For instance, the Jamaican Parliament passed the Dangerous Drugs Act in 1987; the Narcotic Drugs and Psychotropic Substances Act was approved in Guyana in 1988; Barbados adopted the Drug Abuse (Prevention and Control) Act in 1990; and in 1991 Trinidad and Tobago's Dangerous Drugs Act became law.

Calls have also been made for capital punishment for certain drug offences.[59] But, generally, the new laws impose stiff fines and terms of imprisonment for drug use and trafficking. They also provide for the confiscation of property acquired through drug-trading, and they create or expand institutions to deal with different aspects of the problem. In Guyana, for example, the 1988 legislation imposes heavy fines and prison terms for the possession, sale, dispensing and trafficking of illicit drugs. In some cases the penalty is life imprisonment. The law also sanctions seizures of drug-acquired property, and allows bail for drug offenders only under special circumstances. These laws have been applied fully, as when, in March 1992, Guyana's Chief Magistrate, Claudette La Bennett, refused bail to a heavily pregnant woman accused of possessing six pounds of cocaine and weapons and ammunition. The woman, Sharon Morgan, who had been charged along with Colombian and Venezuelan accomplices, appealed against La Bennett's decision and was released on G$100,000 bail. While on bail she delivered her baby, but then failed to attend for trial on three occasions. She was later convicted and sentenced to four years in prison, *in absentia*.[60]

Some of the provisions of the new laws border on the violation of the civil rights of citizens. Two examples will suffice. Firstly, Section 24(1) of the Jamaican legislation permits *any constable* to search, seize, and detain, *without a warrant*, any conveyance he reasonably suspects is 'being or has been used for the commission of any offense under this Act'. The Guyanese law has a similar provision – Section 93(1). These provisions permit considerable police power; power which, regrettably, has been misused often. Secondly, Section 26 of the Jamaican legislation, Section 78 of the Guyanese legislation, and Section 20 of the Trinidad and Tobago law all place the burden of proof of innocence on the accused. This is an exception to the normal provision whereby the state is required to prove guilt.

There are obvious and not so obvious dangers in all this. As the Jamaican Minister of Justice recently observed:

> In our effort to rid our societies of the scourge of drugs and with some international pressures we are being invited to reverse burdens of proof and adopt a retroactive confiscatory regime. All this is understandable. The perceived danger is real, the consequences of the mischief which we would excise disastrous. As we contemplate effective measures, the nagging question though for all of us remains: Are they just?
>
> I remember too that in Jamaica, the mongoose was imported from India to kill out the snakes. It did a very good job. The snakes were eliminated. The mongoose then turned its attention to the chickens. There is a lesson in this. Effective measures against vermin may be turned to effective use by the ill intentioned against decent and law abiding citizens.[61]

Jamaica's National Security Minister, K. D. Knight, reported to the Jamaican Parliament in July 1991 on a special anti-cocaine trafficking strategy introduced the previous year. It involved identifying organisations in Jamaica and the United States involved in the trade; targeting high risk flights from Panama, Curacao and St Maarten; profiling legitimate Jamaican entrepreneurs suspected of trading; and using the intelligence capability of the newly created National Firearms and Drug Intelligence Centre. Between January and November 1991, more than 2,534 kilos of marijuana, three kilos of cocaine, and 36 kilos of hash oil were seized at the country's two international airports. In 1991, Jamaica also increased the manpower of the Port Security Corps to 900, and allowed the United States National Guard to install a radar station on the island. The success of the initial radar operations, from August to October 1991, persuaded officials in Jamaica and the United States to make the operations permanent.[62]

As a result of the previously mentioned Gallagher Report and investigations by Britain's Scotland Yard following inquiries by the United States Office of the Comptroller of the Currency, drastic measures were also taken in 1991 to curb money laundering in Montserrat. The most dramatic was the revocation in March 1991 of 311 banking licences. Many of the institutions that lost their licences were described as 'little more than a smart title and a letter head', and 'nothing more than a few documents in a lawyer's filing cabinet'. Yet they provided the legal basis for moving money around the world. In addition to the bank closures, Britain also amended the island's constitution, assigning responsibility for the financial sector, previously held by local politicians, to the Governor of the dependency. Further, a British adviser was appointed to oversee a new financial supervisory agency. Montserrat had been using the offshore banking industry as part of a strategy to reduce its economic dependency on Britain. Banking licences had been sold for US$10,000 and the island soon became a haven for money laundering and other irregularities.[63]

At the regional level there have been several joint initiatives undertaken in education, intelligence, rehabilitation, law enforcement and other areas under the auspices of the Caribbean Community (CARICOM) High Level Ad Hoc Group on the Regional Drug Program.[64] One significant initiative was the endorsement by CARICOM leaders, at their 1991 Summit, of Jamaica's proposal for a Regional Training Center for Drug Law Enforcement. The Jamaican plan was for a regional agency to serve as a resource base for technical advice to Caribbean governments and to systematise the region's anti-narcotic law-enforcement training. Jamaica argued that such a centre, 'by helping to establish a common approach to drug control strategies, [will] minimize the possibilities of narco-criminals transferring their activities from one country to another within the region'.[65]

The Center will be financed by the Jamaican government, the United Nations Drug Control Program (UNDCP), the Inter-American Drug Abuse Control Commission (CICAD), and other sources. The plan is to locate it in St Catherine, 134 miles outside the Jamaican capital, Kingston, as part of an existing criminal justice complex that includes the Jamaican Police Staff College and the Jamaican Police Academy. Training at the Center will focus on drug identification, interdiction procedures, surveillance techniques, money laundering investigation, intelligence data collection and analysis, risk assessment, procedures for tracking and seizing drug assets and other subjects.

The UNDCP secured the services of Robert Simmonds, a former Commissioner of the Royal Canadian Mounted Police (RCMP), to advise on the establishment of the institution and he made his first visit to Jamaica in June 1991. Jamaica plans to put at the disposal of the Center some of its own counter-narcotics resources and facilities. These include the computerised National Firearms and Drug Intelligence Center; a Joint Information and Coordination Center with computer links to similar centres in the United States and elsewhere; a Contraband Enforcement Team; and a specially trained anti-narcotics Port Security Corps.[66]

Four Caribbean countries (Jamaica, the Bahamas, Belize and

Grenada) have also signed Mutual Legal Assistance Treaties with the United States in the counter-narcotics effort. These treaties cater for training, joint interdiction, asset sharing, intelligence and material and technical assistance. Air Jamaica and the United States Customs Service signed a further agreement in December 1991 to bolster trafficking countermeasures and in August 1992 the United States agreed to give Guyana an additional US$50,000 to help combat transshipment. The sum augments the US$300,000 given in 1989 and is to be used to repair the Guyana Defense Force Coast Guard's radar equipment and to upgrade army and police computer facilities.

Other bilateral narcotics treaties have been signed too. Belize, for example, has four agreements with Mexico for improved narcotics cooperation, including intelligence exchange, and the provision of Mexican assistance for prevention and rehabilitation programmes. Another agreement between the Bahamas and Canada, for example, took effect in July 1990. There is also one between the Bahamas and Britain, and one between Jamaica and Mexico. Also of interest is the fact that, during July 1991, Trinidad and Tobago and Venezuela agreed to establish joint air and naval operations. Moreover, in September 1991, the Bahamas and Cuba initiated talks about joint countermeasures and, in April 1992, Guyana and Venezuela agreed on joint measures, dealing with both drug use and trafficking. There have also been some multilateral treaties. The Bahamas, Britain and the United States, for instance, signed one in July 1990 providing for joint law enforcement involving the Bahamas, the Turks and Caicos Islands, and the United States. This treaty extends the basing network of OPBAT – Operation Bahamas and the Turks and Caicos – from three bases to four. The new base is on Great Inagua, the southernmost island of the Bahamas.[67]

Yet for all the successes of eradication and interdiction programmes, there is a certain futility to efforts to halt drug trafficking completely. One writer explained this in very practical terms:

> Even if the United States can increase the risk of capture and conviction for traffickers, drug smuggling's tremendous profitability guarantees that there will be thousands of willing replacements for the traffickers that are successfully prosecuted. A payment of $50,000 per trip to the masters of these ships is common. The engineers make about $25,000 and each of the crewmen receives between $5,000 and $10,000.[68]

Indeed, the way the United States pursues its drug eradication and interdiction policies in the Caribbean has itself been a problem for many countries in the region. United States law enforcement officials have often pursued suspects into Caribbean territorial waters, arresting individuals in Caribbean jurisdictions, sometimes without even courtesy notification of their arrests. There has often been virtual coercion by United States agencies in the selection of personnel for local drug enforcement units, and in the planning and directing of drug operations. Caribbean governments consider all of these to be affronts to their sovereign authority, and indicated this to President Reagan. On behalf of CARICOM leaders, the then Chairman of CARICOM, Prime Minister Vere Bird Sr of Antigua-Barbuda, wrote to Reagan in July 1988, protesting 'attempts to extend domestic United States authority into the neighbouring countries of the region without regard to the sovereignty and independent legal systems of those countries'.[69] Such affronts have, in fact, been greater in relation to Latin American countries.[70]

At the international level, Caribbean countries are party to several agreements designed to facilitate information sharing, education and joint combat measures. Among these are the 1961 Single Convention on Narcotic Drugs; the 1971 Convention of Psychotropic Substances; the 1972 Protocol amending the 1961 Convention; and the 1988 United Nations Convention Against Illicit Traffic in Narcotic Drugs and Psychotropic Substances. Indeed, the Bahamas has the distinction of being the first country to ratify the 1988 Convention. States in the region have also participated in many hemispheric and international agencies and networks. These include the OAS Money Laundering Experts Group; UNDCP; CICAD; the United Nations Fund for Drug Abuse Control (UNFDAC); the International Narcotics Control Board (INCB); the Caribbean Drug Money Laundering Conference; the Meeting of Heads of National Law Enforcement Agencies (HONLEA); and the Maritime Security Council.

CONCLUDING REMARKS

It is fairly obvious from the above that the threat posed by drugs is a multidimensional one. Its scope and severity vary from country to country, but – to paraphrase Martin Carter, the distinguished Caribbean poet from Guyana – the situation is such that 'all are involved; all are consumed'. The Caribbean narcotics dilemma is not only linked with the socioeconomic circumstances within the region; there are aspects of the phenomenon that extend beyond its geographical and political confines, making the situation all the more complex. As we saw above, Caribbean countries have been engaged in several initiatives and measures to help counter the problems of narcotics production, abuse, trafficking and money laundering. However, there is a central problem with this response: namely, a 'capability deficiency' within the region that limits both the scope of the countermeasures and the prospects for their success. This deficiency exists not only in terms of finance, but also in terms of personnel, skills and technology. Caribbean governments and decent law-abiding citizens have nevertheless to remain engaged in the counternarcotics battles. They have to pool resources and continue to adopt a positive attitude. The consequences of losing the battles are too horrendous even to contemplate. Indeed, it is clear already that, when the final reckoning is done, the people and governments of the Caribbean will have sustained severe political, military and economic casualties in the war on drugs.

NOTES

1. For a useful discussion of the reconceptualisation of security, see E. Azar and C. Moon, 'Third World National Security: Towards a New Conceptual Framework', *International Interactions*, 11, 2 (1984), 103–35; P. Mische, 'Ecological Security and the Need to Reconceptualize Sovereignty', *Alternatives*, 13, 4 (1989), 389–427; B. Buzan, *People, States, and Fear* (2nd edn, Boulder, 1991); J.T. Mathews, 'The Environment and International Security', in M.T. Klare and D.C. Thomas (eds.), *World Security: Trends and Challenges at Century's End* (New York, 1991); and K. Rupesinghe, 'The Disappearing Boundaries Between Internal and External Conflicts', in E. Boulding (ed.), *New Agendas for Peace Research: Conflict and Security Reexamined* (Boulder, 1992).
2. Cited in A.P. Maingot, 'Laundering the Gains of the Drug Trade: Miami and Caribbean Tax Havens', *Journal of Interamerican Studies and World Affairs*, 30 (Summer–Fall 1988), 171.
3. 'Sandiford Addresses Caribbean Coast Guards', *New York Carib News*, 31 July 1990, 36; and 'Statement of Honorable Michael Manley, Prime Minister of Jamaica', in US Congress, Senate, Committee on the Judiciary and the Caucus on International Narcotics Control, *U.S. International Drug Policy – Multilateral Strike Forces – Drug Policy in the Andean Nations*, Joint Hearings, 101st Cong., 1st and 2nd Sess., 6 Nov. 1989, and 18 Jan. and 27 March 1990. Manley's testimony was given on 6 Nov. 1989.
4. The West Indian Commission, *Time for Action: The Report of the West Indian Commission* (Bridgetown, 1992), 343.
5. United Nations General Assembly, *Political Declaration*, XVIIth Special Session, A/RES/S-17/2, 15 March 1990, 2.
6. See J. Scherer, *Crack Cocaine: The Rock of Death* (Minneapolis, 1988), esp. 4–12; and M. Massing, 'Crack's Destructive Sprint Across America', *New York Times Magazine*, 1 Oct. 1989, 38–41, 58–62.
7. United States Drug Enforcement Administration (DEA), *Drugs of Abuse* (Washington, DC, 1989), 30–31.
8. DEA, *Drugs of Abuse*, 40. I am grateful to Francille Griffith, RN, for explaining the fatal consequences of the abuse of cocaine and other substances.
9. DEA, *Drugs of Abuse*, 45.
10. G. Persaud, 'Police, Army Uncover Biggest Ganja Plot Yet', *Stabroek News* (Guyana), 15 March 1992, 1; and F. Gilbert, 'Police Discover G$1 Billion of Ganja in Berbice', *Stabroek News*, 23 May 1992, 1.

11. S.B. MacDonald, *Dancing on a Volcano: The Latin American Drug Trade* (New York, 1988), 89.
12. A.H. Young, 'Territorial Dimensions of Caribbean Security: The Case of Belize', in I.L. Griffith (ed.), *Strategy and Security in the Caribbean* (New York, 1991), 142–3; and US Department of State, *International Narcotics Control Strategy Report*, March 1991, 135. This document is referred to hereafter as *International Narcotics Report*.
13. Department of State, *International Narcotics Report*, 1991, 133.
14. Ibid., 198–9.
15. 'Ganja Growers Finding New Ways to Harvest', *Sunday Sun* (Barbados), 5 Nov. 1989, 24A; and Department of State, *International Narcotics Report*, 1991, 195.
16. MacDonald, *Dancing on a Volcano*, 90.
17. Ibid., 91.
18. Department of State, *International Narcotics Report*, 1991, 182.
19. Department of State, *International Narcotics Report*, 1992, 142. Also, see Howard Frankson, 'An Upsurge of Crime in Belize', *Caribbean Contact* (Barbados), July–Aug. 1992, 5, 8.
20. 'Police Reports Alarming Increase in Cocaine Seizures', *Guyana Chronicle*, 15 Dec. 1989; R. Sanders, 'The Drug Problem: Social and Economic Effects – Policy Options for the Caribbean', *Caribbean Affairs*, 3, July–Sept. (1990), 20; and 'Crack Bases On the Rise', *Jamaican Weekly Gleaner*, 18 May 1992, 4.
21. C. Stone, *National Survey on the Use of Drugs in Jamaica (1990)* (Kingston, Jamaica, 1990), 35.
22. Stone, *National Survey*, 40.
23. Ibid.
24. See R. Singh, 'Barbados Named in Trinidad Drug Reports', *Daily Nation* (Barbados), 3 Feb. 1987; R. Morris, 'Bajan Connection Arrested in London Cocaine Catch', *Daily Nation* (Barbados), 16 May 1990, 1; 'Ten Arrested in Drugs Shootout [in St Lucia]', *New York Carib News*, 16 Oct. 1990, 4; R. Sanders, 'Narcotics, Corruption and Development: The Problems in the Smaller Islands', *Caribbean Affairs*, 3 (Jan.–March 1990), 79–92; 'Bellyful of Dope is Fatal', *Barbados Advocate*, 11 April 1990; '$30 Million in Cocaine is Seized in Trinidad', *New York Carib News*, 29 Feb. 1990, 4; '$30M in Illegal Drugs Seized Last Year', *Sunday Chronicle* (Guyana), 6 Jan. 1991, 6, 7; G. Persaud, 'Witness Tells of Cocaine Found in Soap Powder Box', *Stabroek News*, 14 Jan. 1992, 1, 12; and 'Cops Tell of Finding Cocaine Among Panties', *Stabroek News*, 15 Feb. 1992, 3.
25. J. Griffith, '$6 M Ganja Haul', *Sunday Sun* (Barbados), 5 July 1992, 1; 'Trinidad and Tobago Police Make Big Cocaine Seizure', *Stabroek News*, 29 July 1992, 7; and 'Cops in US$12M Cocaine Timehri Haul', *Stabroek News*, 12 Sept. 1992, 1.
26. For a detailed examination of the use of Bimini and other areas for trafficking, see Government of the Bahamas, *Report of the Commission of Inquiry into the Illegal Use of the Bahamas for the Transshipment of Dangerous Drugs Destined for the United States* (Nassau, the Bahamas, 1984), 9–51.
27. Maingot, 'Laundering the Gains of the Drug Trade', 168.
28. Government of the Bahamas, *Report of the Commission of Inquiry*, 31.
29. Ibid., 7–8.
30. Government of the Bahamas, Ministry of National Security, *Summary Report on the Traffic in Narcotic Drugs Affecting the Bahamas in 1990* (Nassau, the Bahamas, 28 March 1991), 13–14, 66.
31. Ibid., 31; and Government of the Bahamas, Ministry of Foreign Affairs, *Bahamas Narcotics Control Report 1991* (Nassau, the Bahamas, March 1992), 7.
32. Department of State, *International Narcotics Report*, 1992, 141.
33. 'Jamaica Under Drug Seige', *New York Carib News*, 2 May 1989, 4; 'Questions Surround Air Jamaica Drug Find', *New York Carib News*, 16 May 1989, 3; and 'Politicians United Against Drugs', *New York Carib News*, 16 May 1989, 3.
34. US Congress, Senate, Committee on Foreign Relations, *Drug Money Laundering, Banks, and Foreign Policy*, Report by the Subcommittee on Narcotics, Terrorism,

and International Operations, 101st Cong., 2nd Sess. 27 Sept., 4 Oct., and 1 Nov. 1989, 5.

35. Department of State, *International Narcotics Report*, 1991, 364–5.
36. See M.D. Roberts, 'Grenada's Second Invasion', *New York Carib News*, 12 Nov. 1991, 3.
37. Department of State, *International Narcotics Report*, 1991, 366–7. See also Steve Lohr, 'Where the Money Washes Up', *New York Times Magazine*, 29 March 1992, 27ff.
38. Department of State, *International Narcotics Report*, 1991, 367–8, and 1992, 421–2.
39. Interview with Commissioner Phillips, Police Headquarters, Castries, St Lucia, 16 Aug. 1988.
40. See Morris, 'Bajan Connection'. Also see 'Two [Bajan] Cops Detained Following Ganja Bust', *Guyana Chronicle*, 21 Jan. 1992, 7; 'Bahamas Policeman Charged for Cocaine', *Stabroek News*, 18 March 1992, 7; and 'Corruption, A Cancer in Customs Officers', *Jamaican Weekly Gleaner*, 30 March 1992, 5.
41. Government of the Bahamas, *Report of Commission of Inquiry*, 35.
42. MacDonald, *Dancing on a Volcano*, 120–22; and D. Cichon, 'British Dependencies: The Cayman Islands and the Turks and Caicos Islands', in S.W. Meditz and D.M. Hanratty (eds.), *Islands in the Commonwealth Caribbean* (Washington DC, 1989), 579–81.
43. C. Marajh, 'Police "Drug Control" Charges Made in 1991 – Murray Told NAR Gov't', *Sunday Guardian* (Trinidad and Tobago), 12 April 1992, 1, 5; A. Thomas, 'DPP to Act on Suspended Cops', *Daily Express* (Trinidad and Tobago), 14 April 1992, 1, 10; and 'Scotland Yard to Investigate Trinidad Drug Cartel', *Stabroek News*, 10 May 1992, 24.
44. See, for example, testimony by Anthony Maingot in US Congress, House of Representatives, Select Committee on Narcotics Abuse and Control, *Drugs and Latin American: Economic and Political Impact and U.S. Policy Options*, Report of the Seminar held by the Congressional Research Service, 101st Cong., 1st Sess., 26 April 1989, 13.
45. Sanders, 'Narcotics, Corruption, and Development', 84.
46. V. Tulloch, 'Terrorism/Drugs Combination Threatens Security', *Sunday Gleaner* (Jamaica), 15 Jan. 1989, 10A; and F. V. Harrison, 'Jamaica and the International Drug Economy', *TransAfrica Forum*, 7 (Fall 1990), 55–6. Also see 'Gang Wars: Drug Menace Rearing its Ugly Head', *Nation* (Barbados), 10 June 1988.
47. Louis Blom-Cooper, *Guns for Antigua: Report of the Commission of Inquiry into the Circumstances Surrounding the Shipment of Arms from Israel to Antigua and Transshipment on 24 April 1989 En Route to Colombia* (London, 1990), 2.
48. US Congress, Senate, Committee on Governmental Affairs, *Arms Trafficking, Mercenaries, and Drug Cartels*, Hearings, Permanent Subcommittee on Investigations, 102nd Cong., 1st Sess, 27 and 28 Feb. 1991, 127–30.
49. Blom-Cooper, *Guns for Antigua*, 47–52; 120–21.
50. Ibid., 116.
51. Ibid., 117.
52. Ibid., 58.
53. 'GAC Fined 1.2 M (U.S.) for Transporting Ganja', *Guyana Chronicle*, 29 Jan. 1992, 3.
54. US Congress, *Drugs and Latin America*, 12–13; and J.A. Cumberbatch and N.C. Duncan, 'Illegal Drugs, USA Policies, and Caribbean Responses: The Road to Disaster', *Caribbean Affairs*, 3 (Oct.–Dec. 1990), 166–8.
55. US Congress, *Drugs and Latin America*, 12–13; Cumberbatch and Duncan, 'Illegal Drugs', 168; and 'US Customs, Air Jamaica Sign Anti-Drug Pact', *Jamaican Weekly Gleaner*, 23 Dec. 1991, 5.
56. For an examination of Caribbean capability limitations and reliance on foreign assistance, see I.L. Griffith, *The Quest for Security in the Caribbean: Problems and Promises in Subordinate States* (New York, 1993), chapter 3.

57. US Congress, Senate, Committee on Foreign Relations, *International Narcotics Control and Foreign Assistance Certification: Requirements, Procedures, Timetables, and Guidelines*, Report prepared by the Congressional Research Service, 100th Cong., 2nd Sess., March 1988, 1–2.
58. US Congress, *Drugs and Latin America*, 129.
59. See, for example, 'Trinidad Senator Advocates Hanging for Drug Traffickers', *Stabroek News*, 29 Aug. 1991, 9; and '[Dominica Prime Minister] Charles Says No to Drugs: Hang Them', *New York Carib News*, 28 July 1992, 3.
60. See 'Court Refuses Bail to Nine-Month Pregnant Accused', *Stabroek News*, 3 March 1992, 16; and 'Drugs Accused Sentenced to Jail in Her Absence', *Stabroek News*, 14 April 1992, 16.
61. Government of Jamaica, Ministry of Justice, *Crime and Justice in the Caribbean (Keynote address by the Honorable R. Carl Rattray, Q.C., Minister of Justice and Attorney General of Jamaica)*, 10 May 1991, 7.
62. Government of Jamaica, Parliament, *Sectoral Debate Presentation of the Honorable K.D. Knight, Minister of National Security*, 3 July 1991, 72–4; 'U.S. Customs', *Jamaican Weekly Gleaner*; and Department of State, *International Narcotics Report*, 1992, 210.
63. J.B. Treaster, 'On Tiny Isle of 300 Banks, Enter Scotland Yard', *New York Times*, 27 July 1989, A4; 'Montserrat: Stormy Weather', *Economist*, 9 Dec. 1989, 41; 'Oh, My Brass Plate in the Sun', *Economist*, 16 March 1991, 84; and J. Evans, 'Montserrat, in a Cleanup, Pulls Licenses of 300 Banks', *American Banker*, 28 March 1991, 21.
64. See CARICOM Secretariat, *Report of the Third Meeting of the High Level Ad Hoc Group on the Regional Drug Programme*, REP. 90/3/34 RDP, 3 Oct. 1990.
65. Government of Jamaica, *Memorandum Submitted by the Government of Jamaica on the Establishment of Regional Training Centre for Drug Law Enforcement Officers in Jamaica* (Kingston, Jamaica, 1991), 4.
66. See Government of Jamaica, *Memorandum*, 2–4; and Government of Jamaica, Parliament, *Sectoral Debate Presentation*, 64–83.
67. Department of State, *International Narcotics Report*, 1991, 133; 'Trinidad and Tobago, Venezuela Consider Joint Air Operations', *Trinidad Express*, 24 July 1991, 2; Government of the Bahamas, *Bahamas Narcotics Control Report 1991*, 5; 'Venezuela, Guyana Agreed on Joint Anti-Drug Plan', *Stabroek News*, 12 April 1992, 1; and 'US Worried About Guyana Coke Trafficking', *Stabroek News*, 15 Aug. 1992, 1.
68. J.E. Meason, 'War at Sea: Drug Interdiction in the Caribbean', *Journal of Defense and Diplomacy*, 6, 6 (1988), 8.
69. See Sanders, 'The Drug Problem', 22; and The West Indian Commission, *Time for Action*, 348–9.
70. See, for example, B.M. Bagley, 'The New Hundred Years War?: US National Security and the War on Drugs in Latin America', *Journal of Interamerican Studies and World Affairs*, 30 (Spring 1988), 171–4; and L. Greenhouse, 'High Court Backs Seizing Foreigners for Trial in U.S.', *New York Times*, 16 June 1992, A1, A18.

The Politics of Small State Security in the Pacific

ANTHONY PAYNE

The geographical definition of the Pacific is no more precise than that of the Caribbean. The ocean itself is a vast area covering one-third of the world's surface. Its waters wash the coasts of North and South America to the east, Japan, China and South-East Asia as a whole to the west, the Aleutian Islands to the north and Australia and New Zealand in the south. Viewed in this way as a Pacific Basin, the region has had no unifying political structure until in the last few years organisations such as the Asia-Pacific Economic Corporation movement (APEC) and the non-governmental Pacific Economic Cooperation Conference (PECC) have emerged to try to give some cohesion to the diverse collection of territories thereby embraced.[1] The driving force behind this search has been the dynamism of so many of the Pacific Basin economies and the consequent need felt by some constituent states, such as Australia, to organise the economic relationships pervading the region. Similar pressures to establish collective security mechanisms across the Basin are also now beginning to be felt, especially in the aftermath of the Cold War. The institutional complexity of Pacific cooperation will thus probably continue to increase, although only slowly, with difficulty and without prospect of effecting the full integration of the Basin into a united economic and political unit.

Scattered around within the Basin are numerous islands (some 25,000 in total) which collectively are sometimes referred to as Oceania or the island Pacific. For all their obvious membership of the Pacific Basin, they have few cultural and linguistic ties with the so-called Pacific Rim countries. The geographical limits of this sub-region are represented by Papua New Guinea (PNG) and the former United States Pacific Trust Territories to the west, Hawaii and Easter Island to the north and east respectively, and Australia and New Zealand to the south. Conventionally, the island Pacific is divided into three main cultural areas: Melanesia, Micronesia and Polynesia. Melanesia includes PNG, the Solomon Islands, New Caledonia, Vanuatu and Fiji, the last of

Anthony Payne is Reader in Politics at the University of Sheffield in England.

which is in reality a transition area between Melanesia and Polynesia. Micronesia lies mostly in the North Pacific and is composed mainly of atolls. It includes the Caroline Islands of Belau, Yap, Truk, Ponape and Kosrae, the Mariana Islands, the Marshall Islands, Kiribati, and Nauru. Polynesia is the most spread out, constituting a roughly triangular area from Hawaii in the north, Easter Island in the south-east and New Zealand in the south-west, and thus including Tuvalu, Western Samoa, American Samoa, Tonga, Tokelau, Wallis and Futuna, Niue, French Polynesia, Pitcairn and the Marquesas Islands. Australia is embraced within Oceania but sits apart from these cultural designations.[2]

All of the countries in the Pacific which can be designated small island and enclave developing states (SIEDS) are situated in the South Pacific. There are nine of them, listed here in the order in which they gained their independence: Western Samoa (1962), Nauru (1968), Fiji (1970), Tonga (1970), Papua New Guinea (1975), the Solomon Islands (1978), Tuvalu (1978), Kiribati (1979) and Vanuatu (1980). PNG is included, even though it is much the largest state in terms of both population and land area (3.5 million and 180,274 square miles). As already indicated, they are not culturally homogeneous, but they mostly adopted comparable liberal-democratic political systems on achieving independence and their pattern of economic development has been similar, PNG's substantial mineral resources again setting it somewhat apart from the others. Most importantly, they all belong to the South Pacific Forum, which first met in 1971 as an organisation representing the heads of government of the self-governing states of the sub-region.[3] The Pacific SIEDS are joined in membership of the Forum by the much larger states of Australia and New Zealand and by four other island territories which enjoy forms of free associated statehood – the Cook Islands and Niue with New Zealand, and the Federated States of Micronesia and the Republic of the Marshall Islands with the United States (the latter arrangement, although negotiated with the US in 1986, was only accepted by the UN Security Council in late 1990, as another minor manifestation of the unfreezing of the Cold War). The Forum does not have a founding document setting out its aims and objectives and it is open to the criticism that it has operated in a rather casual, albeit consensual, fashion (dubbed the 'Pacific Way'[4]). Nevertheless, through the Forum and its associated agencies, the states of the South Pacific have been able to discuss common problems of development and security on an annual basis for more than two decades and, in so doing, have acquired a recognisable collective identity in the international system.

THE REGIONAL SECURITY CONTEXT

The complexities attaching to the definition of the South Pacific testify immediately to the range of considerations which bear upon the specification of the security context of the region. The United States has built its global power after 1945 in good part on the basis of its hegemony over the entire Pacific Basin and is thus foremost amongst the states which shape the geopolitical parameters within which the Pacific SIEDS operate. Other external state actors also influence the geopolitical environment: they include the former and current colonial powers of Europe, particularly France, and the newer powers of Asia-Pacific itself, such as Japan, South Korea, Taiwan and Indonesia. Finally, there is the regional input itself, the activities of the South Pacific Forum. In this respect, the important fact to reiterate from the viewpoint of regional security is that Australia and New Zealand are themselves members of the organisation. They are able to work from within, which is very different from seeking to guide the Forum states in their preferred direction from outside. The perceived security interests of the two 'middle powers' of the South Pacific are therefore central to the whole security context of the region.

The US and the South Pacific

US security interests and objectives in the South Pacific are largely derivative of its concern with the wider region. The Pacific Ocean has, to all intents and purposes, been an 'American lake' since 1945 and the primary US defence interest has accordingly been the maintenance of secure lines of communication to its friends and allies in Asia, to Australia and New Zealand and through the Pacific to the Indian Ocean. Nearly one-half of US foreign trade transits the Pacific, whilst five of the seven defence agreements to which the US is a party are in the Asia-Pacific area.[5] In this context, the importance of some of the North Pacific islands is manifest. Guam, the North Marianas and Hawaii are all strategically located, are under American sovereignty and are the site of major US military facilities, the latter hosting the headquarters of the US Navy's Pacific Command (CINCPAC) at Pearl Harbor. In addition, the Marshall Islands was the scene of US nuclear testing between 1946 and 1962 and still contains the Kwajalein missile range facility which has been closely involved in the development of the Strategic Defense Initiative. The Federated States of Micronesia are not so important in terms of basing requirements, although it was sometimes argued in the latter stages of the Cold War era that Belau could become relevant in this respect if the US was ever to lose access to its bases in the Philippines.

By comparision, the Pacific SIEDS play nothing like the same strategic role in US perceptions. Washington's primary concern in this part of the area has been with the security of sea lanes. In peacetime, most ship movements from the Pacific to the Indian Ocean pass via the Indonesian archipelagic straits or the Strait of Malacca; in wartime, it has long been assumed that these passages might be closed by enemy action and that North Pacific transits to the Indian Ocean would have to shift to the South Pacific, either north or south of Australia. For the bulk of the period after its signing in 1951, the ANZUS Pact with Australia and New Zealand provided a sufficient security umbrella over the South Pacific for US purposes. The US felt no need to establish formal security relationships in the South Pacific. No bases were sought or needed as long as access to key island ports and airfields could be safely presumed. The result has been that US forces have in the main kept a low profile in the South Pacific, confining their activities to participation in disaster relief and civic action programmes throughout the islands and modest defence cooperation (exercises, training and military equipment sales) with Papua New Guinea and Fiji.

Moreover, given the low level of economic development and the broadly liberal character of political development in the independent states of the region, the US has not generally identified economic and political interests in the South Pacific of any great significance to its security. Its diplomatic presence has consequently been limited, something which has at times offended some of the island governments. Very few major US politicians or senior government officials, or even congressmen, have ever visited the region and US development assistance to the islands (excluding the Micronesian states in free association) averaged no more than two per cent of total bilateral assistance flows during the post-1945 Cold War period. As for the US private sector, apart from fishing interests concerned with tuna and mining companies working in PNG, there was widespread ignorance of such potential for trade and investment as the South Pacific offered. In short, the charge of benign neglect has more often and more aptly been made than that of gross interference.[6]

Extra-Regional Powers

Extra-regional powers concerned with the South Pacific can be divided into the old and the new. Of the former European colonial powers, the Netherlands withdrew when Indonesia seized and consolidated control of Irian Jaya (the western half of the island of New Guinea, formerly known as West Irian) in the early 1960s and thus ceased to be a force within the region. Britain remains a member of the oldest regional organisation, the South Pacific Commission, which it founded with the other colonial powers in 1947; still has responsibility for tiny Pitcairn Island, populated by about 60 people descended from the mutineers of the HMS Bounty; maintains a bilateral aid programme; and has taken part in joint naval exercises with ANZUS. But, having withdrawn from 'East of Suez' in the 1960s, it has long been of only limited significance in regional security matters. It has also seen many of its previous trade and aid links with the region subsumed under the auspices of the European Community (EC) which has formed an invaluable link with many South Pacific states under the terms of successive Lome Conventions since 1975.

France is also embraced by the EC link. Yet, in marked contrast to the other European powers, it not only continues to have colonies in the region but gives every sign of regarding itself as being a permanent South Pacific power in its own right. The peoples of its three territories – New Caledonia, French Polynesia, and Wallis and Futuna – voted to stay as integral parts of France in referenda in 1958, with the result that many colonial characteristics have endured in their political, economic, social and indeed psychological make-up. The establishment of nuclear testing facilities in French Polynesia in 1966 further tied this territory to the cornerstone of France's continuing identification of itself as a major world power and, in fact, greatly strengthened its determination to retain its South Pacific presence as a whole. The Pacific territories also form a critical part of France's global network of military bases and give Paris control over an Exclusive Economic Zone (EEZ) of seven million square kilometres of maritime area in the South Pacific. More widely still, much influential comment in France in the mid-1980s identified the Pacific Basin as the new 'centre of the world', providing yet another incentive to stay in the region.[7]

Of the newer powers, Japan stands out for the sheer scale of its potential economic influence amongst the island states, but has the ugly memory of its wartime record in the Pacific still to overcome. Indonesia is involved via its shared border with Papua New Guinea and the intermittent tensions generated, not only with PNG but also with Vanuatu, by the politics of Melanesian separatism in Irian Jaya. Taiwan has traditional linkages with local Chinese communities and has been concerned to protect its position in the area *vis-à-vis* the not inconsiderable efforts of the People's Republic of China to gain greater recognition. South Korea has not moved much beyond the assertion of its fishing interests in the South Pacific and the Soviet Union never sought to develop anything beyond limited diplomatic links with the region. Apart from these powers, Malaysia and, to a lesser extent, India recognise racial links with Moslem and Indian population groups in the region and even Israel now has an ambassador in Fiji accredited to all the Pacific SIEDS. However, none of these new extra-regional powers can yet be said to play an important part in determining regional security: the point is rather that the range of actors which can potentially be brought into play in a crisis has become considerably larger, although it certainly does not follow that any or all will necessarily want to become involved.

The South Pacific Forum, Australia and New Zealand

The South Pacific Forum has, since its inception, come to sit at the centre of a wide-ranging network of regional activities. It was serviced from an early date by the South Pacific Bureau for Economic Cooperation (SPEC) situated in Suva, the capital of Fiji. SPEC has now been renamed the Forum Secretariat and has been joined by many other regional bodies. They include the Pacific Forum Line (PFL); the Forum Fisheries Agency (FFA); the Coordinating Committee for Mineral Prospecting in South Pacific Offshore Areas (CCOP/SOPAC); the University of the South Pacific (USP); the Pacific Islands Development Programme (PIDP); the South Pacific Organization Coordination Committee (SPOCC); and, most recently, the Forum Dialogue Partners Scheme, a mechanism for structuring the region's relations with extra-regional powers. At the level of economic development and functional cooperation, the network is impressive and it cannot be denied that it has contributed significantly to maintaining the viability, or minimising the vulnerability, of the Pacific SIEDS. As one analyst put it, 'the regional institutional network allocates resources – legitimacy, economic rewards, and status. It determines who is in and who is out in South Pacific regional politics'.[8]

As already indicated, Australia and New Zealand are members of the Forum. Although this has had its advantages from the viewpoint of the SIEDS, it has also invited the charge of insensitive and domineering behaviour on the part of the two 'big brothers'. Their presence has inevitably coloured the work of the organisation, most extensively perhaps in the arena of foreign policy and regional security where it has been the norm for Australia and New Zealand to take the lead in Forum meetings on these issues. The fact is, of course, that the interests of the Pacific SIEDS and their would-be protectors are not necessarily congruent on such matters. Australia, in particular, has identified the

South Pacific as being of major importance to its security, certainly ever since the rapid Japanese advance into New Guinea and the Solomon Islands during the Second World War posed a threat to the integrity of Australia itself. In the most direct sense, therefore, its security interests are focused on the Melanesian territories closest to its northern shore which could act as 'stepping stones' for an attack. The more distant Polynesian territories are of lesser concern. More generally, however, Australia has also had an enduring interest in the security of the long sea and air lines of communication across the Pacific to its major post-war ally, the US, which, in turn, has laid the basis in Canberra of a strong incentive to deny potentially hostile powers access to any part of the South Pacific area. For its part, New Zealand has had broadly similar interests: the main distinctions have been, firstly, that its main area of focus has been Polynesia (which from its perspective includes Fiji) rather than Melanesia, and, secondly, that it has always been a lesser military power than Australia.

The outcome of this dual engagement in South Pacific affairs over a 40-year period has been an intricate web of connections binding together Australia, New Zealand and the Pacific SIEDS in almost every aspect of each other's security. The nature and detail of all the ties cannot be set out here. They have been simply too extensive.[9] What should be noted, however, is that they have been grounded in attempts to reduce the economic, political and social vulnerability of the SIEDS, which Canberra and Wellington have, in fairness, always tended to see as the basis for undesirable external interference. Aid has been considerable, with much attention diligently devoted over the years to harnessing supply to real regional needs. Efforts have also been made to promote intra-regional trade by measures such as the signing of the South Pacific Regional Trade and Economic Cooperation Agreement (SPARTECA) between Australia, New Zealand and the Forum countries in 1970. As regards foreign investment, Australia has long been the largest source in the Forum countries. In other words, both Australia and New Zealand have helped to sustain the open economic development strategies widely favoured since independence by South Pacific island governments. More recently, defence cooperation has also developed on a broader basis. Australia has had a special defence relationship with Papua New Guinea dating back to its period of colonial responsibility for the territory and its defence units have frequently visited island countries. New Zealand ships and troops have been similarly visible and both countries, of course, worked together closely within ANZUS for many years. None of this was done altruistically: it reflected perceptions of national security interest held in

Canberra and Wellington rather than in the Pacific SIEDS. Yet, for a substantial period in the 1960s and 1970s, it effectively substituted for a security policy developed and deployed by these states in accordance with their own perception of their interests.

THE THREAT AGENDA

For all the devotion to regional security demonstrated by Australia and New Zealand, on behalf of the Forum, as it were, the question of what were the security threats which faced the Pacific SIEDS themselves could not be ignored indefinitely. Its embrace was a necessary part of the attainment of political independence. The process of decolonisation in the region reached the end of its first phase in 1980 and the ensuing decade saw the emergence for the first time of a genuine debate about security in the South Pacific.

The Debate of the 1980s

The starting point, however, was still external in origin. It was the publication of a monograph by John Dorrance, a senior foreign service officer in the United States Department of State, which was rightly billed as 'the first comprehensive analysis of the South Pacific from the standpoint of overall United States interests, including security'.[10] He noted that the long period of benign neglect of the region by the US since 1945 had recently given way to a more active role, marked *inter alia* by increased aid and cultural exchange programmes, wider and more professional diplomatic representation, more numerous US navy ship visits and the initiation of discussions with Pacific island states about the nature of the US role in the region. Dorrance attributed this increased US interest to the following factors:

> Australia's and New Zealand's concern about Soviet . . . activity in the area in 1976, the parallel acceleration of the region's decolonization processes (including a consequent rundown in the British presence and influence), a growing awareness of the importance of the region's marine resources, and a perception that the region's goodwill toward the US was being eroded by US inattention.[11]

The tenor of his argument as a whole left no doubt that concern about unprecedented Soviet intervention in the region, by which was meant mainly fishing and maritime activity and, in particular, the unconsummated Soviet offer of aid to Western Samoa and Tonga in 1976 in exchange for shore facilities, extended to Washington as much as to Canberra and Wellington. Dorrance was concerned to develop, and make explicit in a way that had not occurred before, a concept of 'strategic denial' in respect of possible Soviet incursions into the South Pacific, and was saying that a modest increase in Western aid and attention was needed to secure the region for the West. The US thus laid down one important position in the emerging debate about South Pacific security, which was that the main danger derived, as everywhere else in the developing world, from the incipient threat of the Soviets.

The voice of the South Pacific itself sang a very different tune when it was, at last, heard. The occasion was a colloquium on the special security needs of small states convened in Wellington in August 1984 as part of the work of the Commonwealth Consultative Group set up to investigate this general problem in the aftermath of the Grenada crisis in the Caribbean in late 1983. The meeting was attended by ministers and officials from Fiji, Tuvalu, the Solomon Islands, Western Samoa and the Cook Islands, as well as several academics from the region, and produced a concluding statement which declared without any equivocation that 'the most acute special need' of Pacific SIEDS was for 'greater economic security'.[12] It went on:

> South Pacific Island states do not see the risk factor for them from great power rivalry and conflict as being as great as in other regions. The South Pacific is not a primary area for such conflict at this time although all participants agreed that the situation could change, perhaps quickly, in the future. Nor do South Pacific states feel physically threatened by any of their neighbours. They do not perceive any imminent threat or military intervention or interference by a power from either within or outside the region.[13]

By contrast, what most worried the representatives of the governments was their sense of excessive economic dependence, to the point almost of helplessness. They stressed that this was as much perpetuated as offset by aid, but nevertheless called for the development of improved trade and aid policies by concerned states as the best means of reducing economic insecurity.

This emphasis on economic security served to polarise the debate, but did not advance it by much. Shortly afterwards, Robert Kiste and Richard Herr, two academics specialising in South Pacific affairs, produced a report for the US State Department on the potential for Soviet penetration of the islands. They reiterated many of the points made by Dorrance, albeit in the course of concluding that the desire of the Soviet Union to exploit the islands, which they took as a given, could not at that time be 'translated directly into a probability'.[14] What was particularly interesting about their analysis was the challenge it attempted to mount against the predominant view of the Wellington meeting. At one point, for example, they quoted a risk assessment offered by the then foreign minister (and later prime minister) of Papua New Guinea, Rabbie Namaliu, in a discussion in 1983:

> intra-regional conflict (slight); an unprovoked attack on an Island country by an external power (also slight); destabilisation of an Island state for profit or ideology – including great power rivalry (rather more likely); conflict over access to the region's marine resources (also moderately possible); domestic instability in New Caledonia (more likely yet); and domestic internal threats to individual states (the greatest security risk).[15]

Kiste and Herr admitted that this designation of domestic instability as the primary threat doubtless reflected PNG's longstanding preoccupation with secession, but they still judged that Namaliu's 'list and the relativities assigned each category' was 'a more conventionally useful assessment' than the Wellington emphasis on economic security and 'would probably be endorsed'[16] by most South Pacific states.

The objection to this line of argument, as with the earlier counterposing of great power rivalry against endemic economic dependence as sources of security threat, is precisely that it too separated economic insecurity from internal threats and henceforth treated them as competing explanations. In a telling review of Kiste and Herr delivered in early 1986, William Sutherland argued that their report – perhaps inadvertently – served to divert attention from the 'structural interrelatedness' of economics and politics and, in so doing, helped to brand pressures for social, economic and political change in the islands as ' "political", "ideological" or "radical" '.[17] He did not doubt the existence in the South Pacific of a pervasive sense of economic insecurity, as argued in Wellington; indeed, in Sutherland's view, this insecurity was already beginning to find political expression in the emergence of tensions over land rights in several regional states and, in particular, in the growing assertiveness of working-class politics in the key island of Fiji. The great benefit of this type of analysis was that it took a dynamic, as opposed to a static, view of security prospects and was thereby well placed to adjust to the quickening pace of political change in the South Pacific which became apparent in the second half of the 1980s.

Indeed, David Hegarty, one of the most experienced of Australian observers of the region, began a review of small state security in the South Pacific, published in 1987, by commenting on how quickly the rather complacent stance fashionable at the time of the Grenada crisis had been undermined. He drew attention to two trends in regional politics. The first reflected Sutherland's line of argument and constituted the claim that 'domestic political pressures have mounted as island governments have sought to accommodate rising levels of expectations, to mediate emerging class tensions, and (in some states) to resolve ethnic and communal strains'.[18] The dramatic first coup in Fiji in May 1987, which had only just occurred as he was writing, was the most obvious evidence of this trend. The second also reflected a familiar argument, that about competition for influence in the South Pacific between external powers. Hegarty suggested here that, at last, 'superpower rivalry has begun to encroach upon the region'.[19] His evidence was various: Gorbachev's Vladivostok speech in July 1986 asserting the Soviet Union's legitimacy as an Asian-Pacific power; the fishing agreements signed by the Soviet Union with Kiribati and Vanuatu in 1985 and 1987 respectively; the rupture within ANZUS occasioned by New Zealand's controversial decision in 1985 to prohibit the entry into its ports of US nuclear-capable warships; and the resultant US efforts to improve its relations with Pacific island states, most notably through the signing of a fisheries accord in April 1987 which alleviated much of the considerable disquiet previously generated within the region by the uncontrolled activities of American tuna fishermen.

What is more, Hegarty went on to argue that the international politics of the region was being complicated still further by the growing activism of several other external powers with interests in the South Pacific – Japan, China and Taiwan, some of the South-East Asian states, Israel and, most controversially of all, Libya. The latter, he noted, had developed connections with some of the militant sections of the Kanak independence movement which had grown up in New Caledonia and with some elements in the government of Vanuatu.[20] On this flimsy basis, a Libyan 'scare' of extraordinary proportions was mounted in the media and in the propaganda of some governments (especially that of Australia) throughout 1987 and 1988. In general too, the notion that the security of the South Pacific was being prejudiced by aggressive, external power-politics acquired a popularity which was never fully sustained by the facts, even at the height of the supposed contest. In all of this, the other strand of Hegarty's original argument, namely, the tendency towards greater domestic political volatility in the region, became uneasily and inaccurately subsumed in many commentaries within the 'external competition' thesis – to the point where even the first and the second coups in Fiji and the domestic unrest which troubled Vanuatu between 1987 and early 1989 were attributed predominantly to external influences. Analyses by such as George Tanham and Owen Harries exemplified this tendency, for which they were rightly chided in a critical paper by the New Zealand intelligence analyst, Ken Ross.[21] In sum, the South Pacific was readily and too easily portrayed as having lost its 'innocence' during the 1980s, a victim like every other part of the developing world of the insidious embrace of Cold War *realpolitik*.

The Real Agenda

Turning to the 1990s, many of the strands in this evolving debate about the security of the Pacific SIEDS already have a dated air. The Libyan threat is no longer seriously discussed and the whole argument about superpower competition has necessarily had to be revised in the light of the disintegration of the Soviet Union. The United States thus no longer has reason to 'raise its game', as Cold War parlance would have it, in the area. Many have been tempted therefore to consign the South Pacific once more to the status of an international backwater. This would be a misjudgement: several real security threats to the stability, way of life and democratic practice of the region continue to exist and some of them promise to escalate in importance very quickly. Attention is drawn in the remainder of this section to some of the most critical of these threats.

Secession. The first is the threat of secession. All island regions experience the potential threat of secession: it is endemic to their geography. Security analyses of the South Pacific have always noted the possibility and usually made reference to the brief attempted secession of Espiritu Santo, one of the outer islands of Vanuatu, at the time of that country's move to independence in 1980. The background here was Vanuatu's difficult birth as a state. Ruled jointly by Britain and France as the Condominium of the New Hebrides, it suffered a kind of colonial dualism on top of the traditional linguistic, cultural and regional factionalism which characterises the South Pacific. French officials in fact resisted the advent of independence and encouraged the Santo rebels. In the event, the country's youthful political leaders, headed by Father Walter Lini, an Anglican priest, weathered the storm and Vanuatu emerged intact, although it remains one of the states in the region (the Solomon Islands and Fiji are others) most likely to experience further secessionist revolts.

The reason, however, that secession presently looms large in any consideration of the security problems of the Pacific SIEDS is to be found in the events surrounding the resurgence of the Bougainville problem in Papua New Guinea in the late 1980s. PNG is an odd political formation: it is a country with limited internal communications which embraces several diverse ethnic groupings that owe allegiance predominantly to a geographical area rather than the nation. Its main achievement since independence has thus been to hang together, albeit loosely and at a cost in terms of centralised authority *vis-à-vis* the provinces. Particular problems of loyalty to the centre always existed with Bougainville, the copper-rich island (strictly the North Solomons province) located to the north-east of the main island of PNG. The situation blew up again in April 1989, inspired by a mixture of dissatisfaction with the share of the resources returned to the province from the huge Panguna copper mine, outrage at the environmental consequences of the rapacious open-cast mining involved, growing ethnic tension between the mainly black Bougainvilleans and the 'redskins' from other parts of PNG who worked in the mine, and political ambition on the part of local island leaders both in local government and at the grass-roots. A Bougainville Revolutionary Army (BRA) declared itself and launched attacks on the mine and police stations. The PNG Defence Force was dispatched to Bougainville to restore law and order, only to be drawn into a nasty counterinsurgency campaign in which several abuses of human rights were perpetrated against the local population. The government in Port Moresby was as embarrassed by the bad publicity as it was paralysed by the loss of revenue from the Bougainville mine which had been shut down by the rebellion. In April 1990, in some desperation, it withdrew all its security forces from Bougainville in favour of a policy of blockading the rebel islands and its inhabitants. The BRA responded by declaring Bougainville's independence from PNG.[22]

Such a move inevitably raised the possibility that other secessions would follow and that PNG would eventually break up. As already indicated, separatist politics existed in other parts of the state, notably the New Guinea island region. Several other major mining enterprises also existed, many with the potential to sustain separate new states. Yet for the moment such fears have not been realised. The Bougainville secession has in effect been allowed to wither. Formal peace talks between the PNG government and the rebels have taken place on a number of occasions but they have not been consummated in any decisive understanding. Part of the problem is that the rebels are themselves divided and lack full control over their own supporters. The blockade certainly caused suffering in Bougainville and, to that extent, displayed to other potential secessionists in other parts of the country a measure of resolution on the part of the central PNG state. The prospect is then that the writ of PNG will very gradually be reasserted in the North Solomons province and that the different geographical areas will continue to adhere together. That said, the nature of PNG is such that the politics of fragmentation cannot be easily, if ever, exorcised.

It is also worth noting briefly at this point that secession has not been allowed to become an issue of dispute within the South Pacific regional system. Relations between PNG and the Solomon Islands did deteriorate sharply as a result of the Bougainville secession in early 1992. The PNG government believed that the Solomons, whose people have strong traditional links with the Bougainvilleans, was allowing the BRA to use its territory to re-group and it permitted the PNG Defence Force to raid a number of villages just over the Solomons border. It looked as if the Solomons Islands government would demand that the issue be discussed at the July 1992 Forum meeting held in Honiara, the Solomons' capital, but in the end the organisation's received position, that secession was an internal matter, was maintained.

Indigenous Militarisation. The second identifiable threat is in some ways linked to secession: it is a tendency towards what can best be called indigenous militarisation – a militarisation of the political systems of Pacific SIEDS engendered not by external pressures or machinations but by internal instability and the incapacity of civilian political institutions to mediate conflicts successfully. The problem is not one of emerging political turbulence *per se*. Hegarty, for example, in a paper delivered in 1989 noted certain new signs of political change in the region.

> In the Cook Islands governments have changed hands (constitutionally) three times in the past four years. In Kiribati [there have been] ructions in domestic politics and the formation of an opposition party. In Nauru a parliamentary stand-off saw the president lose, then ultimately regain power. In Western Samoa an evenly divided parliament led to difficulties in the formation of a government. In the Solomon Islands a prime minister was toppled for accepting French cyclone-relief aid from his electorate, and the next election saw his government out of power. Even in the Kingdom of Tonga there have been stirrings against monarchical rule.[23]

However, as he acknowledged, these instances of tension mostly reflected the developing politicisation of traditional arrangements and cultures with no necessarily worrying implications, as yet, for the survival of civilian forms. In short, the argument in this context is not about political instability, which has always historically accompanied the development and flowering of democracy. It is about the embrace of militaristic solutions to political problems, and here the dangerous precedent in the South Pacific has been Fiji.

The two military interventions effected in Fiji by Colonel Rabuka in May and September 1987 shook the whole Pacific island region. Quite apart from their disastrous impact on Fijian democracy, they were widely seen as forerunners of similar moves in other states, notably Papua New Guinea and Vanuatu, where signs of political unease had been apparent for some time. Yet Fiji is an unusual society, even in the South Pacific context, and the events there were more exceptional than typical. Even in retrospect, there does not seem to have been anything inevitable about the collapse into militarisation. The coups were not historically predetermined by the nature of the racial conflict between Indian and native Fijian in the island; nor did they reflect the simple assertion of the primacy of indigenous Melanesian values over the national political process; still less did they represent the reaction of a beleagured capitalist ruling class confronted by the socialist project of the Fiji Labour Party. All of these explanations were advanced.[24] In fact, race and class factors, as well as generational tensions and provincial disparities, jumbled up against the loss of patronage and the political pique of the incumbent prime minister, Ratu Mara, and those other members of the Fijian elite within the Alliance Party who had grown used to the exercise of political power, to create a complex brew of forces leading towards military intervention.

Despite fears, a third coup in the same sequence was avoided.[25] Instead, Rabuka chose to turn himself into a populist civilian politician, emerging as the country's first prime minister under its controversial new constitution in elections held in May 1992. The constitution effectively ensures indigenous Fijian domination of the political system; yet Rabuka was backed in the post-election bargaining by the Fiji Labour Party whose administration he overthrew in 1987 and whose support is still largely to be found amongst the Indian community. The conventional wisdom in South Pacific political commentary is that this was evidence of a new political maturity and confirmation of Fiji's return to the democratic fold.[26] Such a judgement is premature: Rabuka not only needs to be tested by time in his new civilian and democratic mode, especially in respect of the promises he has made to consider reform of the constitution, but so too does the Fijian army which he has left. Courtesy of the events of 1987, the latter has become an actor on the national political scene and its future re-intervention will not be something that can be ruled out for many years yet.

The question also arises of the extent to which the experience of militarisation in Fiji will be, or already has been, emulated in Papua New Guinea and Vanuatu. According to one widely articulated line of argument, at least in journalistic circles, PNG hovers on the brink of a coup. Indeed, in March 1990 there was an unsuccessful, and in fact rather drunken, attempt to take over the government in Port Moresby made by the country's commissioner of police. Perhaps this event (dubbed the 'Bar-B-Coup' in PNG after the function which initiated the drinking) should not in itself be taken too seriously. Nevertheless, it is still the view of many observers that PNG's political system has displayed a greater degree of stress in the last few years than perhaps ever before. Tony Siaguru, a former MP and now Deputy Secretary-General of the Commonwealth, talked in late 1988 of the country being 'at the crossroads', and warned that, if 'this slippery, sliding situation' was allowed to continue, there was 'very little hope for us to pull out of it'.[27] The argument in essence is that the development process in Papua New Guinea, prompted of late by a mineral exploitation boom, has unleashed new social forces which are beginning to alter the traditional style and conventional rules of political conflict. Evidence is variously drawn from the growing gap between the rich (including many corrupt politicians) and the poor and the consequent emergence of new class tensions, the spread of crime and what is known as 'rascalism', and, most seriously of all as already discussed, renewed secessionist impulses focused upon Bougainville.

The PNG Defence Force is widely held to be discontented and acknowledged to be something of a wild card. It has also never really been a passive bystander in PNG politics. In recent years, for example, in addition to the Bougainville imbroglio, it has been involved, on and off, in exchanges with the Indonesian army on the Irian Jaya border; rebelled against a cabinet decision to move some of its assets to a new base; rioted briefly in Port Moresby over poor pay and conditions; and been drawn ever more extensively into a general policing role in the face of growing crime and civil violence. At the same time, it suffered losses in men, morale and reputation in its attempt to repress the rebellion in Bougainville and the fact is that, for all the apparent threat it represents and the unusual activities with which it has been associated, what it has not yet done is carry out a coup. Moreover, the consensus of most knowledgeable watchers of PNG is that factors of topography, ethnicity, military capability and institutional rivalry seriously inhibit the prospect, certainly along the lines which occurred in Fiji.[28]

Vanuatu constitutes a different situation again from both Fiji and PNG. The Vanuaaku Pati (VP) dominated the country's politics in the period after independence and was opposed in parliament by a coalition of smaller parties, the Union of Moderate Parties (UMP). This essentially two-party system reflected, in the main, the historical cleavage between opposed British and French political traditions, the leaders of the VP being schooled by the British and the UMP by the French. The first real threat to the VP's rule occurred in 1988 when Barak Sope, the party's secretary-general, attempted to bring down Father Lini and take over as prime minister. Sope was sacked from the cabinet in May of that year following anti-government protests in Port Vila for which he was blamed. Later in the year, in December, Sope tried again: the country's ceremonial president, and his uncle, George Sokomanu, illegally announced the dissolution of parliament and the appointment of Sope as prime minister pending new elections. However, the courts upheld the constitution and the police and the small para-military force stayed loyal, rendering Sokomanu's 'coup attempt' (as it was labelled by the press) an embarrassing failure. Since Sope was the man most responsible for the Libyan links which Vanuatu briefly enjoyed, some saw his bid for power as having ideological origins. In reality, it derived from more mundane considerations, such as ambition and personal rivalry, interwoven, as always in the multi-island SIEDS of the Pacific, with longstanding local conflicts and loyalties.

As regards militarisation, the point to note is that the Vanuatu para-military force did give support to the elected civilian leaders, although it could just as easily be said that it gave support to those leaders with whom it identified politically, who also happened to be elected. The key figures in the force were always understood to be closely linked to Lini and the VP. At the same time, the worrying aspect of the affair is that the regime was unquestionably hard-pressed at the time of the May 1988 protests. Lini was forced to appeal to the Australian government for an emergency air-lift of tear gas and might easily have had to request more overt security assistance to hold on to power.[29] In retrospect too, the struggle for power broke the VP's unity. Lini was ousted from office at the end of a long period of internal faction-fighting in September 1991 and by the time elections were held in December three parties (the VP, the Lini faction and the so-called Melanesian Progressive Party led by Sope and Sokomanu) stood against the UMP, the longstanding opposition grouping. The latter took the main jobs in a coalition formed with the Lini faction, although this did not include Lini himself who is in poor health. The new government thus straddles the Anglo-French divide in Vanuatu politics and a period of instability seems likely, although with no necessary implications for military involvement.

In sum, the trend towards indigenous militarisation in the region is not yet firm or widespread, but it is present in some of the key states and, as such, it constitutes a threat to the peace and security of the islands as a group. Some measure of continued political instability can be expected in these and other states, as traditional modes of politics, organised around local or regional rivalries, ethnic tensions and status differences, come under pressure from an accelerating process of social and economic change characterised by urbanisation, labour unrest and middle-class discontent, to name only the most obvious phenomena. To give just two illustrations, the Western Samoan government has recently been forced to concede universal suffrage following a referendum on the issue and even the chiefly Tongan government has been placed on the defensive by a demand for more accountability led by the commoner member of parliament, Akilisa Pohiva. These processes are internal to the region and are a part of its developing history. They cannot easily be stopped and it is not at all obvious that they ought to be stopped. What does not necessarily have to follow – although it may – is the increasing involvement of the defence and police forces of the various island states in managing, reacting to and, worst of all, repressing these inevitable changes.

Incomplete Decolonisation. The third security threat facing the South Pacific in the 1990s is of a different order: it derives from the fact that the process of decolonisation in the region is not yet complete. Indeed, it has not even gone as far as many people tend to think. As has already been noted, of some 21 political entities in the South Pacific, only nine are fully independent and thus qualify as SIEDS. The constitutional status of the rest takes a variety of forms, with New Zealand, the United States and France all retaining links with territories either on the basis of continuing dependence or free association. In general, New Zealand's relationship with its responsibilities is uncontroversial. The Cook Islands and Niue became self-governing in their internal affairs in 1965 and 1974 respectively, with the former also gradually assuming control over its external relations. Both territories may also terminate their links with Wellington simply by amending their own constitutions.[30] As for the tiny population of Tokelau, it still wants to maintain its dependent ties with New Zealand. In marked contrast, the continuing relationships of both the United States and France with their South Pacific territories have been contested, in some places bitterly, and are the source of more general security problems for the whole region, precisely because they bring external sovereign interests directly into the South Pacific.

The problem with the US presence derives from Washington's efforts during the course of the last decade to divest itself of full responsibility for what was the Trust Territory of the Pacific Islands, established under its supervision at the end of the Second World War. The critical moment came in 1986 when the US government unilaterally abrogated the Trusteeship Agreement, re-establishing the Northern Mariana Islands as a US Commonwealth and the Republic of the Marshall Islands and the Federated States of Micronesia as 'self-governing nations in free association with the United States'. The difficulties with this 'solution' were various. Firstly, the free association arrangements for the latter two states contained separate mutual security pacts which specifically prevented full and final decolonisation in the future. Secondly, the termination of the trusteeship was initially approved only by the United Nations Trusteeship Council, not the Security Council, as originally laid down in the UN Charter. As noted earlier, the approval of the latter was not secured until the end of 1990 when the ending of the Cold War and a US promise that neither state would be used as a base removed the prospect of a Soviet veto. Thirdly, the people of Belau have failed to vote by a sufficient majority to enter into the free association arrangement on no less than seven separate occasions (most recently in February 1990) and thus remain within the terms of the Trusteeship.[31] Uncertainty over the question of political status, albeit combined with traditional patterns of conflict, also led to political violence and assassination in the territory. All in all, the situation continues to be awkward, to say the least. It creates the potential for political disturbance in any or all of these US territories, compromises the constitutional integrity of the Forum movement and complicates wider US diplomacy in the region.

These types of problems reappear writ large when attention is turned to France's relations with its South Pacific possessions. The internal political situation in each of the three French territories is very different: in New Caledonia a powerful and well-organised Kanak nationalist movement, supported by the independent Melanesian states in the region, has arisen demanding radical political change leading to independence; in French Polynesia urban discontent exists but has yet to develop into a call for an independent Maohi state; whilst in Wallis and Futuna no real inclination to break the constitutional link with Paris has ever been shown, even though an unease with the relationship has at times been evident. What links all of them is the determination of the French state to maintain its presence in the South Pacific – for indisputable reasons, as France sees it, of prestige, security and global military reach, not to mention the substantial nickel resources present in New Caledonia estimated at around one-third of total world output.

New Caledonia has unquestionably been the focus of the debate in the South Pacific about the continuing French presence. The provocative policies of the Chirac administration in France from March 1986 onwards threatened for a while to turn the demands of the Kanak community in New Caledonia into a major regional crisis. In fact, for all the talk in the mid-1980s of Libyan and Soviet destabilisation of regional security, France was the one external power with the capacity, and perhaps also the inclination, to bring about that outcome. However, the election of a socialist government in Paris in May 1988 brought a change of approach which led within three months to the signing of the Matignon Accord between France and both the pro- and anti-independence forces in the territory. The agreement provided for a massive injection of French development assistance and the holding of a referendum on political status after the lapse of ten years in 1998. It created what has been accurately described as 'an uneasy peace'.[32] This still lasts. France is pouring millions of francs into the territory each year in an attempt to 'rebalance' its economy somewhat in the direction of the Kanaks. Politically, there have also been interesting developments. The leader of the French settler community in New Caledonia has lately called for the construction of a consensus in the country before 1998, arguing that a referendum vote for or against independence would inevitably disappoint a substantial section of the population. This call has brought to light again the longstanding split between radicals and moderates in the Kanak nationalist movement. In the circumstances, New Caledonia's political future cannot but remain uncertain for some considerable time to come. There is inevitably a possibility that renewed political violence will occur in the territory, that France's response could generate wider tensions, and that these could spill over into other islands.

Resource Piracy. The fourth security threat which faces the Pacific SIEDS is that of resource piracy, which is not too emotional a term to describe the ruthless exploitation of the key economic resources of the islands by external powers. There are fears that seabed minerals may become the focus for such piracy in the future, but the problem so far has concerned the tuna fish which are to be found in plentiful quantity in the huge sea areas constituted by the 200-mile EEZs enjoyed under the Law of the Sea by each independent island state. Tuna has long been seen as the major development asset of the region and was a source of conflict in the early 1980s with the United States whose fishermen used to operate illegally in regional waters without paying licence fees until a deal was struck in 1987. The new culprits then became the fishermen of

Japan, Taiwan and South Korea, who not only deployed a growing number of vessels in the region in the late 1980s but used the controversial driftnet technique dubbed the 'wall of death'. This method catches all manner of sea creatures in addition to the desired fully-grown tuna, including the young fish, which results in the swift depletion of the adult stock. By 1990 the scale of the fishing, with Japan and Taiwan admitting to a combined fleet of 120 vessels and probably actually sending out some 180 (compared to no more than 20/30 a year or two earlier), was such that the Forum Fisheries Agency estimated that it would take five years for the stock to be replenished, even if driftnetting stopped immediately. Its continuation would have been economically disastrous for the fishing industries of all the Pacific island states.

The problem was acute because the states did not, and still do not, have the capacity to police and, if necessary, defend their own EEZs. The area is quite simply too vast. In addition, their resolve to resist the threat to their fishing industries was potentially weakened by the fact that Japan and Taiwan, in particular, have become major aid donors to the region. Even as the controversy over driftnet fishing was coming to a head in a series of meetings in the region in May and June 1989, Western Samoa was announcing its acceptance of a Japanese loan to pay for a major port development in Apia, the Solomon Islands was signing a deal with Japan to construct a new fishing project, Fiji was taking delivery of a number of Taiwanese cars provided for members of the government, and Tonga was using a substantial loan from Taiwan to build a prestigious indoor sports stadium.[33] This list could go on and on, for Japanese aid to the Pacific Islands was estimated even then to be approximately US$70 million a year. Japan and Taiwan manifestly intended to use this kind of 'cheque-book diplomacy' to deflect criticism of their fishing policy in the region. Nevertheless, the threat to tuna resources was of sufficient seriousness to override the attractions of aid and the July 1989 Forum meeting adopted, albeit less than unanimously, the Tarawa Declaration. This declared the South Pacific a driftnet-free zone, called upon Japan and Taiwan to cease use of this method of fishing and banned port visits, refuelling and supply of the vessels involved. Taiwan reacted stubbornly but Japan bowed quickly to the pressure, especially when the issue was successfully taken to the United Nations and a resolution banning the practice was adopted in that forum too.

In general, and for the moment, marine resource piracy seems to have been contained as a security problem, although falling prices for albacore tuna may also have something to do with the improvement. Diplomacy has proved to be effective and it has been important that the

Pacific SIEDS have stood together on the issue. They have been helped too by the fact that none of them, nor Australia or New Zealand, their Forum partners, pose any threat to the fishery resources of the others. The general point is nevertheless well made: the question of resource protection is an issue of security in the South Pacific and could quite possibly re-emerge as a problem during the 1990s in relation either to tuna again or perhaps the logging of the valuable tropical hardwoods located in Papua New Guinea.

Environmental Deterioration. The next security threat to the Pacific SIEDS which needs to be considered is not unrelated to the question of resources: it is the matter of the wider environmental deterioration of the South Pacific as part of the global commons. Notwithstanding the area's reputation for natural beauty and remoteness, which is not exaggerated, major threats confront its environment. Some, in fact, derive from that very remoteness from the major population centres of the developed world. The British, the Americans and the French were all drawn to the South Pacific as a site for nuclear testing for that reason. Despite longstanding and widespread protests from Australia and New Zealand, as well as the island states, the latter continued to engage in underground tests on the outlying atolls of Moruroa and Fangataufa in French Polynesia until it temporarily suspended its programme in mid-1992.[34] (The future testing policy of France is unclear.) The longer term human and environmental consequences of French intransigence on this matter can only be imagined, although the evidence of illness, abnormalities and deaths from the early US experience of testing in the Marshall Islands is horrific. The siting of some nuclear weapons in the region, and the passage through it of others, also risks nuclear contamination of the environment in the event of war or accident, whilst the proposals of some Japanese and US companies to use South Pacific islands as locations for the disposal of nuclear and other forms of toxic waste add yet another dimension to the problem.[35] A recent crisis is the most ironic of all – the plan of the US military announced in 1990 to burn off an old stockpile of chemical weapons from West Germany, unwanted in the light of the ending of the Cold War, on Johnston Atoll, a US restricted-access island south-west of Hawaii. These types of environmental threat may seem distant and intangible at one level, but they affect the very fundamentals of life for the indigenous peoples of the region, with the result that the nuclear question in particular is an issue of great political sensitivity everywhere. It is not irrelevant too from the point of view of the region's prospects of economic development that its tourist potential may be damaged irreparably by a popular fear of nuclear pollution.

Yet perhaps even more threatening to the immediate environment is the new spectre of the 'greenhouse effect'. Although most countries of reasonable wealth and substantial land mass will be able to adapt to the climatic changes likely to be brought about by global warming, the predicted rise in the sea level will mean potential disaster for some South Pacific islands. As the former President of Kiribati, Ieremia Tabai, put it, 'if the Greenhouse Effect raises sea levels by one metre it will virtually do away with Kiribati. In 50 or 60 years my country will not be here'.[36] Similarly threatened are Tuvalu, the Marshall Islands and Tokelau, all of which are composed solely of low relief atolls. They may all cease to contain any habitable land, thereby forcing a policy of total emigration. In this situation the peoples of Tokelau and the Marshalls are better placed, because the former have the right to go to New Zealand (where most Tokelauans already live) and the latter can turn to the US under the terms of the compact of free association. By comparison, the inhabitants of Kiribati and Tuvalu, as citizens of independent states, have to rely on their own capacity to negotiate a solution. If the worst scenarios advanced by the scientists come true, a new wave of 'boat people' will be created and the security of one or two Pacific SIEDS will literally no longer be an issue.

To their credit, the Pacific Islands have responded energetically to the threat posed by environmental deterioration. One development has been the decision to strengthen the South Pacific Regional Environment Program (SPREP). With significant financial support from New Zealand, the programme was separated off from the South Pacific Commission in Noumea and re-established independently and under new leadership in Apia in Western Samoa. It already shows signs of becoming the effective environmental watchdog the region badly needs.[37] The other initiative of relevance has been the formation in 1990 of the Alliance of Small Island States (AOSIS) designed to promote the signing of a climate change convention. Several South Pacific states were instrumental in forging this new body which has been led since its inception by Vanuatu's ambassador to the UN, Robert Van Lierop. They also played a highly visible role both before and at the UN Conference on Environment and Development held in Rio de Janeiro in June 1992, acting, as one commentator put it, as 'the conscience of the entire negotiating group' on the climate change panel.[38] The weaknesses in the final text of the convention and the fact that much more still needs to be done are not their fault: indeed, the graphic picture they were able to paint of entire island nations slowly disappearing beneath the waves contributed a great deal to the seriousness with which the 'greenhouse effect' was treated, at least rhetorically, by other delegations in Rio.

Crime and Drugs. Finally, mention must be made of the threat to the security of Pacific island states which is beginning to emerge from organised crime. The fear has been raised that criminal syndicates, operating variously from Australia, Hong Kong, Japan or the west coast of the United States, could actually gain control of a particular state and use it as a base for their activities. Nothing so dramatic has yet occurred, but several territories – the Cook Islands, Tonga, Vanuatu, the Marshall Islands and Nauru – operate as tax havens with extensive offshore banking facilities of a type which inevitably attract criminal money. Rumours of the involvement of various syndicates thus abound. The geographical location of the islands and the links which some of them have with the United States constitute a further temptation, especially to drugs traders. In the last few years Guam and Belau have both witnessed the break-up of major drugs rings which were importing heroin and marijuana from Thailand and the Philippines and shipping it on to the US. Heroin was also seized for the first time in Vanuatu in May 1989 *en route* to Sydney from Hong Kong. When the case came to court it was revealed that the shipment had been organised by a triad gang in Hong Kong and that Vanuatu had been chosen as the transshipment point because the accused already had some 'legitimate' business interests in Port Vila which were thought likely to provide the required cover. It had also apparently been presumed that the Australian authorities would not expect a consignment coming from Vanuatu. The dangers of the drugs connection for South Pacific states are thus being more fully exposed all the time, but it can still be expected to grow, given the scale of the profits that can be made, the emergence of the highlands region of PNG as a source of marijuana production and the sheer number of tiny islands and atolls which can be used as staging points for transshipment.

THE SOUTH PACIFIC RESPONSE

The response of the Pacific SIEDS to the shifting threat agenda of the last decade or so has generally been undramatic. There has been developed no grand design. Policy has instead been piecemeal and pragmatic. The starting point, perhaps inevitably, has been reflection by the states themselves upon the defence capabilities which they possess. In fact, only Papua New Guinea and Fiji have conventionally maintained military forces of any substance. PNG has a three-battallion army of nearly 4,000 men, with small air and naval support, but it scarcely covered itself with glory in its handling of the Bougainville secession during 1989 and 1990. Prior to this, it had only seen real action once when it intervened, at Vanuatu's request, to quash the rebellion in Santo just after that country's independence in 1980. Fiji also traditionally maintained a force of similar size, virtually all of which was drawn from the indigenous population, but its establishment has been considerably expanded, although from the same ethnic source, since the coups of 1987. Fiji is exceptional too in that its battallions have rotated in service on UN peacekeeping duties in the Lebanon and Sinai, thereby acquiring operational experience and adding to their reputation for discipline and toughness. Of the other states, Tonga has a small force of 300 or so men, mostly in naval units; Vanuatu has a para-military body of about the same size; and the Solomon Islands has a small unit of this sort attached to its police force. All the rest have relied on tiny police forces to maintain law and order and safeguard territorial integrity, one commentator noting, for example, that in the late 1980s there were fewer policemen in Kiribati than inhabited islands![39]

There is, of course, a threat itself contained within the traditional militaristic response to security problems. It is obviously not a coincidence that the trend towards the militarisation of politics in Fiji and PNG (and even, to some extent, in Vanuatu) has emerged in the South Pacific states with the most developed military apparatuses. Military coups can only be made by armies. Most of the governments of the region apreciate this and, Fiji apart, have not been keen to build up their defence systems, even in the era of perceived external threat in the mid-to-late 1980s. They have traditionally relied upon Australia and New Zealand to provide this kind of support and, on the whole, these two powers have not been found wanting. The Australian government still maintains very close defence cooperation with Papua New Guinea, latterly enshrined in a Joint Declaration of Principles signed in 1987 and involving most recently the supply of extra Iroquois helicopters to send to Bougainville; it has equipped several of the SIEDS with patrol boats suitable for fisheries surveillance and policing duties in their EEZs; and it engages in regular P-3 Orion reconnaissance flights over the area For its part, the New Zealand Labour government was concerned to show that the ANZUS dispute did not in any way impair its capacity to defend the South Pacific. It thus put in place in the late 1980s a new 'Ready Reaction Force', trained in intervention in small islands. In addition, New Zealand naturally takes responsibility for the defence of its associated territories and also contributes to the Orion reconnaissance programme. Indeed, the new National government elected in 1990 signalled its commitment to this traditional role by resuming the flights over Fijian waters which had been suspended by Labour at the time of the coups.[40] Although not without flaws and, by definition, offered only on the basis of Australia's and New Zealand's views of their security predicament, the Pacific SIEDS have generally considered it to be in their best interests to rely on their two larger neighbours and traditional protectors to supply most of the hardware needed for their security. Again, Fiji is the only significant exception, embarking after the coups on a wide-ranging, and to some degree successful, search for new sources of military support (including France and even Israel) in the light of the embargo on the provision of military assistance imposed by Australia and New Zealand.

The other important dimension of the recent response of the Pacific SIEDS to their perceived security problems is the consideration which has intermittently been given over the past decade to the idea of establishing some kind of standing regional peacekeeping force. The proposal is usually attributed to Papua New Guinea's then prime minister, Sir Julius Chan, following the Santo crisis in Vanuatu in 1980. It was initially supported by Walter Lini on behalf of Vanuatu and placed before the South Pacific Forum meeting in August 1981, only to receive a cool response from the other leaders, many of whom were suspicious of PNG's motives. The idea surfaced again after the invasion of Grenada in 1983 and was discussed, and once more rejected, at the Commonwealth-sponsored security colloquium held in Wellington in 1984. The Fiji coups brought it to life once more, especially in the minds of supporters of the ousted coalition government, but there was little taste for getting too involved in the situation in Fiji in any of the other SIEDS and the Australian and New Zealand governments quickly realised the political (and military) difficulties attendant upon any intervention, even under regional auspices. Nevertheless, Greg Fry of the Australian National University has cogently argued in a recent paper that the events in Fiji, in conjunction with the Port Vila riots in 1988 and the Bougainville crisis of 1989–90, serve again to make the notion of at least an *ad hoc* intervention force capable of giving 'assistance to a legitimate and effective government' in the South Pacific attractive to policy-makers in Canberra and Wellington.[41] It is significant that the case for such a force was made in terms of its potential appeal to Australia and New Zealand, rather than the South Pacific states themselves, and it is far from clear that, if seriously proposed, it would gain their endorsement.

This does not mean that the Pacific SIEDS have not seen the benefits of regionalism as a response to their security problems. The reverse is, in fact, the case. The governments of the region have worked hard to build the Forum into a valuable support mechanism for their various national strategies. Strains have been largely confined to the traditional Melanesian/Polynesian divide. For a period in the mid-1980s the Melanesian governments, with PNG setting the pace for the Solomon Islands and Vanuatu, found themselves at odds with what they perceived as the diplomatic conservatism of the Polynesian states on issues such as French nuclear testing and policy towards New Caledonia. A sub-regional grouping, the Melanesian Spearhead, was thus formalised, with the signing of 'agreed principles' between the three states in question in 1988. In the event, it rather lost its rationale with changes in government in both Port Moresby and Paris in 1988 removing the main internal and external forces behind its emergence. The Polynesian states were even more unsuccessful in their attempt to create a sub-regional organisation, the project ending in humiliating fashion in 1989 when an inaugural meeting in Tonga was called off due to lack of attendance.[42] The consequence of these failures has been to enhance the standing of the Forum as the overriding organising unit of the South Pacific. The energetic and able former president of Kiribati, Ieremia Tabai, was appointed as the new secretary-general in February 1992 and he can be expected to maintain and probably extend the Forum's work.

This focuses primarily on joint action on development issues and the pursuit of collective diplomacy, including matters which have security implications such as fisheries and environmental protection. Traditional security cooperation has been approached more cautiously. The South Pacific Nuclear Free Zone Treaty, signed at Raratonga in the Cook Islands in 1975, is a case in point. In essence, it remains only a minimal agreement, prohibiting the possession, testing and stationing of nuclear weapons on territories in the zone whilst upholding the principles of freedom of navigation and overflight and affirming the right of signatory governments to make their own decisions about nuclear ship visits.[43] That said, it set out the region's position on this issue and forced other external states to react to it. For example, the United States government lost standing in the region by refusing to ratify the treaty. A Forum Regional Security Committee (FRSC) was set up at the end of the 1980s and has devoted its attention predominantly to issues of crime, drug trafficking and terrorism. Thus far, the main product of its deliberations has been the so-called Niue Treaty on fisheries surveillance and law enforcement cooperation agreed at the 1992 summit.[44] However, notwithstanding considerable pressure from the Australian and New Zealand governments, which are increasingly worried about the development of crime in the South Pacific, both PNG and Fiji, the two most important Pacific SIEDS, refused to sign it on the grounds that it represented a challenge to their sovereign competence in the critical matter of national security. Their action exposed only too clearly the political difficulties which still lie in the way of overt security cooperation amongst the islands.

To sum up, then, the Pacific SIEDS have responded in a generally low-key way to the security threats they have faced during the last ten years or so. They have, for the most part, not acted in ways which would have made their predicament worse. Indeed, they have understood that their own capacity to respond has been limited by their size, dependence and general vulnerability, and that in consequence almost every response is more effectively made at the regional level. The key exception to that rule, in contrast to the experience of the Caribbean, has been the disinclination of the governments to build up a South Pacific 'regional security system' in any of its possible forms, either as a regional army, or intervention force, or even a joint memorandum of understanding on the use of national forces. That has been a positive decision, reiterated on several occasions, and it does not look as if it will be easily or quickly overturned.

NOTES

1. For a good general discussion of these issues, see G. Segal, *Rethinking the Pacific* (Oxford, 1990).
2. For a general portrait of the characteristics of the region, see R.C. Kiste, 'Overview', in F.M. Bunge and M.W. Cooke (eds.), *Oceania: A Regional Study* (Washington DC, 1984), 1–53.
3. The classic account of the emergence of the South Pacific Forum, albeit unpublished, is G. Fry, 'South Pacific Regionalism: The Development of an Indigenous Commitment', MA thesis, Australian National University, Canberra, 1979.
4. For a sense of this concept, see R. Crocombe, *The South Pacific: An Introduction* (Auckland, 1987).
5. See J.C. Dorrance, *Oceania and the United States: An Analysis of US Interests and Policy in the South Pacific*, National Security Affairs Monograph Series 80-6 (Washington DC, 1980).
6. See, again, Dorrance, *Oceania and the United States*, 77–82.
7. See R. Aldrich, 'France in the South Pacific', in J. Ravenhill (ed.), *No Longer an American Lake?* (Sydney, 1989), 76–105.
8. G. Fry, 'The Politics of South Pacific Regional Cooperation', in R. Thakur, *The South Pacific: Problems, Issues and Prospects* (London, 1991), 171.
9. The literature here is considerable. The most useful accounts consulted were G. Fry (ed.), *Australia's Regional Security* (Sydney, 1990); D. Hegarty, *South Pacific Security Issues: An Australian Perspective*, Australian National University Strategic and Defence Studies Centre Working Paper No. 147 (Canberra, 1987); and S. Hoadley, 'New Zealand's South Pacific Strategy', unpublished paper delivered to a conference on Strategic Cooperation and Competition in the Pacific Islands, National Defense University, Washington DC, May 1989.
10. Dorrance, *Oceania and the United States*, v.

11. Ibid., 28.
12. 'Concluding Statement', unpublished summary of the South Pacific Colloquium on the Special Needs of Small States, Victoria University of Wellington, Wellington, 13–14 Aug. 1984, 1.
13. Ibid.
14. R.C. Kiste and R.A. Herr, 'The Potential for Soviet Penetration of the South Pacific Islands: An Assessment', unpublished paper prepared for the US State Department, December 1984, 66.
15. Ibid., 12.
16. Ibid., 12–13.
17. W.M. Sutherland, 'Economic Dependence, Geopolitics and the Postcolonial State', in R. Walker and W. Sutherland (eds.), *The Pacific: Peace, Security and the Nuclear Issue* (London, 1988), 42 and 47.
18. D. Hegarty, *Small State Security in the South Pacific*, Australian National University Strategic and Defence Studies Centre Working paper No. 126 (Canberra, 1987), 5.
19. Hegarty, *Small State Security*, 2.
20. See D. Hegarty, *Libya and the South Pacific*, Australian National University Strategic and Defence Studies Centre Working Paper No. 127 (Canberra, 1987).
21. G. Tanham (with E. Weinstein), *Security Trends in the South Pacific: Vanuatu and Fiji*, Rand Note prepared for the Office of the Under-Secretary of Defence for Policy (Washington DC, 1988); O. Harries, *Strategy and the Southwest Pacific: An Australian Perspective*, Pacific Security Research Institute Occasional Paper No. 1 (Sydney, 1989); and, for criticism, K. Ross, *Prospects for Crisis Prediction: A South Pacific Case Study*, Australian National University Canberra Papers on Strategy and Defence (Canberra, 1990).
22. For background, see S. Dorney, *Papua New Guinea: People, Politics and History since 1975* (Sydney, 1990); and R.J. May and M. Spriggs (eds.), *The Bougainville Crisis* (Bathurst, NSW, 1990).
23. D. Hegarty, 'Political Stability and Instability in the South Pacific', unpublished paper delivered to a conference on Strategic Cooperation and Competition in the Pacific Islands, National Defense University, Washington DC, May 1989, 4–5.
24. For differing accounts of the Fijian coups, see E. Dean, *Rabuka: No Other Way* (Suva, 1988); B.V. Lal, *Power and Prejudice: The Making of the Fiji Crisis* (Wellington, 1988); R.T. Robertson and A. Tamanisau, *Fiji: Shattered Coups* (Leichardt, NSW, 1988); and D. Scarr, *Fiji – Politics of Illusion: The Military Coups in Fiji* (Kensington, NSW, 1988).
25. See S. Lawson, *The Prospects for a Third Military Coup in Fiji*, Australian National University Strategic and Defence Studies Centre Working Paper No. 202 (Canberra, 1989).
26. See *Pacific Islands Monthly*, June 1992, 7–10.
27. A. Siaguru, cited in D. Hegarty, *Papua New Guinea: At the Political Crossroads?*, Australian National University Strategic and Defence Studies Centre Working Paper No. 177 (Canberra, 1989), 1.
28. For a fuller discussion of this prospect, see Hegarty, *Papua New Guinea*, 22–3.
29. See Ross, *Prospects for Crisis Prediction*, 61–116 for a comprehensive and insightful discussion of politics in Vanuatu.
30. See P. Sack (ed.), *Pacific Constitutions* (Canberra, 1982).
31. See S. Firth, 'Sovereignty and Independence in the Contemporary Pacific', *The Contemporary Pacific*, 1, 1 & 2 (1989), 78–83.
32. S. Henningham, 'Keeping the Tricolor Flying: The French Pacific into the 1990s', *The Contemporary Pacific*, 1, 1 & 2 (1989), 99.
33. *Pacific Islands Monthly*, July 1989, 8–9. The general point is also made in R. Alexander, 'Security Issues of the Pacific Island States', in Y. Satow (ed.), *Prospects for Demilitarization and Autonomy in the South Pacific*, Hiroshima University Institute for Peace Science Research Report No. 16 (Hiroshima, 1991), 79.

34. See B. and M.-T. Danielsson, *Poisoned Reign: French Nuclear Colonialism in the Pacific* (London, 1986).
35. For a discussion, see Y.S. Ogashiwa, 'Regional Protests against Nuclear Waste Dumping in the Pacific', *Journal of Pacific Studies*, 15 (1990), 51–66.
36. Cited in J. Connell, 'The Greenhouse Effect: Where have All the Islands Gone?' *Pacific Islands Monthly*, April/May 1989, 17.
37. See, as illustration, *The Pacific Way*, reported prepared by the South Pacific Regional Environment Programme for the United Nations Conference on Environment and Development (Apia, 1992).
38. J. Cameron, Director of the International Environment Law Centre in London, cited in J. Garrett, 'No French Flattery', *Pacific Islands Monthly*, May 1992, 35.
39. Hegarty, *Small State Security*, 12.
40. Useful recent information on Australian and New Zealand policies can be found in R.W. Baker, *The International Relations of the Southwest Pacific: New Visions and Voices*, East–West Center Occasional Paper No. 4 (Honolulu, 1992), 2–10.
41. G. Fry, *Peacekeeping in the South Pacific: Some Questions for Prior Consideration*, Australian National University Department of International Relations Working Paper No. 7 (Canberra, 1990).
42. See N. MacQueen, 'Pacific Microstates: Regional and Security Issues', unpublished paper delivered to the British International Studies Association Conference, University College, Swansea, December 1992.
43. See G. Fry, *A Nuclear-free Zone for the Southwest Pacific: Prospects and Significance*, Australian National University Strategic and Defence Studies Centre Working Paper No. 75 (Canberra, 1983).
44. See *Pacific Islands Monthly*, August 1992, 29.

An Infinite Capacity to Muddle Through?
A Security Audit for Papua New Guinea

NORMAN MACQUEEN

The passing of the Cold War has had little real impact on the security situation of the island states of the South Pacific. The widely held assumption of the later 1980s, that the region faced a loss of international innocence with the magnetic force of the bipolar system belatedly but inexorably coming to bear, proved misguided. Ironically, this concern over impending embroilment derived in part from the very forces that were to put the region once and for all beyond superpower competition. The 'threat' was read into Gorbachev's 1986 Vladivostok speech, translating a proposal for greater Soviet participation in the international economy into a statement of expansionist intent. In reality the speech was part of the process which was to end the entire contest. In the climate of the times, however, reformist intentions all too easily generated suspicions of *realpolitik* manoeuvring. Soviet attempts to establish fisheries agreements and other functional arrangements in the spirit of Vladivostok were thus interpreted in Washington (and to a lesser degree in Canberra and Southeast Asia) as part and parcel of the bipolar contest.[1] As a further complication, Libya's reported interest in the region, via the diplomatic loophole of Vanuatu's non-aligned foreign policy, also greatly concerned Australian strategic analysts in 1987 and 1988.[2]

Even at the time these Western security concerns were not widely shared by the island governments themselves. In many of the islands, particularly in the Melanesian sub-region, a more pressing external security threat was posed by France in its unresponsiveness to the independence movement in New Caledonia and in its continued nuclear testing in Polynesia. This gap in perceptions was a source of considerable frustration in the island capitals. Nevertheless, whichever view of the region's security environment is taken, the collapse of the Soviet side of the bipolar divide, the concern on the part of Libya to shrug off its outlaw status, and the fundamental change in French policy

Norman MacQueen is Reader in International Relations at the University of Sunderland in England.

in New Caledonia following the fall of the Chirac government in 1988 should have collectively transformed the situation, ending the preoccupation with security which they had created.

Yet for Papua New Guinea (PNG), by far the largest, the most populous and potentially the richest of the island states, the disappearance of these externally generated security concerns coincided with the emergence of major internal anxieties. PNG remains a major focus of security analysis – but no longer as key spokesman and diplomatic broker in the international relations of the region. Interest now lies in the way PNG's experience points to 'national security' in the islands as primarily a domestic phenomenon. 'Security', in short, has been reconfigured in PNG as an issue affecting first and foremost the legitimacy of the state and its agencies within, rather than beyond, national frontiers.

Why? Public disorder, hitherto seen as an extension of the country's chronic crime problem, acquired an increasingly political dimension in the later 1980s. Violent protest by various factional interests was rationalised and legitimised by reference to the manifest corruption and lack of accountability of the political leadership in parliament. The pressures of rapid development, far from dissipating traditional clan conflicts in the Highlands and other areas through modernisation, instead increased them as land and other scarce resources were brought into the monetised economy. In other words, sub-national regionalism, the subtext of much state action and inaction in the years after independence, emerged with new vigour in the late 1980s as underlying inter-ethnic conflicts were sharpened by mistrust of national politics and suspicion about the distribution of national resources.[3]

These elements of internal instability came together most dramatically from 1988 onwards with the rebellion and subsequent *de facto* secession of Bougainville, the largest island of the North Solomons Province and the source of a major part of PNG's realisable wealth in the Panguna copper complex. The initial success of the rebellion of the 'Bougainville Revolutionary Army' (BRA) against the central government focused attention, both in Papua New Guinea and the wider South Pacific region, on the whole concept of security: on what it meant and on what strategies best achieved it.[4] The idea of security 'imploded', geographically and ideologically, and the view of the island state as a 'rational actor', preoccupied with the pursuit of 'national security' in the international system, became increasingly untenable. This is not to say that, as the largest of the island states, PNG did not have a pro-active role in regional diplomacy, nor to deny that it had the capacity to affect significantly the foreign policies of larger states. But the limitations on its ability to move beyond regional activism and to determine the nature of its effect on others' policies were increasingly accepted in the country itself. Moreover, given the internal crisis of authority and stability facing the Papua New Guinea state, these traditional indicators of international importance were more and more viewed by politicians and officials as marginal to the country's 'real' security interests.

What then are the proper components of a post-Cold War security audit for Papua New Guinea? An inventory of resources is a necessary preliminary. Beyond this, what are the tasks to which these resources should be devoted? It is the case, firstly, that since independence in 1975 the most frequently perceived 'conventional' threat to Papua New Guinea's national security has been that posed by Indonesia with which PNG shares a 750 kilometre land border. How real is this threat in the 1990s and how far should resources, both material and diplomatic, be committed to meeting it? Secondly, what of the South Pacific region which encompasses PNG's relationship with its former colonial metropole and with the other island states? What is the significance of Australia in PNG's security agenda? More specifically, what is the impact of Australia's perception of PNG's significance to *its* security? Is there a broader Pacific dimension to be considered? Does the island Pacific region in particular offer a role for PNG in the post-Cold War period from which benefits – or threats – to security might accrue? Finally, how do these 'traditional' inter-state considerations connect with the major internal challenges facing Papua New Guinea in the 1990s? Firm answers to many of these questions are impossible to establish. However, an exploration of them should at least clarify the security issues which confront Papua New Guinea in the present period of unprecedented global, regional and domestic uncertainty.

THE PHYSICAL COMPONENTS OF NATIONAL SECURITY

An audit of the tangible assets which Papua New Guinea is able to exploit in pursuit of security must begin with its defence force manpower and resources. In addition to the military, the police force, traditionally an important element in such internal stability as PNG has enjoyed, needs also to be considered. Lastly and quite apart from these formal agencies of the state, the country's physical geography cannot but be a key factor in any assessment of national security, whether internal or external.

The Papua New Guinea Defence Force (PNGDF) has an approximate strength of 3,800. This is its strongest complement since independence and reflects an expansion in numbers since the beginning of the Bougainville emergency. It represents a revision of the figure of 3,050 maximum laid down by the government in 1983. As well as its infantry and engineer battalions, the PNGDF includes an air squadron used principally on transport, maritime reconnaissance and search and rescue duties. However, since the outbreak of fighting in Bougainville, the air squadron has added four Australian-supplied helicopters to its ageing fixed-wing capacity and aroused fierce controversy over its activities in the conflict. The Defence Force also contains a small naval section equipped with landing craft and six advanced fast patrol boats, again supplied by Australia.

The origins of the PNGDF lie in the Pacific Island Regiment (PIR) formed and incorporated into the Australian army during the Second World War. Disbanded after the defeat of Japan, it was re-formed in stages in the 1950s and early 1960s as Indonesia's policy of regional *konfrontasi* caused increasing concern in Canberra. At PNG's independence in 1975, the PIR simply became the PNGDF, little thought being given to the differences in nature and function between the colonial division of an established power and the defence force of a small Third World country.

The history of the PNGDF since independence has been one of gradual decline. The reasons for this are various but all can be traced more or less directly to that initial failure to reassess its fundamental role. Reflecting its origins as a force formed to repel territorial invasion, it remained, in training and self-perception, a conventional standing army. The problem was that such a force did not meet any national requirement. Invasion remained a most distant prospect. Even had it occurred it is unlikely that a force of the size and limited resources of the PNGDF could have offered significant resistance as a conventional 'stand and fight' army. The consequence of this misdirection of security resources was twofold.

Firstly, irrelevance inevitably led to demoralisation and lapses in discipline. In the absence of a comprehensible, unifying and energy-engaging role the perennial seeds of regional division flourished. This inhibited the development of an *esprit de corps* and undermined the chain of command. Such institutional identity as there was tended to express itself in negative and anti-social ways. Street-level conflict with civilians and, more particularly, the police force – with which an intense and often violent rivalry emerged – became increasingly frequent. The 'regionalisation' of the PNGDF also opened the way for its politicisation, along with the rest of the public service, in the 1980s. The term 'politicisation' is used here not to indicate the pursuit of political objectives by the military, but rather the expropriation of its senior positions for purposes of political patronage.[5]

Secondly, the PNGDF's role as a traditional standing army based in battallion-strength barracks denied it a more 'integrative' role in civic action and infrastructural development programmes. Such a role might have provided both a general sense of purpose and a closer relationship with the population. One close observer has made the point that because PNG came to independence without any dramatic or protracted anti-colonial struggle, the PNGDF, in contrast to many other Third World military establishments, has had no distinctive historical role and therefore occupies no place in the national 'myth'.[6] The assumptions of post-independence military planners certainly did nothing to repair the omission.

In fairness, however, it must be acknowledged that events in the region at one crucial juncture did serve to justify the very force structure and strategic assumptions that denied the PNGDF an obvious role at home. The crisis surrounding Vanuatu's independence in 1980 saw the PNGDF intervene decisively at the request of the new government. The operation was a quick, inexpensive and totally successful exercise of *force majeur* by the PNGDF. Its success (against a small, poorly armed and led separatist movement) distracted attention from underlying questions about national security and the role of the PNGDF in its preservation. An assumption of operational competence and relevance of purpose was allowed to develop in the wake of the Vanuatu intervention and was not finally dispelled until the PNGDF's abject failure to tackle the homegrown separatist crisis in Bougainville a decade later.[7]

While the PNGDF may have been lacking as a *tool* of state authority, it has also failed to make of itself an *alternative* to state authority. The reasons for the military's evident reluctance to intervene in politics (thus leaving the politicians to intervene in the military) are varied. At the time of the military coup in Fiji in 1987 much attention was focused on comparisons between the two countries and the prospect of the PNGDF following its Fijian counterpart down the road of intervention in politics. Mounting dissatisfaction with the parliamentary system and its practitioners, growing social and regional tensions and ever-rising crime rates were cited as conditions capable of justifying military intervention. And, perhaps crucially, it was thought that Colonel Rabuka had broken the supposed taboo in the South Pacific region on such interventions. The situation was given added piquancy by the backdrop of a disorderly general election campaign which highlighted the obvious limitations of the parliamentary system in PNG.

However, there were, and remain, a number of key differences between the two countries and their military forces. In particular, nothing comparable to the obvious, sharp cleavage dividing Fijian society and politics between 'indigenous' Melanesians and the ethnic Indian community exists in PNG. Sub-national regionalism exists, but is multifaceted with no single region enjoying any sort of dominance either in society generally or the military specifically. By the same token, the presence of regional loyalties within the military undermines the group identity necessary for effective military intervention. The institutional cohesion of the Fijian military has always been stronger than that of the PNGDF and was further consolidated by extensive overseas experience on peacekeeping duties in the 1970s and 1980s. Moreover, Fijian society as a whole – ethnically Melanesian but strongly marked by the cultural influences of its Polynesian neighbours – has a hierarchical character largely alien to Papua New Guinea. This has affected both the capacity of the military to act in a centrally directed manner and its ability to make its writ run throughout a stubbornly egalitarian society. Geographical differences add to the problem. The terrain of Papua New Guinea is among the most difficult in the world; Fiji's is much more favourable to the exercise of central authority. Finally, the relative sizes of the two military forces are hugely disparate. While in Fiji there is one soldier for approximately every 142 civilians, in Papua New Guinea the figure is one to 1,012.[8] This fact alone has obvious implications for physical control.

Nevertheless, measurement by the Fijian yardstick is inevitable. It was Fiji's departure from one of the unquestioned norms of South Pacific politics which first provoked serious discussion of the PNG situation and the evident success of the Fijian military's project which gave added urgency to the discussion. And, dissimilarities notwithstanding, it would be unwise to dismiss the prospect of *some kind* of serious military intervention in PNG. In the main, the points of difference militate against the achievement of a *successful* coup rather than an unsuccessful attempt. It is certainly conceivable that a combination of discontent with material conditions, the absence of a clear and achievable purpose, and resentment at the misbehaviour of civilian politicians could lead to some kind of intervention. All of these 'provocations' have been present at some level of intensity since the mid-1980s. However likely the ultimate failure of such an attempt might be, it could be hugely destabilising to the already fragile civil institutions of the state.

The other main agency of national security, the Royal Papua New Guinea Constabulary, is approximately 4,700 persons strong –

considerably larger than the Defence Force. Although essentially a civilian body, the police have certain military characteristics. These derive from both administrative and operational circumstances. Firstly, the lower ranks live, for the most part, in barracks or other special accommodation and this has unquestionably affected their self-image. Secondly, public order duties, which have become increasingly common and increasingly violent, have contributed to the development of a quasi-military attitude of mind extending beyond the explicitly paramilitary mobile and riot squads. On the other hand, while morale in the police force has suffered as a result of deteriorating pay and conditions and the seemingly unwinnable struggle against rising crime, it has had one advantage over the army and that is a clear sense of purpose. Its upper ranks have also escaped much of the politicisation that has overtaken the Defence Force.

It is interesting to note in this regard that the only challenge to civilian politics to have been mounted since independence (and that a distinctly feeble one) came from within the police rather than the military. This followed the sudden withdrawal of central government forces from Bougainville after the escalation of the BRA's secessionist campaign in March 1990. The national Commissioner of Police, Paul Tohian, who was also the controller of the state of emergency on Bougainville, reacted to this 'humiliation' by using police radio frequencies in an attempt to rally support for the overthrow of the government. Despite an initial panic reaction on the part of the political leadership and some limited support from elements in the police, the 'coup' ended in farce with the arrest of the inebriated Tohian by loyalist officers. (Tohian's action, following as it did a particularly convivial social function, was quickly dubbed the 'Bar-B-Coup' in Port Moresby.) The affair nevertheless underlined the significance of the hostility between police and army as a restraint on intervention. The military, arguably even more humiliated by the Bougainville withdrawal, showed no interest in participating in any police-initiated action.

Beyond these security agencies, however, it must be acknowledged that one of Papua New Guinea's principal 'resources' in defence of its external security is a purely inanimate one: the physical nature of its frontiers and interior terrain. The importance of geography has already been touched on in relation to the prospect of military intervention. Similar factors affect the issue of territorial integrity. The South Pacific, among all Third World regions, has enjoyed a unique degree of regional stability and security. The reasons for this lie in a range of factors related to political culture and economic organisation. Underpinning them, however, is the simple reality of South Pacific geography. If high

fences make good neighbours, expansive sea areas certainly contribute
to good regional relations. The geographical logic of the region's
borders – and the acceptance of this logic by the imperial powers –
spared the island states much of the trauma of post-independence
territorial adjustment experienced by their counterparts elsewhere in
the world.[9]

There is nevertheless one crucial exception to the rule of naturally
guaranteed borders which affects PNG. The island of New Guinea, by
virtue of its enormous size, was not entirely immune from the arbitrary
demarcations common in Africa and Latin America. The outcome of
the First World War removed one such division with the exclusion of
Germany from the north-eastern quarter and the coupling of this with
Australian Papua in the south. There remained, however, the larger
east–west division between Papua and New Guinea and Dutch New
Guinea. The eventual success of Indonesia's claim to this territory after
the Dutch withdrawal and its assimilation as the Indonesian province of
Irian Jaya created the conditions for future tension. Papua New Guinea
thus found itself at the time of independence with an extensive land
border with a neighbour whose possible intentions would at various
times cause considerable concern in Port Moresby. Have such worries
been justified and do they any longer have a place in PNG's security
priorities?

INDONESIA AND THE BORDER

1975 was in some respects an unfortunate year for Papua New Guinea to
begin its relationship with Indonesia. April saw the fall of Saigon, a key
event in the perceptions of Southeast Asia's domino theorists, amongst
whom the Indonesian leadership was prominent. December then saw
the Indonesian invasion of East Timor. Jakarta's seizure of East Timor
was motivated by a combination of heightened ideological nervousness
in the wake of developments in Vietnam and a fundamental concern
with the integrity of the archipelago. It certainly added considerably to
the suspicion of Indonesia bequeathed to Papua New Guinea by both
left and right in Australian politics.[10] It was understandable, then, that
PNG should have been concerned for the survival of its sovereignty in
this delicate perinatal phase.

Confidence in PNG over border security was not enhanced by
Indonesia's problems in Irian Jaya. The suppression of any expression
of Melanesian political aspirations and the anti-guerrilla campaign
against the small separatist *Operasi Papua Merdeka* (OPM, or Free
Papua Movement) created two related points of friction in the

Moresby–Jakarta relationship. Firstly, a natural sympathy existed for the plight of the indigenous population in Irian Jaya as it was squeezed by pressure on both its culture and its land. Jakarta's uncompromising centralisation and its transmigration programme, which brought settlers from the over-populated islands of Java and Bali, involved the alienation of tribal land, something viewed with particular horror in Melanesian society. Secondly, anti-OPM operations led to frequent border violations as the Indonesian army pursued suspected guerrillas across the poorly marked frontier with PNG. Serious incidents took place in 1978 and again during 1983–84, causing considerable tension between the two governments.[11]

However, the relationship stabilised in 1986 after the government of Paias Wingti concluded a 'Treaty of Mutual Respect, Friendship and Cooperation' with the Suharto regime. While the terms themselves were not far-reaching, the fact of the treaty's signing was an important statement of good intentions.[12] More ambivalently, evidence was soon to emerge of considerable 'informal penetration' by the Indonesians of key parts of the PNG political and military elite. In 1987 it emerged that the then foreign minister (and former commander of the Defence Force), Ted Diro, had received a 'personal gift' from the Indonesian army commander, General Benny Murdani, of $US140,000 to help with his election expenses.[13] Another important link came to light at the beginning of 1988 when the PNGDF commander, Brigadier-General Tony Huai, was obliged to resign following an outburst against Australia's supposed encouragement of anti-Indonesian feeling in PNG.[14]

Whatever Jakarta's motives in buying such influence, preparation for expansion was not among them. Although the post-independence concerns of PNG politicians and planners were entirely understandable, territorial aggrandisement on Indonesia's part has never been a realistic option. Evidently incapable of imposing its will on the relatively tiny territory of East Timor, it was always inconceivable that Indonesia could contemplate a successful occupation of Papua New Guinea with its awesome terrain and assuredly intractable population. These factors have already been adduced, it will be recalled, as militating against a successful *internal* challenge to the state. Beyond this, the over-stretch involved in the attempt might very well have undermined Indonesia's existing political and territorial cohesion. It was also unlikely that serious contemplation of expansion into PNG territory could have survived any consideration of likely international reaction. East Timor was an enclave formed from part of an island in the middle of the national archipelago. It was also under the effective control of an indigenous, implicitly pro-Soviet liberation movement. Even then the Indonesian *fait accompli* was fiercely disputed internationally. With what hope of diplomatic success could Indonesia have embarked on an attack on Papua New Guinea, an affectionately regarded, diplomatically well-connected and fundamentally pro-western state?[15]

Indonesia, in short, did not, and does not, pose any fundamental challenge to the territorial security of PNG, despite its frequent disregard of the border in anti-separatist operations. How should it be placed in our audit? Jakarta's fundamental interests would seem to lie not in undermining the security of the PNG state but rather in underpinning it. Indeed, the general stability of its neighbour remains a central security concern for Indonesia, for both specific and unspecific reasons. Firstly, the situation in Irian Jaya requires a neighbour sufficiently stable to manage the border relationship with what the Indonesians themselves might describe as pragmatic understanding. A secure central government in Port Moresby is seen by Jakarta as the best guarantee of this. Secondly, instability, particularly the instability of separatism, could be infectious. A weak, insecure centre confronted by the demands of a fractious periphery touches on one of the Indonesian regime's most basic and longstanding fears. While the threat of infection should not be overstated, it is an element in Jakarta's perceptions of its security interests in PNG. The security of Papua New Guinea, defined as the stability and authority of the centre, therefore constitutes a desirable 'forward defence' for Indonesia.

The management of this defence interest is clearly a delicate undertaking. How can Jakarta contrive to enhance the security of Papua New Guinea without arousing counter-productive suspicions in an already wary neighbour? One means, obviously, is through the purchase of influence over decision-makers already described. Another, perhaps more surprisingly, has been the encouragement of intervention by a more 'acceptable' third party. This has been in evidence during the Bougainville crisis. In 1990 General Murdani, now Indonesian defence minister, upbraided Australia for not taking a more direct role in the ending of the Bougainville secession. Canberra's role as ex-colonial metropole and major regional power demanded, in his view, a more assertive policy of support for the central government of PNG.[16]

Beyond these conventional security concerns with the border and the danger of destabilising 'spill-over', the relationship between PNG and Indonesia is affected by the converging interests of their respective economic foreign policies. Each is interested in the possibilities of greater involvement in the other's region. Papua New Guinea has seen Indonesia as a potential bridge to the ASEAN region, a bridge the Port

Moresby government seemed particularly keen to cross in the later 1980s. In the event, the ASEAN states, habitually reluctant to consider enlargement of the organisation, showed no enthusiasm for PNG membership.[17] If anything, though, this failure enhanced the importance of the bilateral relationship with Jakarta. The 'bridge' itself remained significant in a way that it would not have done had it served its initial purpose.[18]

For its part, Jakarta has for some time been interested in a more active relationship with the island South Pacific. Indonesian officials have on occasion expressed interest in membership of the islands' principal regional organisation, the South Pacific Forum. Jakarta was also quick to exploit the opportunity of the Fijian coup and the ensuing disruption of Suva's established diplomatic relations to attempt to create a 'special relationship' with the new regime there.[19] This did not in the end prove especially productive for Indonesia, for in the period of post-coup adjustment the military regime appeared more concerned to reconstruct its existing relationships than initiate new ones which might have jeopardised this normalisation. But Indonesia's interest in the South Pacific, in particular as a market for its increasing manufacturing output, remains. In fact, the positions of Papua New Guinea and Indonesia closely shadow each other. Each sees the other, in the absence of alternative means of access, as a route to broader desired ends. There is at least an indication here that the 'realist' high politics of conventional security concerns might already be bound up with the low politics of economic interest – and, if the signs point anywhere, it is to the further ramification of this functional relationship.

AUSTRALIA AND THE SOUTH PACIFIC

The other principal dimensions to PNG's external security are Australia as the former colonial power and the island South Pacific as a whole. The impact of Australia on PNG's post-independence politics and economy has obviously been enormous. The Papua New Guinea state is, to a much greater degree than most in the Third World, a colonial artefact. Moreover, Australia remains a dominating regional presence with continuing interests much greater than those of most former metropoles elsewhere in the world. At the same time, whatever the extent of PNG's interest in opening economic windows westwards to Southeast Asia, it remains, in all essential respects, part of the South Pacific region. To this extent, the refusal of ASEAN to consider PNG's membership was soundly based.

Australia's loyalty to the Western alliance since the end of the Second

World War has been for the most part unwavering, as expressed above all in participation in the Vietnam War and continuing loyalty to ANZUS. This alliance commitment survived New Zealand's *de facto* withdrawal and, what was for many Australians in and out of government, the worrying drift of American policy in the 1980s. In view of its position as the major agent of Cold War interests in the region, Australia might reasonably have been expected to exert what control it could over the nature and direction of PNG's external relations. Yet there is little to be discerned in Canberra's policies towards PNG in the post-colonial period to support this. These have been characterised by tentativeness rather than diplomatic assertiveness. Sensitive to any suggestion of neo-colonialism, successive governments, particularly since the Labor Party came to power in 1983, have been notably diffident in their policy formulation and execution. In truth, Western interests were never sufficiently threatened in PNG to justify any great robustness on Australia's part. The political culture of Papua New Guinea has always been wholly unencumbered by any ideological baggage recognisable to broader international interests.

The 'universalist' philosophy of PNG's post-independence foreign policy, summed up by the dictum 'friends to all, enemies to none', embraced neither membership of the Non-Aligned Movement nor the establishment of a Soviet diplomatic mission (though a Chinese embassy was opened on independence). While it must be assumed that Australian interests informed the work of those colonial administrators who prepared the way for the assumption of foreign policy responsibilities by the PNG government after independence, there was little sign of any nationalist reaction. Even the more focused approach of 'active and selective engagement' pursued after the publication of a foreign policy white paper in 1982 did not lead to the development of a relationship with any state or movement of political concern to the West.[20] There was no sense, then, in which Australian security concerns could cast PNG in the role of ideological domino.[21] Attention was focused instead on two more specific dangers: first, the possibility of Australian interests within PNG being affected by internal developments there; and, second, the threat of embroilment as a third party in PNG's other external relationships.

The problems of rising crime and public disorder in PNG have clearly been of concern in the light of extensive private Australian investment and its still large expatriate community. The smuggling of drugs into Australia which were either transported through PNG or actually produced there became a cause of increasing Australian attention in the 1980s.[22] The interests of both countries converge in these matters. If the stability of the economic and social environment is important for Australian investment and the welfare of its residents, it is equally so for the well-being of the government in Port Moresby. An increasing proportion of Australian aid, in the form of financial subvention, manpower secondment and training, has been devoted to law enforcement since the mid-1980s and this trend seems likely to continue.[23]

The situation with fisheries protection is similarly characterised by considerable Australian involvement with PNG. The prevention of illegal foreign fishing activities in PNG's 200-mile zone contributes to the overall security of the waters of the South Pacific, with clear implications for Australia's own defence. Maritime security is thus an obvious point at which functional areas of cooperation impinge on more conventional strategic ones. The provision of fast patrol boats to PNG (as part of a broader regional programme) certainly enhances PNG's capacity to prevent illegal trawling, but it also permits (through seconded personnel, subsidy of operating costs and refit provision) a degree of Australian control over a key security resource. Similarly, the extension of Australian airforce Orion surveillance flights over PNG waters is only partly altruistic.[24]

Potentially, though, the most dangerous aspect of the security relationship between Australia and PNG has involved Indonesia and the border issue. Australian relations with Indonesia came under considerable strain at various points in the 1970s and 1980s. Most frequently this was caused by Australian press and parliamentary criticism of Indonesian policy and politics and by Jakarta's refusal to understand and accept the government's powerlessness to control it. Certainly, at the time of PNG's independence Canberra was careful not to give its former colony any specific commitments on defence. A 1977 'statement of understanding' between prime ministers Somare and Fraser merely accepted the need for 'consultations' on matters of mutual concern.[25] Following the 1986 PNG–Indonesia treaty, however, Canberra evidently judged the border situation sufficiently stable to permit a stronger formal commitment. This took the form of a Joint Declaration of Principles (JDP) signed by Wingti and Bob Hawke in December 1987. The JDP committed the two countries to the consideration of joint action in the event of an attack on either.[26] Like the Treaty of Friendship with Indonesia which preceded it, the declaration did not involve any obvious change in PNG's external relations. Like the Indonesian treaty too, it was of considerable symbolic importance as an assertion of equality in the relationship. Over time as well, relations between Canberra and Jakarta have also prospered. Economic cooperation underlay this improvement, most notably in arrangements for joint oil and gas exploitation following the Timor Gap agreement of December 1989. There was similarly a clear change in security perceptions; an Australian parliamentary enquiry was able to report at the end of 1991 that 'Australia and Indonesia increasingly understand each others [sic] perspective on events in Papua New Guinea. Both seek strategic stability'.[27]

Fortuitously, Australia has anticipated the end of the Cold War by making a significant shift in its strategic stance during the 1980s. This involved, in essence, a 'regionalisation' of defence policy with the major focus being placed on a geographically limited 'area of primary strategic interest'. Within this area a 'sense of strategic community' was to be actively promoted.[28] Papua New Guinea naturally forms a key part of this area, and the JDP as well as the patrol boats, helicopters and the wider Defence Cooperation Program must been seen in this context.[29] In view of this relatively recent revision of Australian policy and its evident appropriateness in the post-bipolar system, it would appear that PNG's position in Australia's security agenda is unlikely to change significantly in the medium term. Each country's interests parallel those of the other, with Australia providing the necessary resources to pursue them. This coincidence of interest has been a major asset for Papua New Guinea's own security and, in contrast to other regional security relationships formulated in the Cold War period, it looks set to survive the end of bipolarity.

While PNG was obviously the subordinate partner in the Australian relationship, in the broader island Pacific there at least existed the possibility of playing a more dominant role. Ironically perhaps, the generally improved *regional* security of the South Pacific in the 1990s has reduced the potential for such an external role – and of course the dangers inherent in it. The ending of France's confrontational approach in and over New Caledonia following the fall of Jacques Chirac in 1988 has already been touched on. As the largest and most militant of the Forum states, PNG had taken the lead in anti-French initiatives at the United Nations and elsewhere. Similarly, island resentments at what was seen as heavy-handed and condescending external interference over the dangers, real or imagined, of Soviet and Libyan links tended to be most influentially expressed by PNG. The passing of these security 'threats' ended this incipient leadership role. The same shift of political mood also reversed a potentially damaging trend towards the diplomatic division of the region into politically and ethnically distinct sub-groups. This was the development in 1987 and 1988 of a formal Melanesian inter-governmental organisation called the Spearhead and comprising PNG,

Vanuatu and the Solomon Islands. It was formed in good part as a reaction against the perceived conservatism of the more numerous but less populous Polynesian membership of the Forum on a range of security-related issues from New Caledonia to nuclear testing but inevitably seemed less relevant as the salience of this agenda faded.[30]

A further brake on the process of political sub-regionalisation and the development of a leadership role for PNG was, however, provided by the major problems of internal security which afflicted PNG with the outbreak of the Bougainville crisis. By 1989, as the Bougainville emergency deepened, the Spearhead had already been down-graded in PNG's foreign policy priorities as a result of the change of government the previous year. The enthusiasm of Paias Wingti for Melanesian sub-regionalism was not shared by his successor, Rabbie Namaliu (and even less so by the foreign minister, the country's influential independence prime minister, Michael Somare). With the start of military operations in the North Solomons Province of PNG, relations with the neighbouring state of the Solomon Islands came under strain and, as these two constituted two-thirds of the Spearhead's membership, its viability as an inter-governmental organisation was inevitably affected.

Additionally, Bougainville struck a further blow to PNG's regional standing. A major factor in its increasingly dominant position in regional politics in the 1980s had been its relatively large military capacity in terms both of resources and reputation, the latter deriving from the successful Vanuatu intervention of 1980. Indeed, on this basis the then PNG prime minister, Julius Chan, had launched a campaign in the region for the establishment of a local, multi-national peacekeeping mechanism in which PNG would obviously play a major role.[31] By occupying the PNGDF's capacities and more particularly by exposing its inefficiency and indiscipline, the Bougainville crisis served to end any pretensions to such an international peacekeeping role. The disastrous performance of the security forces exposed the myth of professionalism that grew in the afterglow of the Vanuatu intervention. For the concerns of the Solomon Islands government over the behaviour of the PNGDF were not unfounded. Unauthorised movements by PNG patrol boats in Solomon Island waters led to initial strains in 1990, but deeper tensions still were caused in September 1992 by an amphibious raid by PNGDF commandos in pursuit of BRA guerrillas on Solomons territory in which villagers were killed. More broadly, PNG's reputation for civil and political liberties, which had been virtually unparalleled in the Third World, was severely damaged. The attentions of Amnesty International and other human rights groups, more usually focused on Indonesia, now turned to Bougainville. In this way issues of internal security touched directly on the external environment and PNG's potential role within it.

THE BOUGAINVILLE CRISIS AND 'SECURITY' AS NATIONAL COHESION

Perhaps the most important impact of the Bougainville crisis has been the degree to which it has brought a fundamental change in public and political perceptions of the concept of 'security'. For the first time since independence, security has been seen to do with territorial integrity defined as national cohesion rather than as protection of borders. The economic – and therefore social – implications of this have also affected these perceptions. Prior to its closure Bougainville Copper Ltd provided 45 per cent of PNG's export earnings and accounted for 19 per cent of its overall budgetary revenue. The consequence of the loss of such a resource greatly affected government social expenditure and contributed to a further deterioration in the law and order situation. The growing climate of lawlessness and disregard of conventional restraints on behaviour took on political tones and 'criminality' was increasingly rationalised as social protest. The country's two universities were affected by this (and closed for various periods in 1990 and 1991) and the provincial government system fell victim to violent factional conflicts. Eventually, in 1990, night-time curfews were imposed on urban areas and enforced by the police and the Defence Force.

Significantly, however, the ultimate security nightmare – that the Bougainville 'contagion' would spread to cause a generalised national disintegration – has not been realised. Yet the fear was well-enough founded. Sub-national regionalism had been a potent force in PNG politics even in the colonial period. Influential separatist movements were active not only in Bougainville but in East New Britain as well. While the principal manifestations were in the islands region, the mainland suffered from its own cultural and historical divisions. The coastal Papuans were wary of sharing power in a new state with what they saw as the 'uncivilised' highland region. For their part the highlanders feared domination by the more politically sophisticated Papuans.[32] Divisions were evident too in units much smaller than the formal regions. Concern over this potential for fragmentation was reflected from the outset in the distinctly decentralised nature of the post-independence constitution.[33]

The years of independence have done little to dissolve regional and provincial differences. Indeed, the nation-building process might be said to have gone into reverse since the late 1970s. Independence removed much of the efficiency and all of the perceived neutrality of the colonial state. Specifically, it ended Australia's ability to set the nation-building agenda, something Canberra had exercised to the full in its anxiety to lay the basis for a unified and stable neighbour after the transfer of power. The post-independence constitution, with its devolution of extensive powers to the provinces, in the end encouraged the very geographical factionalism it had been designed to neutralise. At the centre, the failure of the party system to take hold and thus provide an institutional basis for stability, further enfeebled the state at the very time an assertion of state authority was required.[34]

Unsurprisingly, then, the Bougainville secession crisis has been seen by the central government not just as a problem in itself, but as a potential catalyst for a much broader fragmentation. Would the Bougainville example regenerate dormant separatist tendencies, or indeed provoke new ones, in other provinces and regions? Initially the omens seemed worrying. The Panguna mine on Bougainville was the largest and longest established of the extractive operations in PNG, but it was only the first of many. In the late 1980s the notion of a 'mineral boom' dominated national economic forecasting and planning. Mineral extraction was seen as the salvation of the PNG economy. It was to be the ultimate economic panacea, soothing away the dual ills of the time: declining Australian aid levels and falling commodity prices for the country's main cash crops. In addition to Bougainville, major gold and copper extraction is underway at Ok Tedi in Western Province; the Porgera gold mine has begun production in the highlands province of Enga; and preparations for large scale gold extraction are well advanced in Lihir in New Ireland and Misima in Milne Bay. Large oil and gas deposits have been located in the Southern Highlands and a long-distance pipeline is planned to facilitate exports. None of these ventures has been free of characteristic Melanesian wrangles over land rights, with local clans and individuals demanding frequently unrealistic compensation and royalty agreements. Mineral-rich provinces have questioned the right of the central government to derive any benefit from extraction. The state, tolerable as a provider of goods and services, is less acceptable as a beneficiary of local wealth. For, although cultural and environmental concerns were certainly involved in the Bougainville rebellion, a major issue has also been resentment at 'subsidising' a country of which Bougainvilleans had never really wanted to be a part in the first place.

The central government faces a difficult dilemma. Failure to manage local restiveness jeopardises the foreign investment necessary to get the 'boom' properly underway. Yet the state is neither materially equipped nor politically inclined to impose repressive control. But, despite occasional spurts of fractiousness in the mining areas, the dilemma has remained theoretical rather than actual. Confounding the pessimistic voices of 1989 and 1990 the centre has actually held through the Bougainville emergency. The secession itself appears to be disintegrating under the pressures of blockade and as a result of the failure of the BRA to create any sustainable political and social structures in the areas it controls. Formal peace negotiations, although frequently attempted, have come to little in the absence of a clear leadership structure among the rebels and their seeming inability to advance any articulate proposals. In these circumstances the security forces of the central government are quickly but steadily re-filling the vacuum created by their departure in 1990. The major remaining question for the government is whether the demon of fragmentation has been exorcised or merely subdued. Certainly Bougainville was a special case in terms of its geographic position and ethnic distinctiveness. Yet all precedents are by their nature special cases.

SUMMING UP – MUDDLING THROUGH?

The 1992 election provided no evidence of a change in PNG's atomised and parochial political culture. The nation-building enterprise remains to all practical effect suspended. The search for the silver-lining in this ends at the barracks' gates within which the military reflect this broader reluctance to identify with the national unit. Combined with the relative ease with which political ambition on the part of individual officers can be satisfied through the existing system, this continues to militate against unconstitutional action. The rise of Ted Diro from force commander to deputy prime minister before his final disgrace over financial wrong-doing in 1991, and the election of former police commissioner and architect of the 1990 'Bar-B-Coup', Paul Tohian, to the national parliament in 1992 are evidence of the permeability of the civilian elite to those with sufficient local standing. The self-made 'bigman' still dominates leadership in Melanesian society, overlaying more recently imported systems of hierarchy.[35] But, of course, this silver lining lies against another cloud: the ineffectiveness of the army as guarantor of national unity at the disposal of democratic government.

Even by the time of the Bougainville secession, the capacity to 'muddle through' successive crises had become almost the defining characteristic of PNG's political system. Bougainville shook the inevitable complacency which emerged from this. Yet the crisis, ending with a whimper rather than a bang, threatens to validate this

Panglossian confidence in the eventual resolution of all problems through inactivity. Not only has the secession failed, it has failed to the accompaniment of sufficient suffering and destruction *pour encourager les autres*; at the same time the impact has been insufficient to pose any real threat to the survival of the state.

The relative ease of access to political position has already been described as a safety valve against military ambitions. This can also divert separatist agitation, for the pressure to fulfil the 'traditional' MP's function of bringing resources from the centre to the electorate will frequently dissipate separatist fervour. There is, however, a future danger threatened by this hitherto stabilising process. A national economy based on mineral extraction could bring an inversion of this function, requiring the politician to prevent the transfer of 'local' resources to the centre. The defeat of the Namaliu government by a coalition formed by his predecessor, Paias Wingti, in the 1992 election was determined not by 'national' issues like Bougainville. Characteristically, the new coalition emerged haphazardly from local decisions about the resource-attracting skills of individual candidates, largely regardless of party allegiance or policy stance. Putting the point in reverse, no government formed of the ideologically incoherent and opportunistic kaleidoscope of factions that prosper in PNG's political culture could weather a generalised challenge from the periphery.

There is, moreover, no international *deus ex machina* either capable or willing to confront any such fragmentation on the central government's behalf. Both Australia and Indonesia are deeply concerned about the stability of PNG as far as it impinges on regional security and, to date, both have defined stability in terms of territorial integrity and authoritative central government. The prospect of direct military involvement in support of this is, however, inconceivable for a raft of sound historical and political reasons. Even indirect support can carry risks. The Australians found this when the helicopters they provided to the PNGDF were used (contrary to agreement and operated by PNGDF personnel) as gunships in Bougainville. The Indonesians suffered similarly from the exposure of their funding of key PNG leaders – rather more perhaps than the recipients themselves. The allocation of blame in PNG politics does not always follow a readily comprehensible logic.

There is anyway a point at which support for a particular structure may become counter-productive. There is nothing *inherently* superior in central control and territorial unity. They remain desirable only for as long as they are perceived to be stabilising elements. If an adjustment in the status quo in PNG was to be seen by Canberra and Jakarta as having a *greater* stabilising effect on the region, then the ties of sentiment to the central government might quickly fray under the force of pragmatism. The Bougainville secession, partly because of its confused and intractable leadership, never approached this point. This does not guarantee, though, that it could not or would not be reached in future. The fact is that Australian security interests are no longer based on the denial of lodgement on its borders to ideologically hostile forces. Such forces no longer exist. The security 'guarantees' to PNG embodied in the Joint Declaration of Principles are not only very limited but are based on a response to *external* threat. It is also possible to overstate Indonesia's instinctive anti-separatism. Geographical neighbours they may be, but Indonesia and Papua New Guinea still look in opposite directions for their respective regional identities. The anti-centralist ripples of Melanesian separatism are, practically speaking, unlikely to fire dormant tendencies in an utterly different culture thousands of miles to the west. While Jakarta would abhor uncontrolled fragmentation, acceptance of ordered change may be attractive as offering the possibility of future influence.

In sum, the Papua New Guinea state persists in reasonable security. It does so with the benefit of a regional international environment which, despite periodic tensions, has been generally benevolent. More significantly, it has to date survived the separatist challenge from within and has done so with a functioning – though imperfect – parliamentary system in place. It is difficult, nevertheless, to resist the conclusion that this survival is due more to a lack of viable alternatives than any positive qualities of the status quo. Neither centralising authoritarianism nor separatist sub-national regionalism are as yet capable of posing effective challenges to this status quo. If one or other is not to do so in the coming years, however, the government must re-invigorate the nation-building process and strive to make an effective marriage between the national parliamentary system and the prevailing political culture. There can be no underestimating the extent of these tasks. 'Muddling through', seemingly sufficient for the immediate post-independence years, is not a reliable option for the 1990s. While the passing of the Cold War may have done little to change the security environment of the South Pacific, it has done much to clarify it. Papua New Guinea's security agenda is perhaps clearer than at any time since independence; it remains to be seen if the will and capacity exist to confront it.

NOTES

1. See, for example, R. Ayson, *Activities of the Soviet Fishing Fleet: Implications for Australia*, Australian National University Strategic and Defence Studies Centre Working Paper No. 170 (Canberra, 1988).
2. See D. Hegarty, *Libya and the Pacific*, Australian National University Strategic and Defence Studies Centre Working Paper No. 127 (Canberra, 1987).
3. The social, economic and political problems of development in Papua New Guinea are dealt with in two recent general studies by S. Dorney, *Papua New Guinea: People, Politics and History since 1975* (Sydney, 1990) and M. Turner, *Papua New Guinea: The Challenge of Independence* (Melbourne, 1990).
4. For the background to the Bougainville crisis, see Dorney, *Papua New Guinea*, 117–149; and R. J. May and M. Spriggs (eds.), *The Bougainville Crisis* (Bathurst, NSW, 1990).
5. See *Australia's Relations with Papua New Guinea*, Parliament of the Commonwealth of Australia Joint Committee on Foreign Affairs, Defence and Trade Report (Canberra, 1991), 164–5.
6. Y. Saffu, 'Military Roles and Relations in Papua New Guinea', unpublished paper presented to Australian National University conference on 'Armed Forces in Asia and the Pacific', Nov.–Dec. 1989.
7. On the Vanuatu operation, see N. MacQueen, 'Beyond *Tok Win*: The Papua New Guinea Intervention in Vanuatu, 1980', *Pacific Affairs*, 16, 2 (1988), 235–52.
8. Calculation based on data from D. Hegarty and P. Polomka (eds.), *The Security of Oceania in the 1990s Vol. 1: Views from the Region*, Canberra Paper on Strategy and Defence No. 60 (Canberra, 1989), 3 and 8.
9. In the few cases where this logic was disregarded – as in the New Hebrides (Vanuatu) with its Anglo-French dual condominium – troublesome consequences tended to ensue with independence. See G. Molisa *et al*, 'Vanuatu: Overcoming Pandemonium', in R. Crocombe and A. Ali (eds.), *Politics in Melanesia* (Suva, 1982), 82–114.
10. On Australian attitudes towards Indonesia during the colonial period, see I. Downs, *The Australian Trusteeship in Papua New Guinea, 1945–75* (Canberra, 1980), 220–32; J. Verrier, 'The Origins of the Border Problem and the Border Story to 1969', in R. J. May (ed.), *Between Two Nations: The Indonesia–Papua New Guinea Border and West Papua Nationalism* (Bathurst, NSW, 1986), 18–48.
11. At one point, in 1983, the PNG Defence Minister predicted an Indonesian invasion within 'the next ten to twenty years'. *The Australian*, 9 Sept. 1983.
12. The text of the Treaty can be found in E. P. Wolfers (ed.), *Beyond the Border* (Post Moresby, 1988), 177–82.
13. *Papua New Guinea Post Courier*, 10 Nov. 1987. The revelation did not appear to damage Diro's standing in the short term.
14. Huai too had received 'gifts' from Murdani but evidently on a lesser scale to that of Diro. His resignation was reportedly insisted upon by Canberra. *Sydney Morning Herald*, 2 Feb. 1988.
15. For a consideration of Indonesia's options, see J. A. C. Mackie, 'Does Indonesia have Expansionist Designs on Papua New Guinea?', in May, *Between Two Nations*, 65–84.
16. Murdani's views were reported in a leaked Australian Department of Foreign Affairs document. *The Australian*, 26 July 1990.
17. PNG was allowed to accede to the ASEAN Treaty of Amity and Cooperation by way of consolation.
18. On Papua New Guinea's position on ASEAN, see N. MacQueen, 'New Directions for Papua New Guinea's Foreign Policy', *Pacific Review*, 4, 2 (1991), 168.
19. See C. Brown, 'Indonesia, the South West Pacific and Australia', *World Review* (Brisbane), 27, 2 (1988), 37–55.
20. Text of the 1982 White Paper in *Papua New Guinea Foreign Affairs Review*, 1, 4

(1982), 11–126. For a discussion of 'universalism' and 'active and selective engagement', see MacQueen, 'New Directions', 162–3.

21. To the extent that Canberra had any such worries in the region they focused on Vanuatu under Walter Lini, which *was* a member of the Non-Aligned Movement and appeared to be attracting the interest of Libya in the late 1980s. See R. T. Robertson, 'Vanuatu: Fragile Foreign Policy Initiatives', *Development and Change*, 19 (1988), 617–47.

22. *Australia's Relations with Papua New Guinea*, 167–8.

23. Ibid., 67–75.

24. F. A. Mediansky, 'The Security Outlook in the Southwest Pacific', *Australian Quarterly* (Spring/Summer 1987), 271.

25. *Australian Foreign Affairs Record*, Feb. 1977, 90–91.

26. 'Joint Declaration of Principles Guiding Relations between Papua New Guinea and Australia', *Australian Foreign Affairs Record*, Nov.–Dec. 1987, 616–17.

27. *Australia's Relations with Papua New Guinea*, 167.

28. *Review of Australia's Defence Capabilities. Report to the Minister of Defence* (the 'Dibb Report') (Canberra, 1986). The main principles were reiterated by foreign minister Gareth Evans in a statement in December 1989, *Australia's Regional Security*.

29. The Australian Defence Cooperation Programme with PNG involved the following sums in aid:

Year	Million Aus$
1988–89	27
1989–90	41
1990–91	53
1991–92	37.2 (estimate)

The 1989–91 figures reflect the special circumstances of the Bougainville crisis.
Total Defence aid from independence to 1991 is calculated at 500 million Australian dollars. *Australia's Relations with Papua New Guinea*, 175.

30. See N. MacQueen, 'Sharpening the Spearhead: Subregionalism in Melanesia', *Pacific Studies*, 12, 2 (1989), 33–52.

31. For various reasons neither the smaller island states nor Australia evinced much enthusiasm for Chan's idea. See G. Fry, *Peacekeeping in the South Pacific: Some Questions for Prior Consideration*, Australian National University Department of International Relations Working Paper No. 7 (Canberra, 1990). In 1988 on the very eve of the Bougainville crisis, a Defence White Paper proposed a major role for the Defence Force in the widening arena of United Nations peacekeeping.

32. On the politics of sub-national regionalism during preparations for independence, see Downs, *The Australian Trusteeship*, 424–52.

33. See W. Tordoff, 'Provincial Government in Papua New Guinea 1974–82', in P. King *et al* (eds.), *From Rhetoric to Reality* (Port Moresby, 1985), 197–208.

34. On the role of parties and issues in PNG politics, see Michael Oliver's introduction to the study of the 1987 election published under his editorship, *Eleksin: The 1987 National Election in Papua New Guinea* (Port Moresby, 1989), 1–14.

35. See R. J. May, 'Political Style in Modern Melanesia', in R. J. May and H. Nelson (eds.), *Melanesia: Beyond Diversity* (Canberra, 1982), 639–49.

Aspects of Security in Micronesia

ROY H. SMITH

Micronesia means 'little islands'. It consists of four politically distinct island groups in the Pacific Basin: the Commonwealth of the Northern Marianas (CNMI); the Federated States of Micronesia (FSM); the Marshall Islands; and the Republic of Belau.[1] The fundamental characteristic of Micronesia is the relative imbalance between its geographic expanse and its land area. It is a vast oceanic region (roughly corresponding in size with the United States) dotted with small, lowly populated islands.[2] Everything else about these island groups and their relations with other states revolves around this factor. In particular, the security of the islands has been influenced by their smallness, remoteness and lack of resources. This article considers the security interests of each of the four groups, focusing on who determines these interests and what factors influence the relevant decision-makers. However, security issues in the islands have long been complicated by the role of the United States as the administrative authority for the region under the United Nations Trusteeship Agreement of 1947[3] and it is with the initiation of Trusteeship that we begin.

MICRONESIA UNDER TRUSTEESHIP

Since the end of World War Two Micronesia has been under the political control of the United States. Previously held by the Japanese under a League of Nations Mandate, Micronesia has a long history of colonial rule. However, the period since 1947 has been different in that the United Nations system of Trusteeship was designed to lead towards the eventual 'self-government or independence' of the various Trust Territories.[4] Despite this apparently significant distinction the extent to which the Micronesian experience during the US administration has diverged from that under previous colonial regimes has been questioned.[5] Such doubts have arisen because of the unique status of the Trust Territory of the Pacific Islands (TTPI). Unlike other territories the TTPI was designated as a Strategic Trust Territory. This meant that

Roy H. Smith is a researcher in the Department of Peace Studies of the University of Bradford in England.

it came under the authority of the Security Council rather than the Trusteeship Council. As a permanent member of the Security Council possessed of the power of veto, the United States thus had complete control over Micronesian affairs. As there was also no timetable set for eventual independence, the United States could be said effectively to have annexed the TTPI as its own territory.

The designation of Strategic Trusteeship came about as a compromise between conflicting views in the US administration at the end of World War Two. The US Navy Department argued for the annexation of the islands because of their strategic significance for US security interests. The State Department supported the United Nations' plans for Trusteeship and wished to avoid the charge of territorial aggrandisement being made against the United States.[6] Although the Navy Department was unable to realise its initial plans for Micronesia, the subsequent US administration of Micronesia under the UN Trusteeship Agreement produced a situation that more than met US naval requirements. Micronesia was denied as a military base for any power other than the United States. In fact, the policy of strategic denial dominated US relations with the TTPI.

Yet the principle of Trusteeship involved furthering the interests of the TTPI, with the ultimate goal being self-government or independence. The 1947 Agreement gave the administering authority clear responsibilities regarding the advancement of the Pacific Islanders' social and economic well-being, with the promotion of their self-sufficiency as a primary aim. Certainly, US funding has been made available to support Micronesian economies. However, the way in which these funds have been administered has led to claims that the United States worked deliberately to undermine economic development, thereby engendering a dependency relationship which the United States could exploit to further its own interests in the region.[7]

Micronesian economies are all disadvantaged by their remoteness to markets, the distance over which their population is spread, their relatively small resource bases and their lack of capital investment to develop potential resources such as fisheries. Despite these disadvantages, it would be wrong to assume that Micronesia is economically non-viable. Quite the contrary, as was demonstrated during the Japanese colonial period by the achievement of a net export of goods until the outbreak of hostilities with the United States.[8] A further consideration is the type of economy that is being promoted in Micronesia. A basic self-sufficient economy with little or no annual growth is sustainable with local fishing and a few staple crops. However, this type of economy has been rejected by the majority of Micronesians in favour of a model based on consumerism and the accumulation of material wealth. Problems have thus derived from the marked mismatch between Micronesian economic aspirations and the extent to which these can be met from revenue generated by the Micronesians themselves, hence the continuing vulnerability of the Micronesian economies and their longstanding reliance on US funds.

Economic security has always been the major consideration for Micronesians trying to move away from the Trusteeship system towards greater independence. This contrasts with the United States' main concern which revolves around military security. Throughout the period of Trusteeship the United States has adopted a policy of maintaining strategic denial and of trying to ensure that this continues as and when the Trusteeship was eventually terminated. To achieve this end, it has at different times promoted various alternatives for the political status of the TTPI beyond Trusteeship. On rare occasions full independence has been discussed, but this has always been tempered by the recognition of Micronesia's economic dependence on the United States.

THE COMMONWEALTH OF THE NORTHERN MARIANAS

The Northern Mariana chain of islands includes Guam, although Guam has never been part of the TTPI.[9] However, the presence of extensive US military installations on Guam has been significant in the developing relationship between the United States and the rest of the Northern Marianas. Although Micronesia has often been referred to as a homogeneous region there are important differences between the various island groups. For example, the US presence in Guam has had a far greater influence within the Mariana chain than in other parts of the TTPI. A reflection of this was the decision taken in a referendum held in the Marianas in June 1975 to separate from the rest of the TTPI and seek Commonwealth status in association with the United States.

Initially, the United States had proposed Commonwealth status for the whole of the TTPI. However, this option was rejected by the other districts in the Territory.[10] The Trusteeship Agreement called for transitions of political status to be carried out across the region as a whole. Separate negotiations with each district were not envisaged under the terms of the Agreement. Despite the reticence of the United Nations to acknowledge the CNMI's new political status, the United States nevertheless concluded bilateral agreements with the Northern Marianas and proclaimed the Commonwealth status effective from 1976. It was to be another ten years before the United Nations accepted the arrangement. It is indeed a revealing indication of the level of influence the United States had as the administrative authority for the region that it could proceed with this change of status without the cooperation of the United Nations.

It is the extent to which the United States has influenced the Northern Marianas, and the other islands of the TTPI, that raises questions about the decision-making process involved in determining the TTPI's political status beyond Trusteeship. Given the reliance on US funding that has developed in the post-war period, there are doubts surrounding the freedom of choice available to the islanders when voting on their future political status. Complete independence cannot be wholly discounted as investment and patronage from other states, notably Japan, could offset the withdrawal of US funding. Yet such an option is full of uncertainty and insecurity for a newly emerging state with a limited resource base to draw on. In this sense, accusations against the United States of furthering its own interests in Micronesia over and above those of the Micronesians retain credibility. However, it would be wrong to stress this argument to the point that the actions of the Micronesians are overlooked.[11] In the case of the CNMI a clear preference for Commonwealth status was shown by democratic process in the 1975 referendum. The Marianans judged that their interests would be best served by a closer relationship with the United States. This seems to deny the assumption that full independence is the ultimate goal of all potential states. Although it can be argued that the Marianans retain aspirations for greater autonomy, their geographic location, distribution and resource base all mitigate against such plans. The assumption that political independence is a necessary element of the enhancement of security interests can therefore be questioned. For the Micronesian territories the price of security seems to involve concessions on political independence.

Discussion of security interests immediately begs the question of how these are defined. It has already been pointed out that there is a mismatch between the United States' emphasis on military security and the Micronesians' on economic security. Both views are likely to be influenced by the perception of military threat, but in differing ways. The United States views Micronesia as a first line of US defence and a staging post that must be denied to any enemy forces. In the post-Cold War era previous US concerns over potential Soviet expansion in the region have lost their credibility. Yet it is unlikely that US strategists will ignore the continuing significance of these islands as potential 'stepping stones' across the Pacific. Although Micronesia is not obviously threatened by any aggressor nations in the short term, the

United States will not lightly forgo its current strategic advantage in the region.

By contrast, Micronesian world-views are more localised. The perception of military threat centres on the region and traditional concerns of invasion and domination. This has been the experience of the Micronesian people over five hundred years from the time of Spanish exploration through to German and Japanese colonisation. Although it may appear that the period of US administration is a marked contrast to these former regimes, there are Micronesians who view US security policies in the region as an overt military threat.[12] The US administration naturally argues that its military activities in the region are for the protection of Micronesia, but there are clearly several aspects to them which are of greater advantage to the United States than to Micronesians. The most striking example revolves around the US nuclear test programme in the 1950s. Here it is the people of the Marshall Islands who continue to feel detrimental effects of the tests.

THE MARSHALL ISLANDS

In 1983 Marshall Islanders voted to accept a Compact of Free Association with the United States. This political status gave them control over their domestic affairs, such as the local budget, with the United States maintaining responsibility for defence and foreign affairs.[13] Included in the Compact document was a settlement of compensation claims against the US government from Marshallese suffering the effects of the nuclear tests carried out in the region. In particular, the 1954 test code-named 'Bravo' resulted in the contamination of the Marshall Islands atoll of Rongelap.[14] In addition to the radiation exposure suffered by these islanders, they were subsequently relocated to other islands with inadequate resources.[15] Since that time they have pursued their claims for compensation through the US courts.[16] Yet, with the signing of the Compact agreement, the Marshall Islands government effectively precluded any further pursuit of these claims. A fundamental point raised by the compensation cases was the validity of the nuclear test programme in the eyes of the Marshall Islanders. As they saw it, their security was devastated by the nuclear test programme and the US presence in their islands was as detrimental to them as the former periods of colonial rule.

The US argument that its nuclear test programme was a necessary element of its security guarantee to Micronesia has thus been unconvincing to islanders removed from their homeland and suffering from prolonged illness. Similarly, the continuing use of Kwajalein atoll for US missile testing and 'Star Wars' research is not wholly accepted as being advantageous to islanders living there. This base has generated jobs for the Marshallese on nearby Ebeye island. However, with approximately 10,000 inhabitants on the 66-acre island, Ebeye has been described as the 'slum of the Pacific'.[17] Conditions on Ebeye have improved in recent years but the advantages of this US defence project still accrue overwhelmingly to the United States rather than the Marshall Islanders. What is more, with some 3,000 US servicemen stationed at Kwajalein and the US administration seemingly committed to further 'Star Wars' research, a long-term US military presence in the Marshall Islands appears to be planned. This has sometimes been portrayed as providing a degree of economic stability for the islands.[18] Certainly, with the vulnerability of the Marshallese economy, a long-term income of the scale generated by the Kwajalein base cannot be easily discounted and would be difficult to generate in other sectors of the economy.

By the same token, the need for the Marshall Islands government to generate extra or alternative income has led it of late to consider some unusual investment offers. One such scheme involved the dumping of nuclear waste on one of the islands.[19] This may seem a particularly insensitive idea given the islanders' experiences with the US nuclear test programme. However, as the Marshall Islands President Amata Kabua has pointed out, some of the islands are already uninhabitable due to toxic radiation levels.[20] Under such circumstances they are logical sites for nuclear waste depositories. Nevertheless, this argument failed to convince the majority of Marshall Islanders who viewed the scheme as a further example of the United States taking advantage of Micronesia's relative political powerlessness. As with the test programme, and the destruction of chemical and biological weapons on Johnston Atoll, Micronesians resented the unwillingness of the United States to conduct these operations on the US mainland. Such schemes constitute only a small part of the web of US/Micronesian relations but their importance is consistently magnified because of the impression they give of dismissive US attitudes towards the islanders.

Another potential foreign investment in the Marshall Islands involved the dumping of US household waste around the coast of some of the islands. A US waste-management company, Admiralty Pacific, offered US$140 million for disposing of 15.5 tonnes of waste.[21] Initially, the use of waste as landfill to increase land area and protect against rising sea-levels was viewed favourably in the islands. In the end, the scheme was rejected because of fears that toxic wastes could not be adequately removed and would be likely to contaminate ground water and harm in-shore marine life. However, the fact that such schemes have been considered at all illustrates the trade-off between economic and other forms of security that the Marshall Islands' government may find it necessary to indulge in future. Indeed, the landfill scheme brings together two key security issues facing the government. First, the need to promote foreign investment in the islands means that potentially high-risk schemes are being given serious consideration. Second, the fear of rising sea-levels is now acute in these low-lying territories. At the 1990 meeting of the South Pacific Forum, the most pressing issue on the agenda was the Greenhouse Effect and its implications for small island states. Again it was noted that this problem could be linked to the energy policies of the United States, and the other major industrial powers.

Issues such as global warming are universal problems. Yet it is revealing that there is a perception on behalf of the Marshall Islanders that their security is suffering as a direct and particular result of US policies. This perception should be viewed in the context of other aspects of the US–Marshalls relationship. The period of US administration in the islands has always involved an extremely asymmetrical power relationship. The move to the status of Free Association has offered some more flexibility to the Marshall Islands government but without altering its fundamental dependency relationship with the United States. Although it can be admitted that there are positive aspects to the income generated by both the direct investment of the military base at Kwajalein and the funding under the Compact agreement, they have manifestly come at some cost to the Marshall Islands with regard to their political autonomy. The islanders have achieved nominal political independence under the Compact, as demonstrated in their acceptance into the United Nations.[22] Yet they remain closely tied to the United States in the degree to which the US controls their security and foreign affairs. To date, the Marshall Islands government has not exercised its quasi-independent status to the point of infringing US security interests in the region. With the end of the Cold War, and the suspension of US paranoia about Soviet infiltration, it is difficult to see what action the Marshall Islands government could take to threaten the United States. The only possibility would be a rejection of the US military presence in the islands. With the importance of the Kwajalein base to the 'Star Wars' programme this would be strongly resisted by the United States, probably to the point of the collapse of the Compact agreement.

However remote the possibility of a fully independent Micronesia may appear, it is worthwhile to consider what options are open to Micronesian governments should they break away from their longstanding relationship with the United States. The US military presence makes this possibility particularly unlikely for the Marshall Islands, but the experience of the Federated States of Micronesia does provide interesting evidence of the problems that may arise if greater independence was to be pursued.

THE FEDERATED STATES OF MICRONESIA

The Federated States of Micronesia voted in favour of a Compact of Free Association with the United States at the same time as the Marshall Islands. Although negotiation of the terms of the different Compact agreements took place separately, the principle of internal self-government, and the abdication of military security responsibilities to the United States, was common to both agreements. Beyond this, though, the differing circumstances of the two island groups have led to different experiences under Free Association.

The lack of major US military bases in the FSM has had a two-fold effect on the islands' economies. First, it has reduced direct investment from the United States; second, it has encouraged the FSM government to look elsewhere for foreign investment. The lesser strategic value of the FSM compared with the Marshall Islands also means that the United States may be less stringent in its monitoring of foreign investment in the FSM. Nevertheless, the period of Trusteeship under US administration has left the FSM in an economic dependency relationship with the United States similar to that of the Marshall Islands. The terms of the FSM Compact agreement provide US$1.3 billion in US funding over a period of 15 years. This is calculated on a sliding scale with a reduction in funds over time aimed at eventual self-sufficiency for the islands. A report by the Bank of Hawaii estimates, however, that, despite sound economic potential, the FSM remains too dependent on US funding to be able to progress to self-sufficiency within the 15-year forecast.[23]

One of the main problems facing the FSM is that there remains a lack of internal cohesion between the individual federated states. The creation of the political entity of the FSM dates back to 1978 and the attempt to establish a Micronesian Federation Constitution.[24] This was put to a referendum across the TTPI but rejected by the Marshall Islands and Belau which went on to formulate their own Constitutions. The districts which voted for this Constitution were Pohnpei, Truk, Yap and Kosrae.[25] On the basis of this vote the FSM thus became a single political unit. It is important to note that these island groups are not culturally homogeneous, which is a further hindrance to political cohesion beyond the practical difficulties of the geographic spread of the states. FSM's President Haglelgam, from Yap, had therefore what was described as the 'herculean task' of both maintaining internal unity and developing the FSM in the face of a lack of resources and an entrenched dependency economy.[26]

The FSM has been able to take advantage of its free access to US markets to attract certain foreign manufacturing ventures. However, these have not stimulated the local economy to the extent that was expected. An example is a joint Taiwanese/Sri Lankan garment factory set up in Yap in 1989. Although this factory employs 150 Yapese, a further 500 Sri Lankans are also employed. This importation of labour, many of whom send much of their income back to their families in Sri Lanka, has meant that local people have not increased their spending power as much as is necessary to stimulate Yap's economy. Australia, New Zealand, China and Japan have all shown interest in investing in projects based in the FSM. Yet the majority of such schemes see the bulk of the income generated returning to the foreign investors.

The mainstay of the FSM's economy is its fisheries resources. This supplies the islanders with their primary source of protein and also generates export revenues. Indeed, it is in the area of fisheries and other offshore resources that the FSM and the other Micronesian territories have their greatest economic potential. A longstanding grievance of Micronesian governments has been that other states have been able to exploit fisheries, particularly tuna, in Micronesian territorial waters. The government faces a double problem: other states have more advanced fishing fleets with the capability to catch more fish and it has few patrol boats to guard its fisheries. The United States has entered into an agreement with the Micronesian governments to regulate US-registered tuna boats. Although this has helped to reduce the problem of the poaching of Micronesia's resources, it remains the case that Micronesian governments do not have the capital investment necessary to take advantage of their potentially most profitable resource.

In considering the economic viability of the Micronesian islands it is clear that there is a crucial disjunction between potential and achievement. Self-sufficiency at a basic subsistence level can be maintained on most of the inhabited islands and, as such, the most immediate security concerns can be met. However, the islanders are not as remote from western culture as their geographic position might suggest. They have aspirations to raise their living standards well beyond subsistence. The period of US administration has presented them with a model of consumerism at odds with the traditional lifestyle of the islands. Most of the islands now have access to television and videos, showing predominantly American programmes. There has, as a result, been a fundamental shift in what represent symbols of status in Micronesian societies. Automobiles and electrical goods are newly valued, but at the same time cost a higher percentage of Micronesian incomes than of comparable US incomes.

The adoption of an American lifestyle can only be successfully achieved if the island economies do fulfil their potential. Theoretically, if a more efficient exploitation of Micronesia's marine resources could be achieved, Micronesians could attain one of the world's highest per capita incomes. This requires greater use of the fisheries resources, but extends beyond that to deep-sea mining, oil exploration and the utilisation of manganese nodules found on the ocean floor. The last example ideally illustrates Micronesia's inability to take advantage of its resources. The gathering of manganese nodules would require advanced technological equipment and an initial financial investment far in excess of that available to Micronesian governments. The possibility of a joint venture or licensing agreement with another state may allow this resource to be utilised in the future. For the moment, Micronesia's economies are developing along less ambitious lines.

An important expanding sector of the FSM's economy is tourism. However, this is confined to relatively few sites with little of the income generated spread through the economy. Illustrative is the increasing number of divers that visit Truk lagoon to see the remains of the Japanese fleet sunk during World War Two. Although developments in tourism are being encouraged in the FSM, there are limitations to the revenue that can be earned in this sector. Over-development will destroy the features that attract tourists. Given the relative inaccessibility of Micronesia compared with the majority of holiday destinations, it is likely that the emphasis of development will continue to focus on the appeal of specialised holidays such as diving.

Without the capital investment required to exploit its marine resources the FSM has only limited options on how to develop its economy. Elements of Compact funding are reserved for infrastructural development. This will be beneficial to the islanders and may encourage foreign investment, but there are serious doubts about the ability of the government to maintain its budgetary balance as Compact funds are reduced. Although the Compact agreement only allows for 15 years of funding, the United States security guarantee has a duration of 50 years. With the continuation of this relationship, the main emphasis within the FSM's external affairs cannot but continue to be on its dealings with the United States. However, this does not necessarily mean that the FSM can count on US trade and investment to support its economy. Moreover, the ongoing relationship with the United States may act as a deterrent to other potential traders and investors. For this reason, the Micronesian states are seeking to develop broader relations with other states. The Marshall Islands and the FSM are now both members of the South Pacific Forum, which helps to integrate them into the evolution of South Pacific regional trade and development.

The longer term security interests of the FSM thus hinge on its ability to establish itself as an actor independent of the United States. Present forecasts suggest that there is liable to be a critical period as Compact funding is reduced, unless this can be offset by increased foreign investment. If the argument that US funding has fostered economic dependency, and therefore undermined the FSM's security interests, is accepted, it would seem that the catharsis of emerging from US dominance is both necessary and overdue. An alternative view is that the position of dependency is now so entrenched that the FSM's security interests are best served by maintaining the best possible relationship with the United States, especially as the alternatives are at best uncertain and quite possibly deleterious.

THE REPUBLIC OF BELAU

Of the four districts of the TTPI, only Belau remains under Trusteeship. Belau is the smallest of the districts in both area and population. Following its rejection of the Micronesian Federation Constitution in 1978, Belau held its own Constitutional Convention. The resulting document has been at the centre of ongoing negotiations with the United States over the termination of the final Trusteeship.

Despite the overwhelming popular support for the Constitution in Belau, the United States has consistently argued that its terms conflict with those of the proposed Compact agreement. This refers, in particular, to the article of the Constitution banning the 'use, testing, storage or disposal of nuclear, toxic chemical, gas or biological weapons intended for use in warfare'.[27] Although it is the case that this provision has obstructed the passage of the Compact, this is not a reflection of a Belauan wish to reject the Compact. In seven Belauan plebiscites the Compact has been accepted by a majority vote. In the FSM and the Marshalls a majority vote was sufficient to ratify their Compacts. However, in Belau the majority acceptance of the Compact brought into question the details of US security policies under Free Association and their compatibility with the Belauan Constitution.

The US argues that the administration of its security guarantee to

Belau requires it to have full access to Belau with no restrictions on its nuclear-capable vessels. Any admission on behalf of the US military of the presence, or lack, of nuclear weaponry on its vessels would be in breach of its 'neither confirm nor deny' policy. Despite the expressed wishes of the Belauan people not to be defended by nuclear means, the United States has insisted that a two-tier system of defence is an unacceptable policy option. The provisions of the Compact are such that the US security guarantee could be enacted as long as this was not in conflict with the anti-nuclear elements of the Constitution. The significant sticking point in the negotiations has thus always been the difficulty of aligning the US interpretation of how it should implement its security guarantee with Belau's anti-nuclear legislation. A fundamental difference of opinion thereby emerged over what constituted an increase in security. For the Belauan pro-Constitutionalists, the nuclear element of US defence policies represented a threat rather than an enhancement of their security.

A simple majority vote was all that was required to show Belauan acceptance of the principle of Free Association. Problems arose when the United States insisted that it could not enact its security guarantee whilst the Belauan Constitution expressly forbade nuclear weapons inside Belauan jurisdiction. The US answer to this impasse was to call for an amendment of the Constitution to withdraw the anti-nuclear legislation, which would have required a vote of 75 per cent in a referendum specifically asking for the withdrawal of the anti-nuclear provisions. The US attitude was viewed by Belauans as an infringement of their right to determine the provisions of their own Constitution. It should be noted that this Constitution was being hailed as the first act of self-determination by Belauans for over 500 years. With this in mind, the argument for defending the Constitution gained support far beyond the anti-nuclear campaigners in Belau. It became nothing less than a matter of national pride, with it being argued that Belauans should decide how they were to be defended and that the imposition of outside views represented a challenge to the security of the new nation.

Throughout the TTPI there has long been an ambiguity about whose security interests were being promoted. In Belau this point has been central to the negotiation of the Compact. After numerous unsuccessful attempts to alter the Constitution it is clear that, whereas the Belauan people accept the principle of Free Association with the United States over any other future political status, they are not willing to compromise their freely determined Constitution to achieve it. Although the anti-nuclear aspects of the controversy are significant for a few committed campaigners on Belau, the main issue has become the principle of self-determination in the face of pressure from the United States.

Over the past decade there have been numerous interpretations of the difficulty in reaching a settlement between the Compact and the Constitution. A US government report argued in 1988 that the anti-nuclear factor was of concern to a minority of Belauans and had been distorted by anti-nuclear campaigners from outside Belau.[28] It is certainly the case that Belauan concerns about the provisions of the Compact extend beyond the nuclear issue. However, the members of the Belauan Constitutional Convention who formulated the document in the first place were specific in their wishes to preclude all things nuclear from Belau. They were also aware of the implications this would have on Compact negotiations. Some observers have suggested alternatively that the provisions were included as a ploy to increase US funding in subsequent negotiations. It is true that the later rounds of negotiations have brought Belau increased levels of funding, but the consistent resistance to amending the Constitution cannot be fully attributed to mercenary motives.

In addition to all these arguments, there was also concern in Belau over US plans to use up to one-third of the largest of Belau's islands for jungle training for US troops. This was seen as further evidence that it was US interests that were being promoted rather than those of the Belauans. Land ownership is a particularly contentious issue in Belau. Another provision of the Belauan Constitution precludes land ownership by non-Belauans. This has also been interpreted as meaning land cannot be used for activities in the interest of non-Belauans. The use of Belauan land for US troop-training is as ambiguous over whose interests are being served as the nuclear issue. Should Belauans feel more secure for having US troops on their territory? The US government argues that this is further evidence of their commitment to protect Belau. Yet some Belauans are concerned that the militarisation of the islands only increases the likelihood of conflict.[29]

Belauan experience of World War Two is remembered more vividly than in most territories. The debris of war can still be seen, with landing craft and other vehicles remaining after nearly 50 years. In addition to these physical reminders, there is the perception that the devastation caused was the result of a war between Japan and the United States. Belauans were only involved as casualties or bystanders, left to rebuild their ruined islands. Belau's situation is such that it is unlikely to be directly threatened other than as a consequence of a confrontation between other states. By allowing a military base, regardless of which power controls it, the Belauans would be open to being drawn into any conflict involving that power. Under these circumstances, the prospect of a military base being established on Belau is viewed as undermining rather than enhancing security.

Belau does not suffer the disadvantages of population dispersal or geographic remoteness to the same extent as the FSM or the Marshall Islands. The majority of Belau's population of about 15,000 lives on the capital island of Koror. This is not the largest in the chain but it is the administrative and trading centre. Fisheries and tourism are the main export earners. In comparison to the other former districts of the TTPI, Belau is relatively well placed to develop its economy. Despite the existence of conflicting political factions, there is a higher degree of national unity than, for example, between Truk and Yap in the FSM. As with the other districts, the lack of capital investment prevents the full exploitation of its fishing and sea-bed resources. However, its closer proximity to the Philippines does make Belau more accessible for trade and tourism. An area of Belau's coral reefs has been designated as a protected marine nature reserve and an increase in tourism is anticipated, based in part on prospective investment from Japan.

With a relatively small population and a number of foreign investors already interested in developing schemes, it would seem that Belau is the district of Micronesia with the greatest opportunity to prosper independent of US funding. However, there is a major stumbling block. Investment in the building of a major power plant on one of the islands, and the subsequent default on the loans taken out to pay for this scheme, has left Belau with a debt in excess of its Compact funding. This means that Belau is operating from a position of considerable disadvantage with an effectively bankrupt economy. There have been numerous investigations as to how Belau could have got into this position while under US Trusteeship, the most notable being a report published by the US General Accounting Office (GAO) in 1989.[30] With a responsibility under the Trusteeship Agreement to foster Belau's economic self-sufficiency, the United States appears to have presided over the ruination of its economy.

While the Belauan economy has undoubtedly suffered as a result of the power plant deal, it is debatable how much of the responsibility for this can be attributed to the United States. As the administrative authority the United States did have the power of veto over schemes that it felt were not financially sound. Yet, as the Belauan government was moving towards self-government, and the power plant deal did not come under the US jurisdiction on matters of defence, the scheme was, perhaps understandably, viewed as a domestic matter to be dealt with by the Belauan government. Indeed, had the United States acted to block the deal, it would almost certainly have been criticised for interfering in Belau's domestic affairs. Such an example shows the ambiguous nature of how security is defined. Apparently, the United States would act if the islands were threatened by military means, but it was prepared to stand by as Belau's economic security and ability to develop further was seriously harmed.

Suggestions have been made that there was a hidden agenda under Trusteeship to prevent Belau from achieving independence.[31] Certainly, the power plant issue meant that Compact funding became more attractive as a means to alleviate overseas debts. The whole period under Trusteeship could be said to demonstrate a growing dependency on US funding rather than a development of the Micronesian economies. At the same time, there is no firm evidence to suggest that this was the deliberate policy of the United States. A more likely explanation is that the *lack* of US policy to encourage constructive investment in Micronesia allowed the present situation to develop. The GAO report accused prominent Belauan politicians of bribery and corruption in relation to the power plant deal. Conspiracy theorists could and do include these factors as further evidence of US involvement in the destabilisation of the Belauan government, but again there is a lack of evidence to implicate the US government in direct involvement in this corruption.

Since the GAO investigation, the former President of Belau, Lazarus Salii, has committed suicide. This has allowed both Belauans and the United States to acknowledge that there was corruption under the Salii administration and to pin the blame for Belau's position on to the discredited former President. This is convenient for both parties in the context of ongoing Compact negotiations and opens the way for fresh initiatives. However, the fundamental conflict between the terms of the proposed Compact and the Belauan Constitution remains. Despite this, the resolution of Belau's future status does lately seem to be of less immediate concern to both parties.

One of the main reasons the United States had for assuring itself a full range of military options in Belau was the need for alternative bases in the western Pacific in the event of a withdrawal from the Philippines. Although this withdrawal has now come about, the international strategic map has been redrawn with the collapse of the Soviet Union. While the United States will still wish to maintain a strategic denial policy in Micronesia, there is a less pressing need for forward and supply bases in the region. Guam remains as a major air and naval base in the Mariana chain, with the potential for further military developments existing on Tinian and Saipan. The incompatibility between US security policies and the Belauan Constitution still remains to be resolved, but with there being no imminent plans to use Belau as a military base the ratification of the Compact agreement has a lower priority on the US political agenda.

Similarly, the Belauan government appears to be in no more of a rush to resolve the current impasse. Since the Marshall Islands and the FSM entered into their Compacts, it has become apparent that Compact funding does not compare as favourably with the funding received under Trusteeship as had been anticipated. Several of the governments' budget headings, such as education, had been eligible for US Federal grants under Trusteeship. These have been withdrawn under Free Association. In short, the difficulties that face the Micronesian territories in developing their economies have become more obvious with the gradual reduction of Compact funding and the lack of foreign investment to replace these funds. Having viewed the experiences of the other districts, Belau can see that there may be advantages to continuing with the relative security of Trusteeship funding.

CONCLUSION

In looking at Micronesian security interests it can be seen that these states face a range of problems. Their geographic remoteness mitigates against their full integration into the world trading system. Their lack of investment capital also prevents them from realising the full potential of their marine resources. The dispersal of populations, other than in Belau, further works against economic development. With the transition from the Trusteeship system, these states now face the challenge of surviving without long-term US funding, even though the relationship with the United States continues in a modified form under Free Association. Yet the future of Micronesia seems more likely to depend on developing links with other states, particularly in the Pacific region. US involvement in the islands has been primarily concerned with securing US military interests rather than developing the islands' economies and there are few indications at present that US investment will increase significantly in the near future. Given too that the US security guarantee under Free Association extends well into the next century and with a minimal prospect anyway of military threats to the islands, attention will continue to focus more and more on aspects of economic security.

NOTES

1. The spelling of Belau is the cause of some confusion. Under US administration the territory is referred to as Palau in US government reports and in UN documents. Although the Palau spelling continues to be used by many outside of the Republic, the Belau version is the one promoted by the islanders and, as such, has been used throughout this article except in quotations and references.

2. Micronesia covers roughly three million square miles, consists of over 2,000 islands and has a population of about 150,000.

3. United Nations Trusteeship Agreement 1947, cited in D.F. McHenry, *Micronesia: Trust Betrayed, Altruism vs Self Interest in American Foreign Policy* (New York 1975).

4. United Nations Charter: Article 76.

5. R.H. Smith and M.C. Pugh, 'Micronesian Trust Territories – Imperialism Continues?', *Pacific Review*, 4, 1 (1991), 36–44.

6. The State Department wished to avoid the United States being in breach of the provisions of the Atlantic Charter and the Cairo Declaration of 1941 which specifically renounced any US intention of territorial expansion at the end of World War Two.

7. C. Lutz, 'The Compact of Free Association, Micronesian Non-independence, and US Policy', *Bulletin of Concerned Asian Scholars*, 18, 2 (1986), 21–7.

8. P.B. Haigwood, 'Japan and the Mandates', in W.R. Louis (ed.), *National Security and International Trusteeship in the Pacific* (Annapolis, 1972).

9. Guam has been an 'unincorporated territory' of the United States since the Spanish/ American war of 1898. Guamanians hold US citizenship but are disallowed from voting in US Presidential elections. There is a non-voting Guamanian member of the US House of Representatives.

10. A. Ranney and H.R. Pennimann, *Democracy in the Islands: The Micronesian Plebiscites of 1983* (Washington DC, 1985), 17.

11. A common feature of political analyses of Micronesia is the tendency to see Micronesians as passive actors or victims. A useful alternative to this view can be found in David Hanlon, 'Micronesia: Writing and Rewriting the Histories of a Non-entity', *Pacific Studies*, 12, 2 (1989), 1–21.

12. *Pacific Women Speak* (Oxford, 1987), 23.

13. *Compilation of Agreements between the Government of the United States and the Marshall Islands* (Washington DC, 1987).

14. G. Alcalay, 'The Bravo Cover-up', *Covert Action Information Bulletin*, 29 (1988), 15–17.

15. R.C. Kiste, *The Bikinians*, (Menlo Park, Calif., 1974).

16. J. Weisgall, 'The Nuclear Nomads of Bikini', *Foreign Policy*, 39 (1980), 76–84.

17. D. Robie, 'Dangerous Playground', *Pacific Islands Monthly*, May 1990, 10–13.

18. T.R. Hughes, 'Marshall Islands', *Asia Pacific Review 1991/92*, 156.

19. 'Nuclear Waste: Marshalls as a Dump Site?', *Pacific News Bulletin*, 3, 1 (Feb./Mar. 1988), 5.

20. P. Brown, 'Hell Fire in the Pacific', *The Guardian*, 27 July 1990, 21.

21. 'Marshalls: Garbage, Pressure and Profits', *Pacific News Bulletin*, 4, 2 (Feb. 1989), 6.

22. 'Trusteeship Agreement for three entities of Trust Territory of Pacific Islands terminated', *UN Chronicle*, 28, 1 (1991), 72.

23. Bank of Hawaii report, cited in T.R. Hughes, 'Federated States of Micronesia', *Asia Pacific Review 1991/92*, 146.

24. N. Mellor, *Constitutionalism in Micronesia* (Honolulu, 1985).

25. *Report of the UN Visiting Mission to observe the Referendum in the Trust Territory of the Pacific Islands, 1978* (UN Doc. T/1795, 1979).

26. Hughes, 'Federated States', 145.

27. Belauan Constitution, Art. 2, S. 3.

28. J.D. Berg, *The Political Future of Palau and Nuclear Issues: Myth and Reality* (Washington DC, 1988).

29. *Pacific Women Speak*, 24.
30. US General Accounting Office, *US Trust Territory: Issues Associated with Palau's Transition to Self-Government* (Washington DC, 1989).
31. Women Working for a Nuclear Free and Independent Pacific, *WWNFIP Bulletin*, 23 (Summer 1991), 7.

Climatic Change: A New Security Challenge for the Atoll States of the South Pacific

JOHN CONNELL

No environmental issue has captured public and private imaginations throughout the world in the past few years more than climatic change: global warming and the 'Greenhouse Effect' (GE). Indeed, perhaps no environmental issue has ever stimulated such global interest and spawned such a variety of popular and academic accounts of future scenarios. Scientific studies have increasingly begun to draw important and consistent conclusions about future trends, and point to regions where the GE will cause the most severe problems. This article examines some of these trends in the context of the four atoll states in the South Pacific where the GE is most likely to cause substantial social, economic and political problems, where such problems may begin to emerge around the start of the next century, and where security considerations consequently ensue. Indeed, the security issues that most concern island states are not of the traditional military kind, but are principally those that relate to economic vulnerability, the environment and domestic social and political stability. The GE poses a threat to all of these.

For most coastal dwellers there will be the option of retreating inland to higher ground, if and when the sea level rises, but the most extreme situation will be faced by those island states occupying low coral islands on atolls where high land does not exist: Kiribati, the Marshall Islands, Tokelau and Tuvalu. This paper does not consider, in any detail, the issues that affect atolls which are part of larger multi-island states that include high islands, such as the Federated States of Micronesia (FSM), French Polynesia, or the Cook Islands. This is, firstly, because it may be possible to divert resources from larger islands with stronger economies to provide special funds and strategies for atoll islands, and, secondly, because the existence of high islands or much larger land masses such as in Papua New Guinea and the Solomon Islands provide atoll dwellers with migration options within states. In most cases these options have

John Connell is Senior Lecturer in Geography at the University of Sydney in Australia.

already been taken in part.[1] However, climatic warming will pose problems even for these larger states, setting new tasks of environmental management and planning.

The four atoll states are quite different from each other in language, culture and political organisation. Tuvalu and Tokelau are part of Polynesia; the Marshall Islands and Kiribati are in Micronesia. The state of Tuvalu consists of nine coral atolls and reef islands with a total land area of no more than 24 square kilometres, yet is spread over 590 kilometres. Kiribati has 20 populated atolls (including Banaba) and a land area of 700 square kilometres, but more than half of this is on Christmas Island (Kiritimati), some 3,500 kilometres away from Tarawa, the national capital. The Marshall Islands has 24 populated atolls, but the majority of the population live in the capital, Majuro, or on Ebeye, close to the American missile range on Kwajalein atoll. Tokelau consists of just three populated atolls; its population is smaller and population density significantly less than in the other three states largely because of substantial migration to New Zealand where a majority of Tokelauans now live. Tuvalu became independent in 1978 and Kiribati in 1979. The Marshall Islands has a considerable degree of autonomy having achieved independence in association with the USA in 1986. Tokelau remains a New Zealand territory and Tokelauans are citizens of New Zealand.

DEVELOPMENT PROBLEMS IN ATOLL STATES

> Coral reefs with their low sandy islets provide the most limited range of resources for human existence and the most tenuous of habitats for man in the Pacific . . . The soil is infertile, lacking humus, and fresh ground water is very limited . . . Maintaining a livelihood is a considerable task for man.[2]

Atoll life was always far from that portrayed in images of the supposedly idyllic Pacific. In many island groups hazard, hunger and disease punctuated periods of well-being and warfare; abortion and infanticide also served to reduce population numbers. Population growth was carefully controlled and wars in pursuit of both land and power were common, especially in Kiribati, the Marshall Islands and Tokelau. Subsistence production was often difficult, natural hazards posed intermittent problems to survival, and adequate management of resources was not easily achieved without wide-ranging regulatory practices.[3]

Atolls vary enormously in size, both in land and lagoon areas, and in rainfall, and hence so do their flora and fauna, their ability to support human populations and, most recently, their ability to provide some form of diversified development. Some atolls are small, arid, drought-prone, and overpopulated, as in the central Gilbert Islands chain. Even where such conditions do not occur, the diversity of resources is limited and natural hazards are usually, but not always, more severe in their impacts; recurrent hazards of droughts, hurricanes and tsunamis have had an important demographic and cultural effect within atoll states. In past times, many atolls have been depopulated and repopulated, following hazards and migration movements of various kinds.[4] In recent times Osborne has provided a vivid description of the dying phases of the small community on Merir atoll, Belau: 'the island is dying . . . the women are too old to cultivate taro in any quantity and the men cannot keep the coconut groves clear'.[5] Five years later, the island was depopulated with the few survivors moving to the mainland of Belau, an option open to atoll dwellers in some form of political liaison with larger islands and states. More generally, atoll populations have often developed cultural ties with other atolls so that, during periods of population–resource imbalance, their proximity to each other enabled economic exchange, personnel mobility and, on the negative side, warfare and raiding.[6] Thus atolls were usually part of coral clusters or complexes, though this was less likely to be true on the larger Kiribati atolls.

Beyond these inherent constraints to subsistence production, the modern era has increasingly demonstrated the tyrannies of distance that have restricted contemporary development. Atolls are tiny, with limited resources, often distant from each other and remote from more substantial land masses. Atoll states consequently face a host of development problems, often in more accentuated form than in other island micro-states; these include limited skills, small domestic market size, high costs of imports and exports, restricted diversity of exports and substantial administrative costs.[7] The consequence has usually been large trade deficits, balance of payments problems and considerable dependence on foreign aid and technical assistance. For example, in 1984 exports from Tuvalu were valued at only A\$220,000 whilst imports cost A\$4,050,000; the same figures for the Marshall Islands in 1988 were US\$2.7 million and US\$42.7 million respectively. In Kiribati in 1989 the figures were A\$6.4 million and A\$28.6 million, and in Tokelau in 1984 A\$24,000 and A\$267,000 respectively. In each case the discrepancy has since worsened. Atoll states have thus moved rapidly into situations of extreme dependence on the outside world, primarily for aid, concessional trade, investment and also migration opportunities.

At a very early stage in colonial history these resource-poor islands became quite significantly dependent on the outside world for consumer goods, including foodstuffs. By the 1890s for both Kiribati and Tuvalu, pacification, population growth and changing aspirations had resulted in overseas labour migration being described as 'the only alternative to starvation'[8] in the sense that population and domestic resources were already recognised to be in some degree of imbalance. Indeed, it has been in Kiribati and Tuvalu that the Malthusian spectre has been sighted most frequently in the South Pacific; mid-nineteenth century Tuvaluans 'were genuine Malthusians. They feared that unless the population was kept down they would not have sufficient food'.[9] A century later, 'few countries of the South Pacific serve to remind one so well of the so-called "Malthusian dilemma" as the two countries under consideration with their rapidly expanding population pressing against a limited and non-expanding stock of natural resources'.[10] The situation was and is marginally better in the less densely populated Marshall Islands and Tokelau.

In every case modern health facilities and medicines have resulted in a rapid natural increase of population in most atoll societies; infants are more likely to survive, and diseases are less likely to be fatal, while modern family planning is largely absent. Even during the early 1940s, at a time when the resettlement of Gilbertese islanders in the Phoenix Islands appeared successful, its instigator, H.E. Maude, noted that 'colonization measures are in fact palliatives only and for more permanent means of population control we must look elsewhere. The ultimate hope for the Gilbertese people probably lies in drastic population control'.[11] For a time, in the late 1960s, Kiribati appeared to have established a successful family planning scheme, but it was shortlived. Much the same was true of Tuvalu. The Marshall Islands now has one of the fastest growing populations of any state in the world at around four per cent per annum; widespread adoption has reduced the perceived need for family planning. Kiribati and Tuvalu are not far behind, though Tokelau has exported much of its fertility to New Zealand. As atoll populations increase, so too of course does the problem of satisfying basic needs (for example, housing, water and food) from local resources.

Throughout the atoll states, and atolls elsewhere, the limited agricultural base of the traditional economy has further declined in colonial and post-colonial times. The most dramatic decline has been in the dominant base of that economy, the taro pits that were the basis of intensive agricultural production systems. In urban areas, notably in Majuro, none or very few are now left. Artisanal fisheries have experienced a similar but less dramatic transition following the depletion of in-shore and lagoon species, which thereby indirectly contributed to the necessity for more labour-intensive fishing practices. In every case there appears to have been a decline in local production per capita, paralleled by a transition to imported food, especially rice, which has followed changing tastes, preferences, convenience and so on. This transition has been so substantial that in each state imported foods and drinks now constitute about 35 per cent of all imports by value – a substantial drain on domestic resources. This is most extreme in the Marshall Islands, where as much as 75 per cent of all food consumed in the country is imported, 44 per cent of the total value of imports is food, malnutrition is not uncommon, and Vitamin A deficiency has reached epidemic proportions.[12]

Limited subsistence agricultural production has been dramatically emphasised since the nineteenth century by the 'coconut overlay'[13] that has transformed the economy of atolls by enabling participation, however limited, in the international economy through copra production and sales. This sole historic domestic source of income, copra production, has largely continued into the present, although in recent years production has declined as global prices have fallen. Nonetheless, even on the more urbanised islands, copra is still produced because of its capacity for directly generating some cash income. However, the relative significance of copra incomes for household and national incomes has declined, especially in the post-war years, as atoll dwellers have discovered that they have a one-crop economy and that this single crop suffers from a falling price on the world market. Necessary activities, such as coconut replanting, are often postponed indefinitely, with the result that copra production offers an increasingly fragile basis for the construction of a modern economy.

Though fish and other marine resources have often been domestically marketed, albeit on a very small scale, marine resources have rarely been exported from the atoll states. In recent years there has been some expansion of domestic fishing fleets in the South Pacific states, often through joint venture operations, and fish have become a growing source of national income, principally in Kiribati and Tuvalu. Much more important has been the leasing of fisheries waters for the fleets of overseas fishing vessels. Through various bilateral and multilateral agreements fisheries leases now represent a major source of domestic income for the atoll states, though substantially less than the value of those fisheries. However, even the combination of fisheries and copra incomes does not provide a high income for the atoll states, most of whose national incomes are now externally generated in a non-trade manner.

All atoll states are nevertheless part of the international economy, and the aspirations of atoll people are generally those of people elsewhere, including improved services (health, education), remunerative employment opportunities, and consumer goods (imported food, clothes, outboard motors, motorbikes and so on), although wants are somewhat less than those of occupants of larger islands where imported goods are more familiar. Everywhere, real and perceived differences between places in life-styles, economic opportunities and the range of available services and facilities have increased, especially since the 1950s. It is a truism that new aspirations can be less easily satisfied in atoll environments; it is equally a truism that, as these aspirations increase, the degree to which they can be satisfied on atolls falls.

THE MIGRATION OPTION

The combination of higher post-war rates of population increase, the growing desire for consumer goods, the location of higher education facilities and hospitals either on one central atoll or on a high island, and the concentration of formal sector employment there has, in many cases, resulted in emigration from atolls, especially where there is a central high island.[14] Although the populations of many, perhaps most, atolls are growing at a slower rate than that of the atoll states as a whole, few are actually losing population, and then only the smallest atolls. On small atolls especially, there are very few prospects of formal sector employment; as population and education levels increase, and demand for employment also increases, this is further emphasised. The extent of emigration, especially in youthful age groups, is often substantial as little local wage employment is available and almost all of this is in the public sector. In each of these states the private sector, beyond stores, is conspicuous by its absence. In every case too public sector employment rapidly expanded in the 1970s as urbanisation proceeded. In Tokelau the rapidity of this expansion caused widespread social changes, challenged traditional activities and also disrupted the fiction of egalitarianism as, by 1981 on Fakaofo, public service salaries accounted for 82 per cent of all cash income.[15]

Many atolls are remote from capitals, hence the costs of transportation (either of commodities or medical services) have rapidly increased as oil prices have increased, and transport services have declined substantially in some areas. Migration becomes a cheaper alternative than remaining. When both population and wants have grown together in environments where local production possibilities are limited, the export of labour has become an important means of meeting some basic subsistence requirements, especially food. For example, by 1971, 'the people of Butaritari and Makin [two atolls in northern Kiribati] [were] becoming increasingly dependent on remittances to pay their taxes and their children's school fees, to buy corned beef and rice for feasts, and to purchase even moderately expensive items at the store ... The export of labour [had] become the principal means of *maintaining* the local standard of living'.[16] Migration has thus increasingly become a quest for essentials rather than luxuries.

While emigration may solve the immediate population and welfare problems of some small, densely populated atolls, it may also increase the problems of destination areas in the atoll states. Some of the most difficult and intractable development problems in island micro-states are experienced in the atoll states. Since aspirations to migration are much the same in these countries, and infrastructure (principally for health and education) is often highly centralised, migration has been concentrated in a very limited number of areas. The most extreme examples of this are the Marshall Islands and Kiribati. Tokelau has no 'centre' and much of the administration is actually undertaken from the Office for Tokelau Affairs in Apia, Western Samoa. In the Marshall Islands, the 1988 census recorded a total population of 43,335, of whom 19,695 were on Majuro (at a density of 2,188 persons per square kilometre); less than 36 per cent of the population were on 'rural' atolls. In Kiribati, the 1985 census recorded a total population of 63,883, of whom 21,392 (33 per cent) were on South Tarawa at an average density of 1,357 persons per square kilometre. The 1991 census of Tuvalu recorded a population of 9,043, of whom 3,840 were on Funafuti, at a density of 1,630 per square kilometre. Funafuti's population had almost doubled between 1979 and 1992. A centralised administration has spawned the centralisation of the service sector, hence most formal sector employment is concentrated in the centre. In Tuvalu, 78 per cent of all those employed in the cash economy in 1983 were in Funafuti; in Kiribati 60 per cent in 1985 were in South Tarawa. The figure for the Marshall Islands (for the two centres) is even higher than that for Tuvalu. In each case these populations have grown between the last two census dates, indicating the continued concentration of both the population and contemporary economic activity. Since social services, the 'bright lights', and a significant proportion of relatives are also at the centre, there are powerful attractions to rural–urban migration. This centralisation may be compounded by 'urban bias', where financial and technical resources, aid projects and development bank loans are also overwhelmingly concentrated in the urban area.

This urban concentration has created problems. Many of these problems are no different from those of much larger urban centres elsewhere in the developing world: overcrowding in poor housing conditions with attendant health risks, pollution (to the extent that the lagoon in South Tarawa is a potential health risk and was one cause of a cholera outbreak in 1977), unemployment (even if disguised by sharing in extended families), the growth of squatter settlements, worsened nutrition (as cash incomes are often inadequate to purchase diets based on imported foods), and sometimes very high crime rates and social disorganisation. Since migrants are not always successful in towns they may be unable, or unwilling, to contribute significantly to the needs of their rural kin. Two related problems have also emerged: the relative depopulation and/or economic decline of the smaller, remote atolls and overurbanisation on the principal atoll. In the absence of overseas migration from atoll states, development prospects are even more difficult. For Tokelau, migration to New Zealand is a right since Tokelau islanders are New Zealand citizens, with the result that in terms of ethnicity, a slight majority of Tokelau islanders now live in New Zealand. As has been noted,

> the idea of permanent emigration, involving a severance of many ties with the home island and of seeking one's fortune elsewhere, is well established in Tokelau life and thought. For the past 70 years or so it appears to have been accepted . . . that some of nearly every group of siblings must *tahe* ('emigrate') simply because the local resources are seen as insufficient.[17]

Migration from the Marshall Islands (and from the Federated States of Micronesia) to the USA is possible under the terms of the Compact of Free Association; indeed the island states were anxious to ensure that such a clause be included in the Compact. There are currently few Micronesians in the United States, but this is already changing rapidly, with a steady movement towards Guam[18] and a smaller movement to Hawaii and the US mainland. For the former British colonies of Tuvalu and Kiribati, only temporary labour migration to Nauru is possible at the moment, and this is currently constrained by fixed employment opportunities there and by the eventual closure of the phosphate mine, perhaps by the end of the century. Both countries have sought resettlement opportunities overseas, as well as new overseas employment by training seamen; the Marshall Islands began to send seamen overseas in mid-1989 and Tuvalu has formally located a handful of workers in New Zealand under existing short-term schemes. However, in the immediate future, only the Marshall Islands has satisfactory long-term overseas migration (or resettlement) opportunities; for Kiribati and Tuvalu opportunities are actually declining.

The significance of international migration for Kiribati and Tuvalu is apparent not only in the flow of remittances but also in changing local attitudes to international migration. In pre-war years the colonial administration decentralised part of the population of the more densely populated Gilbert Islands to the Phoenix Islands group to the east. At much the same time groups of villagers from Vaitupu in Tuvalu purchased land in Fiji for their own private resettlement. Local and colonial perceptions of population density and domestic development prospects were both quite similar. For various reasons settlement of the Phoenix Islands was unsuccessful and the settlers were again transplanted, this time to the then British colony of the Solomon Islands, where they and their descendants remain. In Kiribati such settlers are now viewed quite differently from in the past:

> In earlier days they were the unfortunate ones who did not have sufficient land. Now our values have changed. Settling overseas beyond the oceans of our islands is something to be sought after. Why? Because our population is still growing. So now, many consider them, the resettled ones, the fortunate ones and they consider us to be the unfortunate ones.[19]

In short, permanent international migration is increasingly viewed by many, though certainly not by all, as a key solution to many development problems.

Toleration and encouragement of international migration in the Pacific is a function of its impact on the reduction of population pressures on scarce resources, attitudes to individual freedom of movement and, above all, the substantial flow of remittances that follows international migration. The flows of remittances to Kiribati and Tuvalu and, to a rather lesser extent, Tokelau are large and increasingly crucial to household and national welfare. Migration and remittances have tended to create an appetite for the import of consumer goods, and hence expensive imports, which has driven up wages. The conservative use of remittances partially reflects the lack of productive investment opportunities. Although there are widespread assumptions that remittances emphasise dependency and produce rural stagnation, their contribution to the generation of foreign exchange earnings and employment, especially in the service sector, in small islands where there are few other income-earning opportunities, ensures that there are many exceptions to this generalisation. Migration is often linked or sponsored, with households or extended kinship units planning for and encouraging the migration of particular individuals, to the extent that in the smallest states, such as Tokelau and Tuvalu, the growing perception of the household returns to be gained from migration has led to increasing fertility rates.[20] Marcus has pointed to the emergence of a new institution, the 'transnational corporation of kin', allowing kin groups to colonise and exploit economic opportunities across a wide range of environments.[21] Such behaviour is most apparent where domestic sources of income are least adequate. In all South Pacific states, including the atoll states, there have been no attempts to restrict international migration; rather, there have been energetic attempts to gain greater concessionary migration opportunities overseas.

It is scarcely surprising, then, that individual migrants and households and also many observers have viewed the future of the atoll states in terms of increased levels of international migration. Recent reviews of the possibilities for economic growth in the atoll states and other larger, less remote and better endowed countries in the South Pacific concluded that sustained increases in incomes would essentially only be possible through greater dependence on migration, especially in Kiribati and Tuvalu.[22] Specifically contrasting Tuvalu with Tokelau, where of course Tokelauans can move freely as citizens to New Zealand, Bertram concluded:

> For Tuvalu, where the British and the local elite together managed to push through a transition to formal independence, the key role for the new state will now be to recruit a new patron and to seek out new opportunities for Tuvaluan labour and capital to penetrate the rest of the world. Closed country models, whether in the political or economic realm, simply do not fit the Pacific of the 1980s.[23]

Denied permanent overseas migration opportunities, unlike almost all other states in Micronesia and Polynesia, Kiribati and Tuvalu have hitherto found opportunities in Nauru and on foreign ships. A future in which these decline or even disappear would pose immense problems, not only in rehabilitating and accommodating migrant workers but in coping at home without their remittances.

Alongside the contribution of remittances, further substantial financial support for the national incomes of atoll states comes from overseas aid, welfare payments, subsidies and compensation payments of different kinds. So substantial are aid funds that the atoll states of Kiribati, Tuvalu and Tokelau, alongside Niue and the Cook Islands, have been conceptualised as MIRAB states, where migrant remittances and aid are the most important bases of the economy and, through these flows, a government bureaucracy has become the principal source of wage and salary employment.[24] As for the Marshall Islands, direct external (US) support for the economy is even more substantial. Aid dependence has also taken some unusual forms. In 1987 Tuvalu established an aid Trust Fund of A$27 million composed of direct cash donations from Tuvalu's traditional aid donors. This fund is managed by a subsidiary of the Australian bank, Westpac, and is intended to enable Tuvalu to be able to live off the annual interest, thus dispensing with conventional annual aid delivery. The money will be invested in a low-risk spread of assets, including fixed-interest funds, equities and property. The fund should enable Tuvalu to clear its recurrent deficit and contribute to long-term financial viability by earning an annual interest almost that of current aid receipts.[25] The donors will have some ability to monitor the effectiveness of this fund in contributing to national development. In some respects the Trust Fund was based on the nearby success of the Revenue Equalisation Reserve Fund (RERF), derived from historic phosphate revenue in Kiribati. This fund is managed by a London merchant bank, supervised by a Kiribati committee chaired by the Finance Minister.[26] In 1989 Kiribati received external aid of A$21.9 million (vastly in excess of its exports) and received A$6 million from the RERF; a further $A512,000 was generated from the lease of a tracking station on Christmas Island. Tokelau received New Zealand aid for the same year to the value of A$5.6 million, and, in 1985, Tuvalu received aid of A$4.6 million. The Marshall Islands received a vastly greater sum than all of these from the United States alone: around A$90 million. Indeed, only a very small proportion of the national income of atoll states is generated within those countries, mainly through commodity exports, mainly copra, fish and also postage stamps, but even this income is often dependent on concessionary external support. That said, the concessionary trade agreements of the South Pacific Area Regional Trade and Economic Cooperation Agreement (SPARTECA) have proved of no use to countries that manufacture little, and none of the atoll states has any manufactured exports.

In sum, atolls and atoll states have moved a very long way from any semblance of self-reliance and, in doing so, have gone well beyond the traditional support of local coral clusters to dependence on much more distant nations.

THE IMPACT OF CLIMATIC CHANGE

Previous sections have examined the difficulties of development in atolls and atoll states and noted how, over time, there has been increasing recourse to the option of migration as the preferred individual and household solution to the challenge of development, whilst the states themselves have tended to become more dependent on overseas aid. Rising sea-levels can only worsen, in a number of ways, the problems of achieving development in atoll states. It is apparent that there will be climatic changes in terms of differences in rainfall and storm frequency and rises in air and sea temperatures, that coastal erosion will increase as sea-level rise accelerates beyond the upward growth of corals, and that this erosion will probably be accentuated by the greater frequency of storms. Slowly but inexorably, there will be critical environmental changes but of an unknown rate and dimension.[27]

The basic effect of a rise in sea level is for low-lying lands to be inundated and for coasts to erode. A gradual rise of mean sea level will progressively lift the zone of flooding and increase the impact of storm waves, so eroding areas hitherto considered safe. Human responses will vary, depending on the value of the coastal land under attack and the resources available to provide protective measures. In states where resources are very limited and small populations thinly spread, the provision of expensive engineering works will not be a commonly available option.[28]

Island ecology, in terms of the capacity to support human habitation, is closely tied to the existence of a permanent ground water system. Islands above a certain size, about 1.5 ha, contain a permanent lens of fresh water surrounded by salt water. The volume of the lens is roughly proportional to the surface area of the atoll, hence a decline in the surface area of an atoll would have a disproportionate impact on the volume of the lens. During droughts, water-table levels fall and the ground water may become brackish. Environmental stress is manifested by trees losing leaves, not fruiting and even dying. In Kiribati, where ground water is the main source of drinking water on most islands, populations have already been forced to migrate temporarily to areas with higher rainfall. In fact, the most severe threat to permanent water supplies is not from climatic factors directly, but rather from marine processes that cause coastal erosion and increase the frequency of storm overwash.

Increased ground water salinity will reduce its potability which for most atolls is currently of considerable significance. It would also reduce the productivity of agriculture, since no plant species will gain from increased salinity. In drought conditions access to ground water on atolls is crucial, although on some atolls with reasonably high rainfall construction of better cisterns may enable the use of ground water to be minimised or even ended. If increased salinity is combined with any long-term decline in rainfall, as is possible in some areas, the results will be even more serious, since the cost of water purification and desalination is extremely high. If and when ground water becomes no longer potable, human habitation will be effectively impossible, as occurred on the Phoenix Island group (Kiribati) in the 1960s. Fresh water is most scarce after cyclones or tidal waves have swept over the atoll, salting soils and wells, a situation which is likely to increase under GE conditions.

Erosion will reduce the areas of land and, where there is minimal elevation, such losses may eventually be extremely severe and increase the swampiness and salinity of areas that do still remain above sea level. Areas immediately at risk will be those that have previously been reclaimed from the sea, including parts of Kiribati and the Marshall Islands now used for urban housing. This loss of land will directly affect agriculture, housing, roads and airstrips in these areas. Land losses will inevitably lead to a decline in agricultural production, increased competition for scarce land, and a related decline in handicraft materials (such as wood and pandanus) and firewood, which is already in extremely short supply in urban areas such as Tarawa. Such changes will further threaten the already limited subsistence base of the atoll states and introduce new environmental problems. Erosion of fringing reefs may seriously disturb their ecology and reduce the distinctiveness of lagoon ecology as lagoons increasingly become indistinguishable from the surrounding ocean. Mangrove habitats may also be damaged. This would reduce the artisanal fishing potential of many areas, especially where large lagoons currently provide fisheries diversity.

The GE is likely therefore to lead to a substantial decline in agricultural production, a possible decline in fisheries production, and a loss of vital water, timber and firewood resources, thus reducing the potential of the few areas in which island states currently demonstrate a degree of self-reliance. These effects will occur alongside continued rapid population growth and hence an increase in population pressure on resources, further encouraging rural–urban migration in search of the 'fast money' of wages and salaries rather than the increased unpredictability of agricultural and fisheries incomes.

Much of what is currently known about the impact of the GE is derived from conjecture and speculation, since the order of magnitude of future physical events cannot be determined and there is no real precedent for what is likely to follow. Though the post-glacial marine transgression that ended around 6,000 years ago must have had a similar effect, it occurred in a vastly different social and economic context, leaving few records of its human impact. The causes and consequences of the GE are complex and interrelated, involving changing natural processes and necessitating a variety of human adaptations to those changes; it is effectively an uncontrolled experiment on a global scale. Whatever the precise outcome, it is nonetheless apparent that the GE offers nothing positive to tropical island states and, because all their land is low-lying, poses grave potential dangers to atoll states.

THE CHALLENGE TO DEVELOPMENT AND SECURITY

There are alternatives to the prevailing trends of population migration, growing aid dependency, declining exports and overurbanisation in the South Pacific atoll states, but the GE will make them exceptionally difficult to realise. Only in Kiribati has a series of policy choices evolved in an attempt to achieve more balanced development, including, in the long term, improved rural education (including traditional and practical skills), increased copra prices (by subsidy), the development and expansion of district centres (involving decentralisation of government), and perhaps the resettlement of the distant and sparsely settled Line Islands. In each of the other atoll states there has been a focus on improved fisheries and agriculture, to increase self-reliance, but success has been minimal; popular attitudes have moved away from agriculture and marketing infrastructure is minimal. Development plans in each of the states have thus been exceptionally difficult to translate into practice.

It is improbable that the atoll states can ever achieve a significant degree of self-reliance (unless they discover new sources of mineral wealth); yet they are capable of moving away from their present massive dependence on migration, aid and trade. The elements of such a policy redirection are clear: agricultural development policies that stress diversification and food crop production (while simultaneously encouraging the extension of new coconut varieties and replanting schemes to ensure some necessary cash income); land tenure reform and the taxation of unused agricultural land; increasing concentration on the exploitation and development of the marine resources that are the only obvious base of both export growth and improved nutrition; transport and energy policies that move away from the use of non-renewable resources; job decentralisation; improved infrastructure (especially wharfs and aid posts); and increased emphasis on family planning. Self-reliance entails a more selective approach to external influences of all kinds. However, there is no denying that the necessary steps are extremely demanding, fly in the face of the development trends of the post-war decades, demand stable political authority in exceptionally 'soft' states and are therefore for all these reasons inherently unlikely to occur. Many have been unsuccessfully entrenched in advisory reports and development plans for years. They are not likely to occur just because of the influence of the GE.

In most atoll states, especially those in the South Pacific, movement toward the self-sufficiency that a reduction of aid and remittances implies would undoubtedly be difficult and painful, especially for the young. In most places aspirations are firmly directed towards the acquisition of modern goods and, as has been argued for the small island of Rotuma, 'with the prestige given to "foreign" goods, it is doubtful, therefore that Rotumans would *want* to be self-sufficient, even if that were a possibility'.[29] In other small islands the same kind of situation exists; in Tikopia it has been suggested that 'from such a level of dependence on imported goods it becomes difficult to retreat without unease and a sense of deprivation'.[30] In Ponape, too, villagers are not interested in adequate subsistence, nor even 'the right to subsistence', but rather they desire 'continued and increased access to the goods and prestige provided by employment'.[31] While these statements refer specifically to small islands rather than atolls, such attitudes are apparent in most atolls and emphasise the reality of relative deprivation. Policy presciptions that focus on self-reliance, rather than on interdependence, are therefore unlikely to be taken for several reasons: the constraints of more than lingering demands for the prestige associated with modernisation and Westernisation, the difficulties attached to establishing rural projects (which are rarely prestigious), and the fact that concerted comprehensive policy formation in loosely structured, democratic states is difficult to achieve.[32]

This last point is important. Present socio-political systems have limited capacity and inadequate will to control global events such as the unique Greenhouse 'experiment'. Meyer-Abich, in a paper with the suggestive title 'Chalk on the White Wall – On the Transformation of Climatological Facts into Political Facts', has argued that there are three options for response – prevention, compensation and adaptation – but concluded that, from a political perspective, prevention and compensation are much less practical than adaptation. Adaptation allows the least action in the present and defers expenses into the future.

In addition, adaptation does not require long-term international cooperation or agreement on long-range goals. If adaptation is the most rational political option, the climate problem tends to fade ('Chalk on the White Wall') compared to the already extremely serious and immediate social and economic problems confronting developing countries.[33] As indicated, such problems include rising populations, environmental problems including sewage and garbage disposal, pollution and over-use of underground water supplies, the consumption of energy and pressures on housing space. Infrastructure is already stretched to its limit. Thus climate-oriented policies to cope with climatic change tend to become part of development policies in general, and are unlikely to be prominent amongst them.

Uncertainty over the outcome of the GE has necessarily restricted ability and willingness, both nationally and internationally, to respond to the problem through policy formation. Response is least likely in the atoll states where information is least adequate and where planning offices are small and fully stretched to cope with standard recurrent activities. Indeed, in general planning remains in its infancy; finance, data, continuity and technical expertise are limited, environmental planning is almost non-existent and five years is usually the limit of long-term thinking. As the Prime Minister of Tuvalu, Bikenibeu Paeniu, has pointed out, 'we strongly believe that we have done the least to cause this hazardous problem although we are now faced with the highest possibility of losing the most'. It is extremely difficult to get problems that are distant (in space and time) placed on the political agenda of any country.[34] Atoll states, and other microstates, cannot act individually or collectively to remove or reduce the causes of the GE, though they can call upon international organisations to act on these matters. An international approach is manifestly essential to tackle this global problem, although it still needs to be appreciated that, even at an international level, climatic change is only one element in a complex and integrated set of population, resource, economic and environmental problems.

Despite the individual and collective inability of island states to prevent the GE, they have taken the lead in drawing attention to the problem. The particular threat to small island countries was first articulated in 1988 when representatives from five states from the Caribbean, Indian and Pacific Oceans met in the Maldives. Subsequently, an Alliance of Small Island States (AOSIS) was formed at the Second World Climate Conference in 1990 to promote six fundamental principles on which a climate change convention should be based; these principles stressed that developed countries should take immediate steps to reduce their production of greenhouse gases and move towards improved energy conservation and efficiency. Through AOSIS, the small island states have been innovative in stimulating a global response to the climate change problem. More recently, in January 1992, an inaugural summit of Smaller Island States was held in the Cook Islands – linking that country with Kiribati, Tuvalu, Nauru and Niue – to establish a secretariat to examine the particular social and economic policies, especially relating to the reduction of global warming, that might contribute to the solution of the particular problems of some of the smallest island states. In different ways, then, the GE has contributed to a new unity amongst small island states and strengthened the priority given to international responses.

For any particular state, options range from direct action to avoid or eliminate the risk (which is clearly not possible for the GE), action to reduce vulnerability levels and action to move away from, or abandon, the most risk-prone areas. The GE will eventually overwhelm atolls since everything is coastal (in distance and altitude). Many conventional measures to reduce vulnerability (for example transferring populations, infrastructure and economic activities to higher land) are impossible. Other conventional measures, such as the construction of dikes, sea walls and pumping stations, are extremely expensive (especially when a small population is spread over a large number of islands) and, in any case, because of the high porosity of coral and coral sand, would not solve the problem since the continuous inflow of water underground would necessitate expenditure on land drainage whilst there would be no protection for the freshwater lenses. Similarly, there would be no possibility for the transport of material to nourish island growth on the scale that would be required. Even defending the few urban areas, several of which are themselves spread over wide areas, would be a complex and costly operation, and in itself would be a pointless exercise. Moreover, the finance for projects of this kind is wholly absent within the atoll states and no aid donor would contemplate aid on the scale that would be necessary, even to strategically important states, which those in the South Pacific are clearly not following the end of the Cold War.

Potentially increased emigration must be seen as one response to the GE, a response that builds on existing trends but unavoidably depends almost entirely on the policies of metropolitan states in the cases of Kiribati and Tuvalu and the other independent island states. Nevertheless, as the title of a review of the possibility of a concessionary Australian migration scheme implies, 'Australia's Next Boat People?',[35] islanders could ultimately take migration matters into their own hands.

Based on the experience of existing migration from the South Pacific to Australia and New Zealand, the bulk of potential migrants from Kiribati and Tuvalu would be young, with some education, and would find employment reasonably easily; moreover, only a small proportion of the population would initially choose to migrate. Hastings has concluded that 'it should not be any great economic burden to this country [Australia] to subsidise a substantial proportion of island peoples – perhaps all of them in a few instances – but should we do it?'[36] His concern related to the grave dangers involved in selective migration policies and the fear that much larger countries, such as Papua New Guinea and the Solomon Islands, might subsequently demand the same policies. In a context of recession, both Australia and New Zealand have lately tightened up migration policies to reduce numbers, and have given no preferences to South Pacific island states.

The serious development problems experienced in the atoll states cannot adequately be met even now by internal policies or regional cooperation and higher levels of aid will not contribute to economic growth (as opposed to improved welfare). This is certainly the case in the small island of Niue which has one of the highest levels of per capita aid in the world and also one of the highest rates of emigration. Whilst there is much evidence of the widespread social and economic disadvantages that ensue from high levels of overseas migration, the fact is that, in the smallest states, such as Tokelau, there are substantial gains from migration that cannot be realised by other means. Where expectations of appropriate lifestyles continue to forge ahead of economic realities, the migration response, especially under the impact of the GE, becomes even more probable. In historic times atoll dwellers were extremely mobile and far from insular; men and women moved readily between islands in search of new land, disease-free sites, marriage partners, trade goods, and so on. In this way some islands were populated, depopulated, and later repopulated. Mobility itself was responsible for demographic survival; without mobility, adaptation and change were impossible. It is a phenomenon of contemporary times that atoll state populations are growing, and political boundaries and policies minimise long-distance migration. Without the flexibility that this kind of resettlement migration provides, the uncertainties and limitations of atoll environments are emphasised as both populations and expectations rise. The era of great Micronesian and Polynesian voyages may be over but the future may nonetheless lie on distant shores.

Long before the contemporary implications of the Greenhouse Effect were recognised the choice of appropriate development strategies for atoll states had caused concern. Few world states have ever had such limited prospects for development, have gained so little from contemporary technological change, but have nevertheless become so dependent on the outside world. Now it is even more crucial for a focus on development issues in atoll states to be created. Without further substantial external assistance, there is little doubt that people who were once described as real and potential 'economic refugees' will become 'environmental refugees'. It is extremely unlikely that actions that will or even can be taken within the atoll states alone will allay this gloomy forecast. Some of the most recently populated islands in the world may be depopulated. Some of the most recently formed islands may disappear. Long-term climatic change may be the greatest, yet the most intangible, threat to security in the South Pacific.

NOTES

1. J. Connell, 'Population, Migration and Problems of Atoll Development in the South Pacific', *Pacific Studies*, 9, 2 (1986); and J. Connell, 'The Carteret Islands: Precedents of the Greenhouse Effect', *Geography*, 75, 2 (1990).
2. W.L. Thomas, 'The Variety of Physical Environments among Pacific Islands', in F.R. Fosberg (ed.), *Man's Place in the Island Ecosystem* (Honolulu, 1963), 36.
3. G.A. Klee, 'Oceania', in G.A. Klee (ed.), *World Systems of Traditional Resource Management* (London, 1980).
4. W.H. Alkire, *Coral Islanders* (Arlington Heights, 1978), 28–30.
5. D. Osborne, *The Archaeology of the Palau Islands* (Honolulu, 1966), 49.
6. Alkire, *Coral Islanders*, 94.
7. J. Connell, *Sovereignty and Survival. Island Microstates in the Third World* (Sydney, 1988); J. Connell, 'Island Microstates: The Mirage of Development', *The Contemporary Pacific*, 3, 2 (1991).
8. B. Macdonald, *Cinderellas of the Empire: Towards a History of Kiribati and Tuvalu* (Canberra, 1982), 53; and D. Munro, 'Migration and the Shift to Dependence in Tuvalu: A Historical Perspective', in J. Connell (ed.), *Migration and Development in the South Pacific* (Canberra, 1990).
9. Cited by R. Bedford and D. Munro, 'Historical Background', in *Report on the Results of the Census of the Population of Tuvalu* (Funafuti, 1980), 3.
10. I. Fairbairn, *Employment in the Gilbert and Ellice Islands* (Noumea, 1976), 1.
11. H.E. Maude, *Of Islands and Men* (Melbourne, 1968), 342.
12. J. Connell and M. Maata, *Environmental Planning, Climate Change and Potential Sea Level Rise: Report on a Mission to the Republic of the Marshall Islands* (Apia, 1992), 18–21.
13. R. Bedford, 'Demographic Processes in Small Islands: the case of internal migration', in H. Brookfield (ed.), *Population Environment Relations in Tropical Islands: The Case of Eastern Fiji* (Paris, 1980), 48.
14. J. Connell, 'Population, Migration', 45.
15. A. Hooper, *Aid and Dependency in a Small Pacific Territory* (Auckland, 1982).
16. B. Lambert, 'Makin and the Outside World', in V. Carroll (ed.), *Pacific Atoll Populations* (Honolulu, 1975), 220–21.
17. A. Hooper and J. Huntsman, 'A Demographic History of the Tokelau Islands', *Journal of the Polynesian Society*, 82 (1973), 403–4.

18. F.X. Hezel and M. Levin, 'Micronesian emigration. Beyond the brain drain', in Connell, *Migration and Development*.
19. B. Schutz and R. Tenten, 'Adjustment: Problems of growth and change, 1892 to 1944', in A. Talu (ed.), *Kiribati: Aspects of History* (Suva, 1979), 127.
20. J. Connell, *Sovereignty and Survival*, 28–9.
21. G.E. Marcus, 'Power on the Extreme Periphery: the perspective of Tongan elites in the modern world system', *Pacific Viewpoint*, 22 (1981).
22. L.V. Castle, 'The Economic Context', in R.G. Ward and A. Proctor (eds.), *South Pacific Agriculture, Choice and Constraints* (Canberra and Manila, 1980); and Australia, *Report of the Committee to Advise on Australia's Immigration Policies* (Canberra, 1988).
23. G. Bertram, 'The Political Economy of Decolonisation and Nationhood in Small Pacific Societies', in A. Hooper *et al* (eds.), *Class and Culture in the South Pacific* (Suva, 1987), 29.
24. G. Bertram and R. Watters, 'The MIRAB Economy in South Pacific Microstates', *Pacific Viewpoint*, 26 (1985).
25. E.K. Fisk and C. Mellor, *Tuvalu Trust Fund Appraisal Study* (Sydney, 1986).
26. S. Pollard, *The Viability and Vulnerability of a Small Island State: The Case of Kiribati* (Canberra, 1987).
27. P. Roy and J. Connell, 'Climate Change and the Future of Atoll States', *Journal of Coastal Research*, 7, 4 (1991). The environmental implications in particular island states are discussed in Connell and Maata, *Environmental Planning*, 1992; M. Sullivan and L. Gibson, *Environmental Planning, Climate Change and Potential Sea Level Rise: Report on a Mission to Kiribati* (Noumea, 1991); B. Aalbersberg and J. Hay, *Climate Change and Sea Level Rise, Report on a Preparatory Mission to Tuvalu* (Apia, 1992); and S. Humphries and D. Collins, *Tokelau Country Report* (Canberra, 1991).
28. J.G. Titus et al, 'Greenhouse Effect and Sea Level Rise: The Cost of Holding Back the Sea', *Coastal Management*, 19, 2 (1991).
29. C. Plant, 'The Development Dilemma', in C. Plant (ed.), *Rotuma: Split Island* (Suva, 1977).
30. R. Firth, 'Economic Aspects of Modernisation in Tikopia', in L.R. Hiatt and C. Jayawardena (eds.), *Anthropology in Oceania* (Sydney, 1971).
31. G.T. Petersen, 'External Politics, Internal Economies and Ponopean Social Formation', *American Ethnologist*, 6 (1979).
32. J. Connell, 'Islands on the Poverty Line', *Pacific Viewpoint* 26, 2 (1985).
33. K.M. Meyer-Abich, 'Chalk on the White Wall? On the Transformation of Climatological facts into Political Facts', in J. Ausubel and A.K. Biswas (eds.), *Climatic Constraints and Human Affairs* (Oxford, 1980).
34. D.C. Mercer and J. Peterson, 'Australia and the greenhouse effect: the science/policy debate', in G.I. Pearman (ed.) *Greenhouse: Planning for Climatic Change* (Melbourne, 1988), 716.
35. D. Howlett, 'Australia's Next Boat People? The Need for a Concessionary Migration Policy for Kiribati and Tuvalu' (Brisbane, 1985).
36. P. Hastings, 'Door may open for rush from Pacific slums', *Sydney Morning Herald*, 19 March 1984.

Towards a Security Policy for Small Island and Enclave Developing States

PAUL SUTTON and ANTHONY PAYNE

The differing security environments of the Caribbean and the Pacific point to parallel security concerns for their small island and enclave developing states (SIEDS) but not identical ones. The complex and sometimes divisive experience of the Caribbean in the 1980s stands in marked contrast to the less urgent and comparatively simpler security debate encountered in the Pacific. Similarly, whilst the security agenda for the 1990s in both regions demonstrates a convergence of likely threat, on past record the detailed response in each region is likely to be very different. The regional context, in short, is sufficiently distinctive in the Caribbean and the Pacific to caution against any simple transposition of example from one to the other without appropriate qualification being made.

At the same time, however, the vulnerabilities inherent in SIEDS remain common to both and suggest the wisdom of a broadly similar approach to redress them. There has been less progress in this direction than might have been expected, in part because of differing regional perceptions. But what consensus has emerged, and informs thinking both within the regions and among the small circle of international advisers charged with deliberation on this question, is the necessity of multi-level and multi-dimensional strategies to maintain and enhance security.[1] The security of SIEDS is regarded as not only or even mainly a military or paramilitary question, but much more a political, economic and social matter. It is also one that cannot be realised solely at a national, regional or international level since no one level is optimal for every purpose or eventuality. All must be engaged if there is to be effective security provision.

To ask this of the SIEDS is to demand a great deal from them. Resources, by definition, are scarce and difficult choices have to be made. In recognising this SIEDS (and others) need to keep a sense of proportion. The security need of these countries is security with a small 's'. It is not the accumulation of power but the acquisition of flexibility which is important; not the engine but the steering mechanism which counts. This has long been recognised as a necessary, if not a sufficient, condition for the survival of small states. It now becomes an imperative

– indeed their only plausible expression of sovereignty and guarantee of survival in an increasingly asymmetrically interdependent and globally transnational age. For the SIEDS in the Caribbean and the Pacific this means attention to the following five dimensions of security strategy.

1. Policy Capacity

The promotion of representative and responsive government is vital to the security of the SIEDS. Political systems in such states may be 'robust' and political order rarely disturbed, but when breakdown does occur it is usually sudden, always traumatic, and frequently with effects beyond the borders of the state itself, sometimes ending in intervention and occupation. To guard against this SIEDS need to develop a consensual, adaptive and effective policy capacity.[2] This demands more than the creation of a coherent and efficient executive and administration – important as these are. It also requires a large measure of agreement about the ends and means of security. This requires, in turn, legitimacy and openness in the political system and the ability to combine defence, foreign and domestic policies into one integrated security policy. The former is best served where popular participation in politics (including the opportunity openly to dissent) is assured and the basic rights of citizens (including entrenched provision for the protection of the rights of minority groups) are widely respected and guaranteed by law. The latter occurs when government, centrally and as a priority, establishes publicly accountable mechanisms and procedures through which threats and vulnerabilities are perceived and assessed, resources are allocated, and policies are selected and implemented. This particular provision is an important, but characteristically neglected, aspect of government in many of the Caribbean and Pacific SIEDS. All too often the security of such states is the responsibility of only a few individuals who meet infrequently and respond only to the immediate issues in front of them. A wider vision is lacking. Yet, it should be apparent that such a vision, emanating from and responsive to a broadly based bipartisan security committee, constitutes an indispensable basis for a credible national security policy in the first instance and a necessary basis for upholding an acceptable public order in the last. Where such an arrangement or its equivalent does not exist security is ill served, since it lacks effective oversight and public confidence. It therefore follows that the establishment of such a committee (or equivalent mechanism and procedure) should be subject to discussion and open debate at the earliest opportunity. It also follows that where they are in being they should be reviewed to determine their appropriateness to the overriding necessity of enhancing the political capacity, and not simply the coercive capacity, of the political system as a whole.

2. Economic Growth and Social Integrity

The promotion of economic and social development is frequently cited as the most important factor bearing on the security of the SIEDS.[3] Without it, a series of calamities are expected to descend on them, ranging from economic stagnation through increasing migration to eventual social disintegration and the collapse of the state itself. While this sequence has yet to manifest itself anywhere in the Caribbean and the Pacific in its entirety, the process is discernible enough in several of the SIEDS (Suriname and, prospectively by some accounts, Vanuatu) to act as a warning to others. Political leaders in both regions are therefore very sensitive to the issue and anxious to promote policies that encourage economic growth and social integrity. In current conditions this means two things. First, it requires an economic strategy that is outward-looking and that encourages maximum adaptability to changing circumstances in the world market. This does not mean abandoning policies aiming at greater self-sufficiency, but it does follow that these must be complementary to those favouring export-oriented growth, whether of goods or increasingly of services. Second, it demands the pursuit of social cohesiveness, particularly where ethnicity divides or modernisation increasingly marginalises tradition and custom. Although all groups can be disadvantaged in such circumstances, the youth are likely to feel the effects most keenly. It is therefore imperative that they be actively engaged in both social change and political and economic decision-making. National integration should be encouraged through cross-cultural, cross-racial and cross-religious group projects in the fields of social welfare, education and recreation. Opportunities in education and employment should also be made equal. Indeed, provision of the latter is the *sine qua non* for the continued existence of the SIEDS as viable nation states. Without the creation of job opportunities migration will rise, separatist subcultures flourish and social discontent escalate to damaging heights. The fashioning of an effective employment policy for youth (demographically the major element of the population in most of the SIEDS) is accordingly the single most important guarantee of future political stability in the Caribbean and Pacific SIEDS.

3. Regional Cooperation

Regional cooperation has special significance for the SIEDS. In both the Commonwealth Caribbean and among the South Pacific countries a relatively long-standing tradition of regional cooperation exists and regional arrangements are in place to cater for a range of needs – primarily economic, but also including many areas of functional cooperation such as the surveillance and development of marine resources, sea and air transport, and disaster preparedness and relief. Since some of these relate to security it is apparent that this is also an area where a regional approach can fruitfully be developed further. It does require, however, a sensitivity to context and sovereignty. A regional military force involving all or nearly all the Caribbean SIEDS or a majority of the Pacific SIEDS is presently not in sight. A sub-regional arrangement involving some (where a high degree of regional homogeneity exists) has proved practical in the eastern Caribbean and may in time be feasible in Melanesia and parts of Polynesia. Similarly, while there is a compelling case for a regional intelligence network (including efficient public information services, data banks, commercial and financial assessment, and military and police intelligence), great care must be taken to ensure that national access and control is guaranteed and paramount.[4] In short, regional cooperation in matters of security, narrowly defined, must advance through incremental measures and evolving consensus if it is to succeed. The Caribbean is in advance of the Pacific on this question and the latter can profitably learn from the former, particularly in respect of the RSS and the development of appropriate para-military, coast guard, and police provision. Indeed, these are the most immediately promising areas for expanded security cooperation in both regions. Such provision is universal (even the smallest SIEDS maintain police forces), it is generally well-regarded (especially in areas such as search and rescue, fisheries protection, and environmental protection), and it is proportionate to the threat (which is primarily one of internal instability or when external is less likely to come from neighbouring SIEDS than from organised crime in its various forms). Measures should therefore be taken to encourage the development of regional police solutions (including para-military and coast guard capabilities) to tangible common problems. It will not, of course, in itself prevent threats from arising, but it is an important first step in establishing the necessary trust to move towards a common community approach (in which cooperation to pool resources and coordinate efforts appears natural), as opposed to a collective security approach (which is simply the sum of separate national interests), to security in the Caribbean and the Pacific.

4. Extra-Regional Association

The SIEDS of the Caribbean and the Pacific are all 'new' states. As such, they have until recently been formally tied to extra-regional powers. The responsibilities of such countries could be said to end with independence. However, in respect of the SIEDS there is a case for arguing that in the interests of all concerned some form of loose association should continue, at least in the medium-term. The two areas where this appears most beneficial to security are in respect of the economy and military capabilities. The first addresses the vulnerability of the SIEDS in the international economy. It recognises that without special market access arrangements to sustain and develop their exports; preferential and concessional access to public and private capital markets to stimulate aid and investment; and guaranteed long-term access to the labour markets of larger economies to provide remittances and ease demographic pressures, their economic future is uncertain. The ex-colonial powers are well aware of this. They are usually well-placed and able, by themselves or in association with others, to do something about it. The same applies to the second area, that of military capabilities. Again the question is about offsetting vulnerability, particularly in matters of territorial and political integrity. SIEDS cannot guarantee these except against the lowest level of threat. Accordingly, temporary outside assistance will almost certainly be needed in the smaller SIEDS to repel an invader (including any substantial mercenary action); to defeat secession (especially of remote out-islands); and to quell or contain protracted urban riots, coup attempts, or any combination of these, especially if they are manifested on any scale. In such circumstances regional action is appropriate: so also is extra-regional action. The countries best suited to provide this are Britain and Canada for the Commonwealth Caribbean (the Netherlands for Suriname) and Australia and New Zealand for the Pacific (the United States for Micronesia). They are familiar with the respective regions; have a sizeable diplomatic presence and a substantive aid programme in most of the SIEDS; and presently enjoy the confidence of the United States and the other medium powers which believe they have interests in either or both regions. More to the point, all four countries have recently engaged in foreign policy reviews of their commitments in these regions and have concluded that a continuing and/or expanded presence is necessary.[5] The SIEDS in the Caribbean and the Pacific should take advantage of this fact and the many opportunities it offers by channelling extra-regional associations to their own ends.

5. Diplomatic Coordination

The SIEDS have few economic or military resources at their disposal. As such, diplomacy becomes the primary instrument through which to advance their interests in international relations. In the main this is achieved through a highly selective bilateral and multilateral diplomacy in which national representation is foremost. This will obviously continue. However, diplomacy could be improved, and the security of the SIEDS correspondingly enhanced, if efforts were made to coordinate foreign policy, both within and between regions, whenever possible. This could be attempted in four ways. First, national interest could be promoted through a policy of joint representation where necessary. This is already the practice of some of the smaller Caribbean and Pacific SIEDS in respect of diplomatic missions in London, Ottawa and at the UN in New York. It could be extended with good effect as a general measure for all the SIEDS in establishing a presence in the wider region – Latin America for the Caribbean and East and South-East Asia for the Pacific. Second, coordination of foreign policy within a region can provide an important source of support for one or more SIEDS threatened by aggression, either directly or through misinterpretation. The latter is a situation which can easily arise in respect of major powers or superpowers with substantial regional interests. Initiatives involving closer association with Cuba in the Caribbean or the Soviet Union in the Pacific are past cases in point. In such circumstances effective coordination, and in particular jointly agreed action, could do much to dispel fears and, as importantly, retain regional consensus on sensitive foreign policy issues. Third, common regional projection in regional and international organisations is made possible and more effective through diplomatic coordination. Again, this is already practised to some degree among Caribbean and Pacific SIEDS. It is apparent, however, that it is not as advanced as it should be, particularly in mobilising international support behind specific sub-regional interests or regional candidates for senior positions in international agencies.

Finally, and most importantly, diplomatic action should be concerted between the Caribbean and the Pacific in support of the common problems each has as regions overwhelmingly constituted by SIEDS. The Association of Small Island States (AOSIS), the Commonwealth and the UN are all fora where this could be pursued with some hope of success. The creation of AOSIS at the Second World Climate Conference in 1990 is particularly promising since its 37 members comprise most of the SIEDS. It has been especially successful in focusing attention on environmental issues, particularly the serious threat of flooding resulting from any global warming, and has contributed to raising the profile of small states in the UN system. In this it has been helped by the Commonwealth which has to date been the single most active international organisation working on behalf of small states. The Commonwealth Secretariat has been in the forefront of special assistance provision to small states and while there is no small states programme as such within the Secretariat the fact that many members of the Commonwealth may be so classified serves as a stimulus to keeping the small state dimension as an integral part of its activities. It is, however, to the UN system that small states must ultimately look to safeguard their security. The General Assembly and UNCTAD have already responded to calls for technical assistance and acted as advocates in the cause of small states. The pressing need now is to engage other parts of the system. The final recommendations of the Workshop on the Protection and Security of Small States held in the Maldives in May 1991 are particularly instructive in this regard. They propose, *inter alia*, that the Secretary-General play a more active role in the spirit of Article 99 in responding to incipient and low-level security threats; that serious consideration should be given to the establishment of either a permanent or an ad-hoc UN force that may be activated under Chapter VII for international security needs; and that the Security Council should consider providing collective security guarantees to small states in appropriate circumstances.[6] These are all sound suggestions which deserve further exploration and consideration.

Effective implementation of any or all of the above five themes will require policy innovation. In no instance, however, is this sweeping and to that extent the recommendations made here are feasible. They are also complementary and so mutually reinforcing. All levels of the international system are engaged, with the proviso that the regional is particularly stressed since action here can do so much to redress the weaknesses and vulnerabilities of individual countries. In the end, though, security for the SIEDS is not a matter of national, regional or international action but one for the communities and peoples who live in the islands and enclaves themselves. It may be a truism to state this, but it is the fount of all wisdom and the necessary starting point for policy debate and action in the small states. In the final analysis, the security of the SIEDS rests on the qualities and resourcefulness of their peoples – and in particular their economic, political and social development.

NOTES

1. See, in particular, The Commonwealth Consultative Group, *Vulnerability: Small States in the Global Society* (London, 1985); Sheila Harden, *Small is Dangerous: MicroStates in a Macro World* (London, 1985); Report of the Study Group of the

Commonwealth Parliamentary Association, *The Security of Small States* (Commonwealth Parliamentary Association, London, December 1984); and the papers presented to *The Workshop on the Protection and Security of Small States*, Maldives, 5–6 May 1991.

2. The concept of policy capacity is discussed at length by Edward Azar and Chung-In Moon in 'Legitimacy, Integration and Policy Capacity: The "Software" Side of Third World National Security' in Edward Azar and Chung-In Moon (eds.), *National Security in the Third World* (London, 1988), 77–101.

3. This view is held as axiomatic in all the studies cited in Note 1 above.

4. See, in particular, Commonwealth Consultative Group, *Vulnerability*, paras. 5.35–50 and Neville O. Linton, 'International, National and Regional Initiatives to Enhance Security Through Exchange of Information and Diplomacy – The Commonwealth Report Revisited' in Anthony T. Bryan et al., *Peace, Development and Security in the Caribbean* (London, 1990), 257–80.

5. For Britain, see Address by the Rt. Hon. the Baroness Young, Minister of State for Foreign and Commonwealth Affairs, to the West India Committee Luncheon – 31 Oct. 1984, and 'Britain and the Caribbean: The Way Ahead', speech by Mr Tim Eggar to the Annual General meeting of the West India Committee – 28 June 1988; for Canada, see Statement by Mark MacGuigan, Ministry of External Affairs, Canada, before the Canada/CARICOM Joint Trade and Economic Committee – 15 Jan. 1981; for Australia, see G. Evans, Minister for Foreign Affairs and Trade, 'Australia's Regional Security', Ministerial Statement, December 1989; and for New Zealand, see R. Marshall, Minister of Foreign Affairs, 'New Zealand Foreign Policy', Address to Royal New Zealand Air Force and Staff College, Auckland, 3 Oct. 1989.

6. Final Recommendations of the Workshop on the Protection and Security of Small States, Maldives, May 1991.

www.ingramcontent.com/pod-product-compliance
Ingram Content Group UK Ltd.
Pitfield, Milton Keynes, MK11 3LW, UK
UKHW020412010325
455677UK00029B/868

9 781138 981997